Aristotle on Moral Responsibility

B

Issues *in* Ancient Philosophy

General Editor: *Jonathan Barnes*

Aristotle on Moral Responsibility

Character and Cause

Susan Sauvé Meyer

BLACKWELL
Oxford UK & Cambridge USA

First published 1993

Blackwell Publishers
238 Main Street,
Cambridge, Massachusetts 02142
USA

108 Cowley Road
Oxford OX4 1JF
UK

Library of Congress Cataloging-in-Publication Data

Meyer, Susan Sauvé.
Aristotle on moral responsibility: character and cause / Susan
Sauvé Meyer.
p. cm.—(Issues in ancient philosophy: 3)
Includes bibliographical references and index.
ISBN 0–631–18527–5
1. Aristotle—Ethics. 2. Aristotle—Contributions in concept of
responsibility. 3. Ethics, Ancient. 4. Responsibility.
5. Character. 6. Causation. I. Title. II. Series: Issues in
ancient philosophy (Cambridge, Mass.): 3.
B491.E7M474 1994 170—dc20 93–19147 CIP

British Library Cataloguing in Publication Data

A CIP catalogue record for this book is available from the British Library.

Typeset in 11/13pt Garamond by Pure Tech Corporation, Pondicherry, India
Printed in Great Britain by Biddles Ltd, Guildford, Surrey

This book is printed on acid-free paper

To Milton

Contents

◆

Acknowledgments

———————◆———————

While preparing this manuscript, I have benefitted from the comments and criticism of many colleagues and students. Special thanks are due to John Carriero, Paula Gottlieb, Terry Irwin, Milton Wachsberg Meyer, Elijah Millgram, Tim Scanlon, and Gisela Striker. Seth Fagen and Mitzi Lee provided valuable bibliographical assistance, Mitzi Lee and Mary Sullivan saved me from many errors, and Mary Sullivan helped to prepare the indices. Drafts of various chapters have benefitted from discussion at colloquia at Queen's University, the University of California at Berkeley, the University of California at Los Angeles, and the University of Wisconsin at Madison. For the leisure to prepare the first draft of the manuscript I am grateful to the President and Fellows of Harvard College who granted me a Presidential leave during the academic year 1989–90, and to the National Endowment for the Humanities who awarded me a Fellowship for University Teachers in 1990.

Susan Sauvé Meyer
Cambridge, Massachusetts

Abbreviations of Aristotle's Works

———————————◆———————————

APst.	*Posterior Analytics*
Catg.	*Categories*
DA	*De Anima*
De Int.	*De Interpretatione*
EE	*Eudemian Ethics*
EN	*Nicomachean Ethics*
GA	*De Generatione Animalium*
MA	*De Motu Animalium*
Met.	*Metaphysics*
MM	*Magna Moralia*
Ph.	*Physics*
Poet.	*Poetics*
Pol.	*Politics*
Rhet.	*Rhetoric*
Top.	*Topics*

Tables

Introduction
Moral Responsibility and
Aristotle's Concerns

◆

1 Moral Responsibility and Aristotle's Concerns

In each of his three ethical works, Aristotle interrupts his general discussion of the virtues and vices of character to give an extended discussion of voluntariness (*to hekousion*) and related notions.[1] He indicates that praise and blame are for voluntary actions; that voluntariness is relevant to praise and blame because an agent must be the cause (*aitios*) of any action for which he or she is praised or blamed; and that voluntary actions are the ones of which the agent is the cause.[2] He furthermore insists that the causal relation between agent and voluntary action is one in which the "origin" (*archē*) of the action is in the agent (or the agent *is* its origin), the action is "up to" the agent (*ep' autō(i)*) to do and not to do, and the agent is in control (*kurios*) of whether the action occurs.[3] These features of Aristotle's discussions of voluntariness make it natural to suppose that he intends it to provide an account of moral responsibility: an account of the causal conditions in which an agent merits praise and blame for what he or she does.

There are, however, a variety of reasons why one might doubt that Aristotle's concern with voluntariness is a concern with moral responsibility:

1 First of all, Aristotle's ethical writings focus on the practical question of how we can become morally good (*EN* 1095a2–6, 1105b9–18,

1179a33–b7), and he conceives the task of the politician to be to make the citizens morally good (*EN* 1102a7–10; cf. 1180a1–24). Since he writes the ethical works with a view to instructing the politician in this task (1102a12–26), and since he clearly thinks praise and blame influence the development of good and bad character (1104b16–18, 1113b21–26), we might wonder whether the sorts of praise and blame he has in mind when he discusses voluntariness are justified by purely prospective rather than retrospective considerations. That is, we might wonder whether he thinks praise and blame are justified not on the basis of the agent's merit or desert, but rather on the basis of their contribution to the formation and control of the agent's character. If so, then Aristotle's concern with the conditions of praiseworthiness and blameworthiness is not a concern with moral responsibility.[4]

2   Second, Aristotle insists that voluntariness is shared by children and animals (*EN* 1111a25–6, b8–9). But non-human animals are not morally responsible for their actions, and children are morally responsible only to a diminished degree, if at all (*EN* 1149b31–5; cf. *EE* 1224a27–30). And so, by Aristotle's own admission, voluntariness seems to be an inappropriate category to capture the distinctive feature of morally responsible agents.[5]

3   Furthermore, Aristotle's discussions of voluntariness appear to proceed in ways that belie the suggestion that he is offering a positive theoretical account of responsibility, moral or otherwise. The account in *EN* iii 1 appears to identify the criteria for voluntariness simply by negative contrast with two broadly recognized criteria for involuntariness. Such an unreflective compilation of "commonsense" criteria would suggest that his goal is simply to enumerate the ordinary criteria for imputability prevalent in his day, without attempting to give a philosophical account of moral responsibility.[6] The discussions of voluntariness in *EE* ii 6–10 and *MM* i 9–16 seem equally ill-suited to support any positive theoretical conclusions. They appear hopelessly aporetic and disjointed.[7]

4   Finally, Aristotle in his discussions of voluntariness fails to address a question that has dominated discussions of moral responsibility at least since the time of Epicurus.[8] This is the question of whether causal determinism precludes our actions being up to us (*eph' hēmin*) in the way that moral responsibility requires. Compatibilists over the centuries have argued that we can have the sort of control over our actions that moral agency requires even if everything we do is fully determined by the sequence of causes at work in the rest of the natural world, while

incompatibilists have insisted that the special causal status of the moral agent requires a suspension or interruption of such causal sequences. In a recent twist to an old debate it has been argued that the incompatibilists are right that morality and its claims require us to be independent of the sequence of natural causes, while the compatibilists are right that this causal independence is both unattainable and not worth having. Morality, it is concluded, is an institution of dubious merit, and Aristotle is cited as an example of a thinker who is free of its presuppositions.[9]

These various motives for scepticism amount to the suspicion that Aristotle's goals and concerns in discussing voluntariness, as well as the notions he invokes and the methods he uses, are not those of someone concerned with developing a theoretical account of moral responsibility. The project of this book is to argue, on the contrary, that Aristotle's concerns and aims in his various discussions of voluntariness are precisely those of a theorist of moral responsibility. Aristotle has an account of moral responsibility that is far from being an uncritical recapitulation of commonsense notions. It is a sophisticated philosophical account capable of solving most of the problems that a theory of moral responsibility must address. In this introduction I shall first, by way of response to the initial objections, sketch the view I attribute to Aristotle and the argument of the following chapters. I shall then discuss the textual evidence for Aristotle's views, and sketch the ordinary notions of voluntariness (*to hekousion*) and involuntariness (*to akousion*) in the light of which Aristotle develops his account.

2 Aristotle's Conception of Moral Responsibility

1 Aristotle clearly has the concerns of the moral educator in mind when writing his ethical treatises and he thinks praising and blaming play an important formative role in moral education. But he nonetheless conceives the goal of moral education to be to produce a fully autonomous individual who *merits* praise or blame. The only agents who merit praise or blame are those who are properly subject to the demands, expectations, and evaluations of morality. The first task of a theory of moral responsibility is to identify the features that properly subject an agent to these demands, expectations, and evaluations. An agent who has these features is a morally responsible agent. Aristotle's account of moral character (the condition common to virtue and vice of character)

accomplishes this first task of a theory of moral responsibility. The account of voluntariness, which occurs in the context of his account of moral character, is intended to accomplish the second task of a theory of moral responsibility: to identify the circumstances in which a morally responsible agent is morally responsible *for* some particular action. On Aristotle's view, the property that makes an agent a proper subject of moral demands and evaluations must cause any action for which she is morally responsible. Briefly put, Aristotle thinks we are morally responsible for all and only those actions of which our moral character is the cause.

2   While Aristotle explicitly recognizes that not all voluntary agents are morally responsible for their voluntary actions, he nonetheless thinks that agents with moral character are morally responsible for their voluntary actions; for he thinks that the voluntary actions of such agents are produced by their moral character. He develops his accounts of voluntariness in order to capture the conditions in which this causal relation obtains.

3   Although he develops his accounts of voluntariness by appealing to ordinary criteria for voluntariness and involuntariness, Aristotle does not rely on these criteria uncritically. Rather, he examines them dialectically, and revises them in the light of independent criteria for moral responsibility. The account of voluntariness with which he concludes this dialectical argument has been tested not only against ordinary criteria, but also against rival philosophical accounts. It goes well beyond commonsense criteria and is able to solve the most pressing problems such criteria raise.

4   Finally, Aristotle's failure to ask whether the voluntary exercise of moral character is compatible with causal determinism does not show that his concern with voluntariness and moral character is not a concern with moral responsibility. The question about determinism is not definitive of the topic of moral responsibility. Rather, it is a question whose answer presupposes an account of moral responsibility, and an account of moral responsibility must accomplish the two central tasks described above. Aristotle's accounts of moral character and voluntariness address these tasks.

Aristotle's goal of capturing with his account of voluntariness those actions produced by the agent's states of character might appear to support the view that he is not ascribing to the voluntary agent a causal status ultimate enough to justify holding him morally responsible for his actions. For it is easy to see how actions produced by character can be accommodated into a naturalistic or even deterministic explanatory framework. However, Aristotle also insists, unequivocally, that voluntary actions are up to the agent to do and not to do (*EN* 1113b4–14, 19–21) and that such an agent is an origin of action in the sense that there is no cause (*aition*) of his causation of his action (*EE* 1222b29–41). He therefore attributes to the voluntary agent precisely the causal status that ascriptions of moral responsibility presuppose. Such attributions might appear to conflict with his view that actions caused by character are voluntary; however, the appearance of conflict arises from reliance on modern rather than Aristotelian causal notions. If we understand properly the conception of causation that Aristotle presupposes, we can see that he is able to explain how an agent's acts and omissions are up to him in such a way that he merits praise or blame for them, but without supposing that such agency is an exception to the sequence of causes in a world of which naturalism, or even determinism, is true. His account of moral responsibility is one that contemporary compatibilists would do well to take seriously.

3 Outline by Chapters

Chapters 1 and 2 argue that Aristotle's inquiry into the conditions of voluntariness is reasonably interpreted as an investigation of the conditions of moral responsibility.

Chapter 1 establishes that the general context in which Aristotle's discussions of voluntariness occur, his general account of the virtues and vices of character, is itself concerned with the conditions of moral agency. It focuses on Aristotle's conception of the property common to the virtues and vices of character (*ēthikē aretē kai kakia*) and to the intermediate states of character falling between perfect virtue and full vice. These states are recognizably moral qualities, and Aristotle denies them to animals and small children on the grounds that they have no conception of happiness. The feature distinctive of such a state, on Aristotle's view, is that it expresses the agent's conception of happiness; and so this must be the feature that, in his view, makes an agent properly subject to the expectations and evaluations of morality.

Chapter 2 considers Aristotle's own explanation of why he includes a discussion of voluntariness in his discussion of moral character. The connection he sees between voluntariness and the praiseworthiness and blameworthiness of states of character gives us reason to suppose that the account of voluntariness is intended to capture conditions of moral responsibility for action. He thinks we are morally responsible for those actions and feelings produced by our states of moral character. The account of praiseworthiness on which he relies, however, fails to endorse a common modern assumption about moral responsibility, the view that one's praiseworthiness or blameworthiness for action requires responsibility for the states of character from which one acts.

Chapter 3 offers a detailed textual analysis of the discussions that yield the definitions of voluntariness in the *EE*, *EN*, and *MM*. It shows that Aristotle carries out in these discussions precisely the project that chapters 1 and 2 lead us to expect he will, and that he carries it out in his typical dialectical fashion. The discussions in the *MM* and *EE*, which are not entirely aporetic and inconclusive, and that of the *EN*, which is far more theoretical and critical of ordinary criteria than it initially appears, are, respectively, earlier and later stages in an extended dialectical argument in which Aristotle develops an account of voluntariness by appeal to (a) ordinary criteria for and paradigms of voluntariness and involuntariness; (b) rival philosophical accounts of voluntariness – notably those of Plato and Socrates; and (c) plausible examples of praiseworthy and blameworthy activity. In typical dialectical fashion, Aristotle first generates conflicts between (a), (b), and (c), and then solves the conflicts by revising the initial considerations. He always solves conflicts by revising (a) and (b) in the light of (c), and (c) turns out to express the account of praiseworthiness that emerges from Chapter 2: that agents are praiseworthy and blameworthy for the actions caused by their moral character.

The apparently disjointed stages in the discussions of *EE* ii 7–9 and *MM* i 12–15 are stages in this dialectical argument. The definitions of voluntariness and involuntariness with which they conclude are unstable and open to further criticism from the dialectical considerations. The definitions of voluntariness and involuntariness presented in *EN* iii 1 solve the remaining dialectical problem left over from the conclusion of the *EE*'s and *MM*'s arguments: that of articulating properly the causal role played by ignorance in cases of involuntariness. Aristotle takes care, in *EN* iii, to show that his account fits the two major paradigms of involuntary action because he is concerned to show that he has solved the remaining dialectical puzzle left over from the Eudemian account of voluntariness. Far from being evidence that his account is not theoretical, Aristotle's recapitulation of these ordinary criteria for involuntariness is intended to demonstrate that his theory is dialectically justified – that it preserves "most and the most important" of the initial considerations (*EN* 1145b4–5).

Chapters 4 and 5 consider Aristotle's treatment of two issues of importance to a theory of moral responsibility: the status of actions performed under duress and compulsion, and the significance of responsibility for character. **Chapter 4** considers his differing verdicts, in the different ethical works, on whether compelled actions are voluntary. In the *EE* and the *MM* Aristotle classifies such actions as involuntary, but in the *EN* he insists that they are voluntary. These conflicting verdicts reflect different ways of making precise the basic presupposition guiding his dialectical inquiry into voluntariness, the thesis that agents are morally responsible for the actions produced by their moral character. In the *EE* and *MM* he denies that such actions originate in the agent because he thinks such actions are not expressions of the agent's character, while in the *EN* he insists that such actions are voluntary because he believes they do express the agent's character. Reflecting on these difficult cases forces Aristotle to specify the sort of causal relation between character and action he has in mind, and to do this he appeals to his distinction, familiar from his physical works, between intrinsic (*kath' hauto*) and accidental (*kata sumbebēkos*) efficient causation. He shows that he thinks the agent's moral character must be the intrinsic, not merely the accidental, cause of the actions for which he is morally responsible. His invocation of this distinction allows him to offer a satisfactory defence of the thesis that agents are morally responsible for compelled actions while at the same time acknowledging the ways in which such actions are different from the other actions for which we are morally responsible.

Chapter 5 considers the significance Aristotle attaches to the thesis, for which he argues in *EN* iii 5, that we acquire our states of character voluntarily. This thesis is not, as is often supposed, the linchpin of his account of moral responsibility.[10] Rather, his argument for the thesis plays a subordinate, albeit important, role in a more general argument against the Socratic thesis that only our virtuous actions are voluntary. The scope of Aristotle's thesis that we are responsible for our states of character is, in any case, insufficient to provide an adequate basis for moral responsibility. It ascribes to us a degree of causal responsibility for our states of character sufficient only to make praise and blame appropriate as tools for influencing character formation rather than as attitudes of moral assessment. Once we recognize that Aristotle's argument for the voluntariness of character is not intended to establish our moral responsibility for our states of character, his argument for that claim becomes more persuasive. In particular, it is not undermined by his insistence on the importance of being properly habituated right from birth (*EN* 1104b11–13).

Chapter 6 considers how we are meant to interpret Aristotle's claim that the voluntary agent is an origin of action. Does this claim attribute to the agent sufficient causal control over her actions to justify holding her morally responsible for what she does? And can Aristotle defend it, given that he does not think its truth requires the agent to be responsible for her states of character, and appears to think it is compatible with the action being a fully determinate expression of the agent's character? By appealing to Aristotle's notion of a self-mover, and to the distinction between intrinsic and accidental causation that he has shown to be implicit in his account of voluntariness, we can answer both questions in the affirmative. The conception of moral agency Aristotle uses his account of voluntariness to capture does not attribute to the moral agent causal powers that require the interruption or suspension of the causal sequences at work in the natural world, but it nonetheless captures the distinctive causal role that only morally responsible agents play in that world.

4 Assumptions about Aristotle's Texts

In discussing Aristotle's views, I rely primarily on the discussions of character and voluntariness in the *Eudemian Ethics*, the *Nicomachean Ethics*, and the *Magna Moralia*. While the *MM* is almost certainly not written by Aristotle, I include it for discussion on the assumption that its content is substantially Aristotelian.[11] For simplicity, I will sometimes paraphrase or interpret passages in the *MM* using locutions such as "Aristotle says . . .," but without implying that Aristotle actually wrote the passages in question.

According to the manuscript tradition three books are common to the *EE* and *EN*. I will refer to them by their Nicomachean labels (*EN* v, vi, and vii; = *EE* iv, v, vi). I accept the view that these books were originally composed as part of the *EE*, but may have been revised for inclusion in the *EN* – if the latter is the later work. I make no initial assumptions about the relative priority of the Eudemian and the Nicomachean *Ethics*. However, my examination of the relation between the Eudemian and Nicomachean accounts of voluntariness (chapter 3) supports the conclusion that the Nicomachean account is later.[12] I will also appeal to Aristotle's non-philosophical discussions of these ethical issues in the *Rhetoric* and the *Poetics*, and to his discussions of action in the non-ethical contexts of the *De Anima*, *De Motu Animalium*, and *Physics* viii. In elucidation of the causal notions appealed to in Aristotle's accounts of voluntariness and involuntariness, I will appeal primarily to the *Physics* and *Metaphysics*.

5 Ordinary Notions of *Hekousion* and *Akousion*

Before proceeding to the main discussion, it is worthwhile to pause briefly over a question of terminology. So far in this introduction, I have been following customary usage by using the English terms 'voluntary' and 'involuntary' to translate the pairs of terms Aristotle uses: '*hekousion*' or '*hekōn*' and '*akousion*' or '*akōn*'.[13] Translators and commentators generally consider these translations to be unsatisfactory or at least problematic, and resort to them only for want of a better alternative. I shall continue to use these customary translations, but without the usual apologies. These translations are very apt renderings of Aristotle's terms. Seeing why this is so will help us to appreciate the sort of difficulties Aristotle encounters when he undertakes to give a philosophical account of these notions.

Some object to the customary translations because, according to Aristotle's own account of the *hekousion*, some things which it would be exceedingly strange to call 'voluntary' turn out to be *hekousion*, and similarly with his account of the *akousion*. For example, 'voluntary' and 'involuntary' are predicated of actions, but in *EN* iii 1 Aristotle counts as *akousion* ('involuntary' on the customary translation) things which are not actions of the agent at all but are merely things that happen to him – being kidnapped, for example (1110a1–4). And he claims (1110a15, b5–7) that an action performed under duress or coercion is *hekousion* ('voluntary' on the customary translation), while such actions are naturally labelled 'involuntary' in English.[14]

These considerations do not provide good reasons to reject 'voluntary' and 'involuntary' as translations of '*hekousion*' and '*akousion*'. For when we seek an adequate translation of a term that Aristotle employs in his discussion we should not seek an English term whose extension coincides with the extension of the term as Aristotle defines it.[15] Rather, we should seek an English term that adequately captures the ordinary non-philosophical meaning of the term for which Aristotle is providing a philosophical definition. Otherwise, our translation will mask any controversial innovations that Aristotle introduces in his philosophical definition of the term. In fact, the examples from *EN* iii 1 discussed above, which are supposed to cast doubt on the translation of *'hekousion'* by 'voluntary' and *'akousion'* by 'involuntary', are just such controversial innovations. In his discussions of *hekousion* and *akousion* in the *EE* and the *MM*, Aristotle classifies coerced action and action under duress as *akousion* – a verdict which is more or less in keeping with ordinary Greek usage of his time. His claim in *EN* iii 1 that such actions are *hekousion* constitutes a challenge to and revision of the ordinary notions of *akousion* and *hekousion*. Surely Aristotle does not change his mind, between these different works, about what *'akousion'* and *'hekousion'* mean. He changes his mind about which actions are *hekousion* and *akousion*. But if we tailor our translation of *'hekousion'* and *'akousion'* to fit Aristotle's philosophical accounts of these notions, our translation will render invisible this change in Aristotle's view.

We should not object to the customary translations of *'hekousion'* and *'akousion'* simply because these translations do not render Aristotle's classifications of actions into uncontroversially true English sentences. A good translation will preserve the controversial status of Aristotle's own use of the terms. The customary translations are objectionable only if the English terms 'voluntary' and 'involuntary' do not adequately capture the ordinary non-philosophical meanings of the Greek terms *'hekousion'* and *'akousion.'* But in fact, 'voluntary' and 'involuntary' capture quite nicely most of the range of the Greek terms.

It is often pointed out that the distinction between *hekousion* and *akousion*, or between *hekōn* and *akōn*, in some cases corresponds to the distinction between intentional and unintentional (or witting and unwitting) actions, and in other cases to the distinction between willing and unwilling actions.[16] For example, Oedipus claims he killed his father and married his mother *akōn* on the grounds that he did not know what he was doing (Soph., *OC*, 964ff.). An unwary passerby who disturbs a wasps' nest does so *aekōn* (Homer, *Il.* 16.263–4).[17] And according to Athenian law, someone who kills another unintentionally commits *akousios phonos*.[18] In these cases inadvertent and unintended actions are classified as *akousion*. In other cases, unwilling or reluctant actions which are neither inadvertent nor unintended are classified as *akousion*. For example, the reluctant messenger delivers the bad news to Creon *akōn* (Soph., *Ant.* 274–7), and when Zeus threatens Inachus with the destruction of his entire progeny unless he expels Io, Inachus complies, but *akōn* (Aesch. *PV* 663–72).[19]

'Voluntary' and 'involuntary,' however, are also used to mark these two distinctions. For example, sometimes they mark the distinction between witting and unwitting behavior, as when inadvertent or unintended actions are classified as involuntary (e.g., involuntary manslaughter). But at other times they mark the distinction between willing and unwilling behavior. For example, a patient committed to an asylum against his will is confined involuntarily; someone who hands over her wallet at gunpoint is considered to have done so involuntarily; and a soldier conscripted into the army is not considered to have volunteered. Voluntary euthanasia is euthanasia that accords with the expressed wishes of the patient. Since 'voluntary' and 'involuntary' mark the same two distinctions as '*hekousion*' and '*akousion*', they are very good translations of the Greek terms.

To claim that '*hekousion*' and '*akousion*' are used to mark these two different distinctions (or, for that matter, to claim this of 'voluntary' and 'involuntary') is not to claim that the terms have two irreducibly different meanings – in the way, for example, that '*zō(i)on*' means both 'animal' and 'painting'.[20] To recognize that the use of these terms straddles these two distinctions is simply to recognize a certain vagueness in the notions of the *hekousion* and *akousion*. But vagueness is not the same as difference of meaning. For example, the term 'bald' is vague but has a single meaning. To claim that someone is bald is to claim that he has a hairless head, but what one counts as having a hairless head will vary from circumstance to circumstance.[21] Similarly, to claim that someone's action is *hekousion* rather than *akousion* is to claim that he performed the action 'of himself' – even though what one will count as acting 'of oneself' will vary from circumstance to circumstance, depending on the contrast one has in mind. The fullest degree of commitment one can have to an action one performs involves performing it wholeheartedly, without hesitation or regret. The slightest degree of commitment one can have to an action involves simply performing it in full awareness of what one is doing. Where, on this continuum of commitment, one draws the line between *hekousion* and *akousion* depends on the situation. For example, the Spartan commander who invites the besieged Plataeans to surrender the city to him *hekontes* (Thuc. 3.52.2–3) has in mind the contrast between the Plataeans giving up the city without a fight, and their being physically overpowered by a military assault on the city. He is not inviting them to endorse his capture of their city. Odysseus has roughly the same contrast in mind when he threatens to bring Philoctetes to Troy by means of physical force unless he comes *hekōn* (Soph., *Phil.* 984–5). By contrast, when Io claims her father expelled her from his house *akōn* (Aesch. *PV* 671), she has in mind the contrast between his doing so only under threat of dire consequences, and his doing so gladly and under no such threats.

Because of these different interpretations of the criteria for the *hekousion*, it is intelligible that the same person should describe the same action as both *hekousion* and *akousion*. For example, when Zeus describes his compliance with Hera's wish to destroy Troy as *hekōn aekonti ge thumō(i)* (Homer, *Il.* 4.43), he says he complies voluntarily but with an unwilling (i.e. involuntary) spirit. It is also intelligible that the vagueness in the criteria for the distinction should result in disputes over whether a particular action is *hekousion*, with different parties to the dispute resolving the vagueness differently. Such disputes occur, Aristotle tells us, over cases in which an agent is forced or compelled to perform an action.[22] These cases are generally agreed to be cases of *bia* (force) and *anankē* (necessity). But two significantly different types of cases count as forced or compelled. First of all, cases in which the agent is physically overpowered count as forced (*bia(i)*). For example, the guard overpowered by attackers counts as forced away from his post. But actions whose agent is not physically overpowered may also count as forced. For example, an agent (such as Philoctetes) who is threatened with such physical force if he does not cooperate of his own accord, or an agent (such as Inachus) who acts in order to avoid an extremely unattractive alternative is sometimes described as forced. Both kinds of action are properly labeled cases of compulsion (*anankē*), while the label 'force' (*bia*) is generally reserved for cases of the former sort (physical force), and for cases of the latter sort in which the compelling circumstance is the threat of physical force.[23]

Cases in which an agent is not physically overpowered, but still acts from fear of greater evils, are the sort whose voluntariness Aristotle tells us is disputed. Such actions are relevantly similar to physically forced actions, but also to unproblematic cases of *hekousion* action – action performed knowingly and of the agent's own volition. Depending on which contrast between *hekousion* and *akousion* a speaker has in mind, an agent who performs an action under threat of dire consequences could be described either as *akōn* (since he acts to avoid the threatened alternative) or as *hekōn* (since he is not physically overpowered).

Such disputes become important, and not mere verbal quibbles, when something significant depends on whether the actions are voluntary or involuntary. If agents are praiseworthy and blameworthy only for what they do voluntarily, then it matters whether such actions are voluntary. In most cases, the point of pleading compulsion (*ananke*) or force (*bia*) is to avoid blame or punishment for the action one cla ims one has been compelled or forced to do. Such disputes cannot be resolved simply by appealing to the ordinary criteria for *hekousion* and *akousion*, for the conflict arises from these criteria. To resolve the disputes, a decision must be made between the conflicting criteria yielded by ordinary usage. This decision, and consequent revision of ordinary usage, is the task of the philosopher rather than the translator, and it is the sort of task that Aristotle undertakes in his accounts of the *hekousion* and *akousion*. But in order to see the problems he proposes to solve, we must recognize the ordinary criteria for the application of the terms '*hekousion*' and '*akousion*,' since these criteria generate the problems in the first place. We must seek a translation that captures these ordinary criteria as closely as possible.

'Voluntary' is a suitable rendering of '*hekousion*' because the notion of voluntariness is similar to the pretheoretical notion of the *hekousion* in its imprecision and apparent intractability to non-revisionary philosophical analysis. The difficulty Aristotle encounters in providing an account of the *hekousion* is analogous to a difficulty one has in articulating an account of voluntariness. The difficulty is roughly this. Actions performed under coercion or duress are paradigmatic examples of cases in which agents do not act voluntarily. But when one attempts to present a positive characterization of the conditions in which one acts voluntarily, it is hard to avoid giving an account that entails that coerced actions are voluntary. For example, we are inclined to say that the person who hands over his wallet at gunpoint does not act voluntarily, for he acts against his will. But we are also inclined to say that the person who on a generous impulse sends a cheque to a charity acts voluntarily. It is attractive to say that in the latter case, the voluntariness of the action consists in the fact that the agent's action is caused by his desires, which reflect his assessment about what he has reason to do in the circumstances. But according to this account, our original example of allegedly non-voluntary action turns out to be voluntary, since surrendering the wallet in the face of the threat was an eminently reasonable thing to do, and this is why the agent does it.[24]

In our examination of Aristotle's different accounts of the *hekousion*, we shall see that he encounters precisely this problem with providing an account of the *hekousion*. For these reasons, 'voluntary' and 'involuntary' are very good translations of the terms *'hekousion'* and *'akousion'* respectively.

NOTES

1 *Eudemian Ethics* ii 6–11, *Nicomachean Ethics* iii 1–5, *Magna Moralia* i 9–17. I address the authenticity of the *MM* in section 4 of this chapter, and discuss the suitability of translating *'hekousion'* by 'voluntary' in section 5.

2 Praise and blame are for voluntary things: *EN* 1109b30–5; *MM* 1187a21; for what the agent is the cause of: *EE* 1223a10–13; *MM* 1187a25–8. Voluntary actions are caused by the agent: *EE* 1223a15–19.

3 The origin of action is in the agent: *EN* 1111a23, 1112b28; *EE* 1224b15. The origin is the agent: *EE* 1222b19–29; *EN* 1112b31–2, 1113b18, 1139b5; cf. *MM* 1188b6–14. The action is up to the agent: *EN* 1110a17–18, 1112a31, 1113b7–8; *EE* 1223a2–9, 1225a9–33, b8; *MM* 1187a5–b34 passim. The agent is in control of the action: *EE* 1223a5–7; *EN* 1113b32, 1114a3. Aristotle indicates that these conditions are mutually entailing: *EE* 1223a2–9, *EN* 1110a15–18, 1113b19–1114a6.

4 So Jean Roberts argues (Roberts 1989).

5 So Jean Roberts (Roberts 1989) and Terence Irwin (Irwin 1980b) formulate the objection, although Irwin goes on to argue that Aristotle is concerned with moral responsibility because he presupposes a stronger notion of voluntariness that animals and children do not satisfy.

6 See, for example, Austin 1956–7.

7 Loening 1903, p. 140, n. 30. Kenny 1979, p. 21.

8 See Sedley 1983 on possible earlier occurrences of the question. Pamela Huby suggests that Aristotle is simply unaware of the problem posed by determinism (Huby 1967; reply in Hardie 1968). David Furley does not allege nescience, but suggests that Aristotle has not adequately considered some aspects of the determinist thesis (Furley 1967, p. 194). For a detailed catalogue of interpretations of Aristotle's position on determinism, see Sorabji 1980, p. 3.

9 This general view is developed by Bernard Williams (Williams 1985 and Williams 1986). He diagnoses Aristotle's position in Williams 1985, pp. 38–40.

10 As, for example, Troels Engberg-Pedersen has suggested (Engberg-Pedersen 1983, pp. 240–1).

11 The view is defended by John Cooper in Cooper 1973.

12 Anthony Kenny argues that the differences between the Eudemian and the Nicomachean accounts support a later dating for the *EE* (Kenny 1979).

13 '*Hekousion*' and '*akousion*' modify actions, while '*hekōn*' and '*akōn*' modify agents and sometimes are more naturally rendered into English by adverbial rather than adjectival forms.

14 Kenny makes the point about non-actions (Kenny 1979, p. 28). David Charles and Terence Irwin make the point about coercion and duress (Charles 1984, pp. 61–2; Irwin 1985a, p. 431). Additional criticisms of the translation are offered by Ross 1923; Siegler 1968; Moline 1989; Urmson 1988; and Hardie 1980.

15 This is explicitly how David Charles evaluates the adequacy of alternative translations of *hekousion* (Charles 1984, pp. 61–2, 256–61). Jon Moline criticizes Charles' translation, but accepts the methodological assumption (Moline 1989).

16 For example, Kenny 1979, p. 27; Hardie 1980, pp. 152–3; Irwin 1985a, p. 431. In contrast, GailAnn Rickert rejects the view that the ordinary notions of *hekousion* and *akousion* straddle these two distinctions. She claims instead that the distinction corresponds fairly closely to the distinction between willing and unwilling behavior – that *hekōn* indicates the agent's attitude to the action is strongly positive while *akōn* indicates the agent's attitude to the action is strongly negative (Rickert 1989, p. 128). But this proposal appears to be at odds with certain features of ordinary usage. It does not seem to accommodate those cases in which an agent is said to do something *hekōn* while acting under extreme duress or as the result of a threat: for example when the Plataeans who have run out of food surrender *hekontes* to the Spartans who besiege their city (Thuc. 3.58.2–3), or when Darius demands that the palace guard stand aside *hekōn* or else be forced out of the way (Hdt. 3.72.5). Cf. Odysseus' claim that Philoctetes will be forced to go to Troy unless he comes along *hekōn* (Soph., *Phil.* 984–5), and the chorus' invitation to Cassandra to don the "yoke of necessity" *hekousa* (Aesch., *Ag.* 1071). Rickert, who discusses all these passages (pp. 41–51), argues that the apparent implausibility of ascribing strong positive attitudes to the *hekōn* agent in such cases stems from a suspicion that the agent really does not act *hekōn* (pp. 166–7; cf. 160–4). But surely a more straightforward explanation of these uses is that the agent is called *hekōn* because he or she performs the action of her own volition. The Spartan commander does not invite the Plataeans to endorse his capture of the city when he invites them to *paradounai tēn polin hekontes*; as Rickert herself points out (p. 47), he simply wants to avoid storming the city (Thuc. 3.52.2–3). The invitation to hand over the city *hekontes* is an invitation to the Plataeans to do so of their own accord rather than be physically forced to do so.

17 These passages are discussed in Maschke 1926, p. 55 and in Rickert 1989, pp. 63, 66. While I do not accept all of Rickert's conclusions, I have benefitted from her detailed classification and discussion of uses of '*hekōn*' and '*akōn*' in writers prior to Aristotle.

18 Examples are given in Plato, *Laws* ix. The criteria for *akousios phonos* are disputed. See MacDowell 1963, ch. 6 and Loomis 1972.

19 Discussed by Rickert (Rickert 1989, pp. 55, 133).

20 So Rickert interprets the claim (Rickert 1989, pp. 3–4). Part of her reluctance to accept that unwilling actions can count as *hekousion* is explained by her concern to resist the view that *hekōn* words simply mean the absence of certain external conditions (e.g. external constraint), and to insist that they essentially indicate something morally relevant about the agent's attitude toward the action (pp. 36, 168–9). Compare Alexander of Aphrodisias, *Ethical Problems*, 131. 17–22.

21 A man with very few hairs on his head would be considered bald when the relevant contrast is with someone with a full head of hair. But when the contrast is with someone with absolutely no hairs on his head, the same person would not count as bald. But bald still means the same thing in each case.

22 *EE* 1225a2–9; *EN* 1110a4–8.

23 For a detailed survey and discussion of the evidence, see Rickert 1989, pp. 7–19, 48–55.

24 I do not deny that it would be quite unidiomatic in English to describe such actions as voluntary. This is a case in which conventions of idiom are underdetermined by the stereotypical criteria associated with ordinary usage.

1

Moral Responsibility and Moral Character

◆

The first step toward recognizing that Aristotle's various discussions of voluntariness are concerned with moral responsibility is to acknowledge that their broader context concerns moral responsibility. In each of Aristotle's ethical treatises, the discussion of voluntariness occurs in the context of a general discussion of the virtues and vices of character. On an appropriately broad conception of moral responsibility, Aristotle's inquiry into the conditions common to virtue and vice of character is an inquiry into the conditions of moral responsibility. For it is an inquiry into the conditions of moral agency – the conditions in which agents are subject to the demands and evaluations of morality. Moral responsibility, broadly construed, is the property that distinguishes moral agents from non-moral agents. It makes the behavior of agents virtuous and vicious rather than simply welcome, unfortunate, or regrettable.

1 Moral Responsibility and Moral Agency

On a narrow but familiar construal, the topic of moral responsibility appears to be the concern of the civil and criminal law and, outside these domains, the preoccupation only of the ungenerous and the excessively censorious. It concerns the conditions in which an agent merits praise or blame, or reward or punishment, for an action. An agent merits blame or punishment for an action if and only if she is morally responsible for it, and similarly for merited reward and praise. On this narrow construal, moral responsibility is a relation between an agent and her action, and the topic of moral responsibility, while important, is of limited practical and moral significance.

On its broadest construal, however, the topic of moral responsibility concerns issues of central importance to our conception of morality and to our conception of ourselves as moral agents. Praise and blame are simply two of a wide range of interpersonal attitudes that are of central importance to our lives as moral agents. An agent who does not merit praise or blame for her actions is also an inappropriate recipient of such attitudes as gratitude, resentment, forgiveness, anger, friendship, and love.[1] These attitudes are based on certain expectations of interpersonal regard and they express our reactions to the fulfillment or non-fulfillment of those expectations. To be subject to such reactive attitudes is to be subject to these expectations, and to be subject to these expectations is to be subject to the demands of morality, and hence to be a moral agent. On this broader construal of moral responsibility, moral responsibility is the property of an agent that makes her subject to the demands of morality, and hence subject to moral evaluation in the light of these demands.

We generally suppose that only normal adult human beings satisfy this condition for moral responsibility. While we think non-human animals, small children, and the mentally defective have important claims upon our concern and attention, we do not consider these claims to be reciprocal. While we may praise and blame or reward and punish such agents with a view to controlling or altering their behavior, we do not do so because we think they merit such treatment. In the case of children, we may do so because we expect that they will become morally responsible agents, or because we think that they have already acquired some degree of responsibility. But to the extent that we do not think such agents are morally responsible, we take what Strawson calls the "objective attitude" toward them, and suspend the reactive interpersonal attitudes:

> The objective attitude may be emotionally toned in many ways, but not in all ways; it may include repulsion or fear, it may include pity or even love, though not all kinds of love. But it cannot include the range of reactive feelings and attitudes which belong to involvement or participation with others in inter-personal human relationships; it cannot include resentment, gratitude, forgiveness, anger, or the sort of love

which two adults can sometimes be said to feel reciprocally for each other. If your attitude toward someone is wholly objective, then though you may fight him, you cannot quarrel with him, and though you may talk to him, even negotiate with him, you cannot reason with him. You can at most pretend to quarrel, or to reason, with him.[2]

The features that make us morally responsible agents are central to our conception of what is most important and valuable in our lives. Even if we do not particularly care about whether we fulfill the demands of morality, and even if we do not particularly care about what other people think of our behavior, we think we will have lost something extremely valuable, perhaps even that we will have ceased to exist, if we lose the capacities that make us morally responsible – for example, if we suffer extreme brain damage or advanced senility.

The first task of a theory of moral responsibility is to identify the criteria that underlie our discriminations between agents who are morally responsible, and hence full-fledged members of the moral community, and those who are not. That is, it seeks to explain why we hold normal human adults morally responsible for their actions and make moral claims upon them, but do not make such claims at all upon non-human animals, and do so only to a diminished degree in the case of children. The second task of such a theory is to identify the criteria that explain the discriminations that we make, within the class of actions performed by agents who satisfy these conditions for moral responsibility, between those actions for which the agent is morally responsible and those actions for which she is not. The next chapter will show that Aristotle discusses voluntariness in order to address this second task of a theory of moral responsibility. The present chapter seeks to show that Aristotle's account of virtue and vice of character accomplishes the first task of such a theory: that it contains an account of the features that subject an agent to the demands and evaluations of morality.

2 Virtue and Vice of Character

In all three of the ethical treatises, Aristotle distinguishes two different types of human excellence or virtue (*aretē*): ethical virtue or virtue of character (*ēthikē aretē*) and virtue of intellect (*dianoētikē aretē*):

We call some virtues intellectual and some ethical (*ēthikas*). Wisdom and understanding and intelligence are intellectual virtues, generosity and temperance ethical virtues. For when we speak of someone's character (*peri tou ēthous*) we do not say that he is wise or understanding but rather that he is calm or temperate. (*EN* 1103a3–8; cf. *EE* 1220a8–10; *MM* 1185b3–12)

The virtues and vices of character include, for example, justice and injustice, courage and cowardice, temperance and intemperance, and generosity and meanness. Agents are virtuous or vicious[3] depending on whether they are disposed to act and be motivated properly (*hōs dei*) in situations in which a particular sort of value, the *kalon* (noble or admirable), and its opposite, the *aischron* (base or shameful) are at stake.[4] Particular virtues and vices are distinguished according to the range of activity in which these values are at stake. For example, one is cowardly or courageous depending on how one is disposed to act in situations in which a noble death (*kalon thanaton*) is at stake (*EN* 1115a28–31, 1116a11–12); and one is temperate or intemperate depending on whether one has base appetites (*phaulai epithumiai*, 1178b15–16; cf. 1118a23–b8).

The *kalon* is an impersonal standard of value. It is distinguished from other goods in being praiseworthy (*EE* 1248b18–20), and is typically contrasted with self-interest or expediency (*EN* 1162b34–6; *Rhet.* 1389a32–5, b36–7; cf. *EN* 1169a6). Its pursuit requires one to take proper account of the good of others – hence the prohibition on "overreaching" (*pleonektein*) essential to justice, of which all the individual virtues and vices of character are, Aristotle tells us, specific instances.[5] The impersonality of the standard of value appealed to in evaluating someone's behavior as *kalon* or *aischron*, together with its relation to the expectation of others to be treated justly, give us reason to conclude that to attribute to someone a virtue or vice of character is to subject him to a specifically moral assessment. It is to assess how well he lives up to the demands and expectations of morality. If we can identify the conditions that Aristotle thinks are common to both virtue and vice of character (*ēthos*), we will understand the conditions that, in his view, subject an agent to these demands.[6]

On Aristotle's view, the properties essential to the virtues and vices of character are properties whose possession distinguishes human agents both from the other animals and from the gods:

> Just as there is neither virtue nor vice of a beast, so too there is neither virtue nor vice of a god. Rather, the condition of the one is more

honourable than virtue, while that of the other is of a different kind from vice. (*EN* 1145a25–7)

The gods do not have the virtues and vices of character because they do not engage in the sorts of activities that these virtues and vices concern:

> We think that the gods are most blessed and happy, but what sorts of actions (*praxeis*) do we properly attribute to them? Just actions? But will they not seem ridiculous engaging in business and returning deposits and such things? What about courageous actions – withstanding fearful things and undergoing dangers because it is noble? Or shall we attribute to them generous actions? But to whom will they give, and surely it is absurd to suppose that they have money or anything of the sort! And concerning what could they be temperate? Is it not vulgar to praise them for not having base appetites? Upon consideration, it appears that all things concerned with actions (*ta peri tas praxeis*) are trifling and unworthy of the gods. (*EN* 1178b8–18)

Aristotle explains here that the gods fail to be virtuous or vicious because they have nothing to do with "things concerned with actions" (*ta peri tas praxeis*, b17). These "things" include both actions one might perform (risking danger, returning a deposit, making a gift) and feelings in the light of which one might act (e.g. appetites). Like the virtuous person, the gods do not perform base actions or have base appetites, but unlike the virtuous person, the gods do not have any appetites or engage in any actions at all. Their whole activity is theoretical contemplation (*EN* 1178b18–22).

The capacity for "passion" (*pathos*) is the faculty possessed by humans whose lack renders the gods incapable of the range of activities in the domain of virtue and vice of character (*Pol.* 1286a17–20, 1287a28–30). Socrates failed to define virtue of character adequately, Aristotle complains, because he defined it purely in intellectual terms, leaving out "passion and character" (*pathos kai ēthos*, *MM* 1182a22–3). Aristotle's illustrative lists of the "passions" (*pathē*) show that he includes in this general category a wide range of occurrent psychological states – emotions such as anger and envy, feelings such as friendliness and enmity, and desires such as appetite.[7] In each of the three ethical works, he defines virtue or vice of character as a state or disposition (*hexis*) of the aspect of the soul to which these passions belong:[8]

> Let us now seek what virtue is. Since there are three sorts of things that occur in the soul – passions, capacities, and states – virtue must be one

of them. I call passions appetite, anger, fear, confidence, envy, delight, friendliness, hatred, yearning, emulation, pity and in general what pleasure or pain accompanies. Capacities are those things according to which we are such as to undergo these – for example, according to which we are able to be angry or pained or to pity. States (*hexeis*), on the other hand, are those things according to which we are well or badly disposed towards the passions; for example, towards being angry, if we are disposed to be angry violently or slackly, we are badly disposed, but if we are disposed in the intermediate way (*mesōs*), we are well disposed. And similarly too for the others. (*EN* 1105b19–28; cf. *MM* 1186a9–22; *EE* 1220b10–20)

Aristotle here claims that the virtues and vices of character are the sorts of state or disposition (*hexis*) that determine when and at what objects one's capacities for the passions will be exercised. For example, the virtue or vice concerning anger determines what we get angry at, and how strongly (1105b25–8). Aristotle tells us that these dispositions are acquired by exercising one's capacities for the passions in certain ways, and that, once acquired, they are in turn responsible for the fact that these capacities are exercised in these ways.[9] For example, if one repeatedly satisfies one's appetites and does not resist any of them, they grow larger, stronger, and harder to resist (*EN* 1119b3–15). By becoming used to standing one's ground in certain initially frightening situations, one can cease to feel fear at such situations and find it easier to stand one's ground (1104a35–b3). Aristotle's examples of the sorts of activities from which the various virtues and vices of character are acquired and his detailed discussion of the various activities typical of these states of the soul show that he considers the exercise of one's capacities for the passions to include not only the experience of the emotions, feelings, and desires themselves, but also the actions one performs in the light of or as a result of these feelings.[10] That is, he considers the exercise of the capacities for passion to include all the activities he denies of the gods when he explains why they do not have virtues and vices of character (*EN* 1178b10–18). Henceforth, I shall refer to these activities as "feeling and doing".

While the fact that virtues and vices are dispositions of our capacities for feeling and doing explains why the gods are not virtuous or vicious, it does not explain why Aristotle excludes animals from virtue and vice (1145a25–6). For he claims that the capacity for passion is common both to human beings and non-human animals (*Pol.* 1287a30).[11] The latter creatures fail another of his requirements for virtue and vice. They lack reason, the capacity that human beings share with the divine:

We do not call beasts either temperate or intemperate, except metaphorically when one kind of animal differs from another in violence and wantonness and in being ravenous. For they do not have decision (*prohairesis*) or reasoning (*logismos*), but rather are outside of ⟨this⟩ nature just like the mad among human beings. (*EN* 1149b31–1150a1; cf. 1117a4–5)

The reason Aristotle gives here for excluding non-human animals and the insane from virtue and vice of character is also a reason for him to exclude children from these categories of moral evaluation. For, on his view, children do not yet possess the capacity of reason:

In a human being there is both reason and desire – that is, at a certain age, the one at which we attribute action (*praxis*). For we do not say that a child acts, nor that a beast does, but only that someone who is actually acting due to reasoning does so. (*EE* 1224a27–30; cf. 1222b19)

Because children and non-human animals lack reason, they do not "act" (*prattein*) in the strict sense in which only agents acting according to reason (*ēdē dia logismon prattonta* a30) can act.[12] The specific sort of reasoning whose lack makes both children and non-human animals incapable of "action" (*praxis*) is decision (*prohairesis*) (*Ph.* 197b4–8). Since Aristotle denies that non-human animals can have virtues and vices of character because he thinks they lack decision (*EN* 1149b31–5, quoted above), he is committed to saying the same about children.

Although Aristotle never, in so many words, denies that children are virtuous or vicious, this is clearly his view. For example, when arguing that none of the so-called "natural virtues" is a genuine (*kuria*) virtue, he appeals to the fact that the natural virtues can belong "even to children and beasts" (1144b8–9), implying that children and animals do not have genuine virtues. And in *EN* i 9, he indicates that a child's lack of reason makes him incapable of virtuous (and presumably also of vicious) activity:

Political science takes great care to make citizens of a certain sort, that is to make them good and productive of noble actions (*praktikous tōn kalōn*). So we deny, quite reasonably, that an ox or a horse or any other of the animals is happy. For none of them is able to participate in activity of this sort. For the same reason, neither is a child happy, for due to his age he is not yet such as to perform such actions (*praktikos tōn toioutōn*). Those who do call children happy are calling them blessed on the basis of expectation. (*EN* 1099b30–1100a4)

The first sentence of this passage indicates that virtuous activity is the performance of noble actions, for the good (*agathoi*) are such as to perform noble actions (*praktikous tōn kalōn*) (cf. *EN* 1129a8, 1134a2). The third sentence indicates that neither animals nor children can perform noble actions (*praktikos tōn toioutōn*). This is to deny that children or animals are capable of virtuous activity.[13] Aristotle here indicates that children are excluded from virtue and vice of character for the same reason that animals are excluded (*dia tautēn de tēn aitian oude pais*, 1100a1–2). They do not yet have *prohairesis*, the ability to act according to reason.

In allowing that children and non-human animals possess the so-called "natural" virtues and vices, Aristotle allows that these agents can have dispositions (*hexeis*) that govern the exercise of their capacities for feeling and doing (*EN* 1144b4–9; *EE* 1234a23–34; cf. *EN* 1117a4–5).[14] He denies that these dispositions are genuine virtues and vices of character on the grounds that their possessors lack decision (*prohairesis*) (*EE* 1234a24–6). He articulates the requirement that a genuinely virtuous or vicious agent must have decision by claiming that a genuine virtue or vice of character is a *hexis prohairetikē* – a state (*hexis*) involving decision (*prohairesis*) in some way (*EN* 1106b36, 1139a22; *EE* 1227b8, 1230a27). In order to understand the role he thinks decision must play in a genuine virtue or vice of character, we need to understand Aristotle's account of decision, and the distinction he draws between it and another kind of rational desire, wish (*boulēsis*).

3   Rationality and Morality

In contexts where he is not discussing his specific conception of virtue and vice of character, Aristotle generally follows Plato in recognizing a single kind of rational desire. His name for this desire is "wish" (*boulēsis*). When articulating his own account of virtue and vice of character, however, he distinguishes wish from decision (*prohairesis*) and insists that decision is the desire most important to virtue and vice of character.[15] Let us first examine the feature that, on Aristotle's view, makes both wish and decision rational desires, and then examine his distinction between them.

Following Plato, Aristotle takes rational desires to be desires directed at the good (*to agathon*). He makes this claim about both wish and decision.[16] The good in question is happiness (*eudaimonia*), the greatest good for a human being. Happiness is the ultimate object of pursuit, for it includes all the goods worth pursuing for their own sake (*EN* 1097b14–21). It is the goal of rational activity (*EE* 1214b6–11; *EN* 1094a18–22). Our rational actions are the actions that we perform because we think they will contribute to our happiness, and our rational desires are for objects we want because we think they will contribute to our happiness. We may be mistaken about what our happiness consists in, but insofar as we act on rational desires, we pursue what we think will make us happy (*EN* 1113a15–26).

According to this conception of rational desire, the goal of any rational desire is happiness. Aristotle generally distinguishes wish (*boulēsis*) from decision (*prohairesis*) by saying that wish is more of the goal, while decision is of the things that promote that goal (*ta pros to telos*) (*EE* 1226b7–17; *EN* 1111b26–9; *MM* 1189a7–11). A decision is a desire arrived at by reasoning about how to execute a wish:

> Decision (*prohairesis*) is deliberative desire for something that is up to us. Having arrived at a judgment on the basis of deliberation, we desire according to wish (*kata tēn boulēsin*). (*EN* 1113a10–12)[17]

A decision is therefore a desire to execute in one's actions the conception of happiness expressed in one's wishes.[18] Wish also differs from decision in that it need not be for something one can bring about by one's own actions. For example, one might wish to be immortal, or wish that the government of a distant people be of a certain sort (*MM* 1189a6–7; *EE* 1225b32–4; *EN* 1111b22–4). But even if one wishes for something that one can bring about through one's own actions – for example, if one wishes to be healthy (*EN* 1111b27) – such a wish need not move one to act. One might not know how to execute that wish. And even if one does know how to execute it, one might prefer to do something else. For example, a wish may simply take the form "I ought to do such and such" (*EE* 1226a4–7) – a resolution which need not result in any effective decision to do such and such. As Aristotle says, "Everyone or almost everyone wishes (*boulesthai*) for noble things, but decides upon (*prohaireisthai*) beneficial things" (*EN* 1162b34–6). A wish may simply be a favourable evaluative attitude toward an opportunity that has no actual effect on one's inclinations to act. A decision, by contrast, is a determinate intention to act that actually moves the agent to act. It is not always successful, for it can be impeded by an opposing desire, as in the case of continence or incontinence. However, it always yields some impulse (*hormē*) toward action. This is the impulse that non-rational desire opposes in the case of incontinence, and that overcomes non-rational desire in cases of continence (*EN* 1102b21; *EE* 1224a31–3). It is an "origin of action" (*archē praxeōs*) (*EN* 1139a31).

In insisting that a virtuous or vicious disposition must involve decision, and not simply wish, Aristotle makes it clear that such a disposition must not simply dispose one to have desires based on a conception of happiness. It must dispose one to execute those desires in one's actions. Aristotle thinks that the distinctive feature of moral agency is not simply the possession of a conception of happiness, or even the ability to form desires based on a conception of happiness, but rather the disposition to act in accordance with that conception. In calling a virtue or vice of character a *hexis prohairetikē*, Aristotle means that it is a disposition in which one's capacities for feeling and doing are disposed to be exercised in a way that expresses one's conception of happiness. The distinctive feature of the moral agent, on Aristotle's view, is that he acts for the sake of his happiness.

The primacy Aristotle accords to the pursuit of happiness in the virtuous person's motivation often strikes modern readers as exceedingly strange, or even antithetical to the moral enterprise. It is often objected that in claiming that a rational person acts for the sake of his own happiness, Aristotle attributes to him a motivation, pursuit of self-interest, that is fundamentally at odds with a truly moral motivation.[19] According to this objection, the essentially moral motivation is to perform the virtuous action for its own sake, regardless of whether it contributes to or detracts from one's interest.

As a preliminary response to this objection, it is worth noting that Aristotle does not claim that the virtuous person's orientation toward happiness is what makes his motivation moral. For, in his view, it is a necessary condition for a disposition's being vicious no less than virtuous that it be a *hexis prohairetikē* (cf. *EN* 1117a4–5, 1149b31–1150a1) – i.e., that it express the agent's conception of happiness. The orientation toward happiness characteristic of rational activity makes both the virtuous and the vicious person's motivation and activity morally significant. Activity can be neither moral nor immoral, in Aristotle's view, unless it proceeds from a disposition that expresses the agent's conception of happiness. An agent cannot be classified as just or unjust, temperate or intemperate, cowardly or courageous, unless he has such a disposition. In Aristotle's view, the pursuit of happiness is distinctive not of morality, but of moral responsibility. It is the feature that subjects an agent to the demands and evaluations of morality.

Of course, even if one recognizes that the pursuit of happiness is common to both the vicious and the virtuous person's motivation, one might still object that such an orientation is incompatible with a genuinely virtuous motivation. For the truly virtuous person, it is objected, does not perform the virtuous action as an instrumental means to some further end, such as happiness, but rather takes it to be an end in itself. This criticism, however, construes much more narrowly than Aristotle does the scope of activity in pursuit of happiness. Aristotle thinks one's conception of happiness is a conception of the set of goods one deems worth pursuing for their own sake (*EN* 1097b14–21; cf. *EE* 1215b15–1216a27), and he specifically includes virtuous activity among such goods (*EN* 1097a30–b5). On his view, to claim that the virtuous person performs the virtuous action for the sake of happiness is not to claim that the virtuous action is merely an instrumental and contingent means to some independently specifiable activity or condition.[20] Rather, it is to claim that the virtuous person considers virtuous activity to be a constituent of his happiness,[21] which is to say (as Aristotle himself claims – *EN* 1105a32) that he performs the virtuous activity for its own sake.

While Aristotle insists that the happiness one pursues is good for oneself, he does not think this good coincides with one's narrow self-interest. His account of the virtue of courage provides a vivid illustration of this. He insists that the courageous person acts on decision (*prohairesis*, *EN* 1117a5), which is to say that he does what he thinks promotes his happiness. Yet, he also claims that the courageous thing to do in certain circumstances is to submit to death when it is noble (*kalon*) to do so and shameful (*aischron*) not to (1115a28–35). The pursuit of his own happiness actually requires the virtuous agent to violate his own self-interest, narrowly construed. The goods that are part of my self-interest narrowly defined (health, wealth, honour, for example) are goods that, on Aristotle's account of happiness, are less important than virtue and hence not to be pursued when they conflict with virtue. The person who has a correct conception of happiness will sacrifice his own narrow self-interest when this conflicts with the demands of virtue. Aristotle's conception of rational agency, therefore, does not attribute to the rational agent a fundamentally amoral motivation. While a person who pursues his own happiness may very well think virtue is not worth pursuing for its own sake, the person who chooses the virtuous action for its own sake is thereby acting for the sake of happiness.

Doesn't make distinction between immediate self interest of dying &
the post death conception of his eudaimonia (pur/distal).

4 The Scope of Moral Agency

What makes an agent a fit subject of moral evaluation and expectation is a feature that, in Aristotle's view, makes a distinctively human life desirable and worth living. For activity according to reason, which he identifies as essential to virtue and vice of character, is distinctively human. If carried out properly and successfully, it yields happiness (*EN* 1098a3–18), the goal we all value and aim at in our actions (1094a1–2, 1095a14–20). So, on Aristotle's view, agents who are incapable of being virtuous or vicious are also incapable of happiness. The feature that Aristotle thinks makes us morally responsible agents is intimately connected with the "attributes that are the subject of our most humane concern with ourselves and the source of what we regard as most important . . . in our lives".[22]

It is important to recognize at this point the wide range of agents whom Aristotle thinks achieve the degree of rational activity distinctive of moral agency. He attributes to the person who has achieved full and complete virtue of character the virtue of practical wisdom (*phronēsis*). Such a person acts "according to right reason" (*kata ton orthon logon, EN* 1138b25). In describing the activity of such a person, Aristotle says:

> First of all he knows what he is doing. Second he decides to do it, and decides to do it for its own sake. And third, he acts from a stable and unchangeable disposition. (*bebaiōs kai ametakinētōs echōn*) (*EN* 1105a31–3)

The fully virtuous person, who has a correct conception of happiness, has correctly identified what he should do and the reasons for which he should do it. In both these ways, the fully virtuous person's reason is "correct". Aristotle's third point here indicates that this correct conception of happiness and the disposition to execute it correctly must also be firmly, indeed unshakably, embedded in the dispositions of the fully virtuous agent. These conditions for full virtue of character are, Aristotle admits, extremely difficult to fulfill and rarely achieved; yet, he insists that agents whose states fall short of this condition (and its mirror opposite, perfect vice) are still praiseworthy and blameworthy for what they do (*EN* 1109a30–b26; cf. 1110b28–32).[23]

Agents who fall short of perfect virtue will do so for a variety of reasons. For example, their conception of happiness may be mistaken (as in the case of those who pursue pleasure or material goods as happiness: *EN* 1095b16–17, 1113b1–2, 1168b15–19) or, if not mistaken, may still not be fixed firmly enough in their dispositions for feeling and doing. Nonetheless, since Aristotle thinks the less than fully virtuous agent is subject to moral assessment, he must think that these agents count as acting "according to reason" (*kata logon*). He is committed to claiming that they act from some conception of happiness, which is fixed firmly enough in their dispositions for feeling and doing to make that disposition count as a *hexis prohairetikē*. Such agents include those whose conception of happiness is merely implicit in the life they lead (*EN* 1095b14–17), and might even be disavowed if it were articulated for them explicitly (*EN* 1153b25–32). It might even vary from time to time and from circumstance to circumstance (1095a22–5, 1113a21–2). However vaguely and incompletely Aristotle has specified the minimal conditions for rationality satisfied by these agents,[24] these minimal conditions, rather than the maximal conditions satisfied by the perfectly virtuous person, subject agents to moral evaluation and expectation. I will refer to all dispositions that satisfy these minimal conditions for rationality as "states of moral character".

Aristotle sometimes restricts the terms 'virtue' (*aretē*) and 'vice' (*kakia*) to apply only to states of moral character that are perfectly fixed and unchangeable dispositions, as, for example, when he distinguishes vice from incontinence (*akrasia*) (*EN* 1150b32) and virtue from continence (1128b33–4). However, even in these contexts, he allows that incontinence is a vice in some sense of the term (*pē(i) isōs*, 1151a6). And in other contexts, he uses 'virtue' and 'vice' with wider scope, in which he explicitly includes continence and incontinence (*EE* 1223a37, b12; cf. *MM* 1188a15).[25] I shall henceforth follow the wider scope Aristotle assigns to 'virtue' and 'vice' and will use these terms to refer to all the dispositions that satisfy the conditions for being states of moral character.

Although Aristotle allows that incontinence and continence are especially unstable dispositions – one tending to develop into full vice, the other into full virtue – the fact that he is nonetheless prepared to call them virtues and vices indicates that he does not require immutability or irreversibility of states of moral character. A good index of the degree of stability and fixity Aristotle thinks sufficient for a state of moral character is his frequent claim that the virtues and vices of character are states (*hexeis*) of the soul in the way health and sickness or strength and weakness are states of the body.[26] While it is an enduring rather than a transitory condition, a state of character (like a state of health) is still susceptible to being altered by the sorts of activities in which the person engages. While Aristotle thinks that some states of moral character, just like some states of the body, are incurable (*EN* 1114a12–21, 1165b18), he does not think that all states of moral character need be.

5 Conclusions about Moral Agency and Moral Character

Aristotle thinks that the behavior of all animals, including human beings, is determined by a set of dispositions (*hexeis*) that collectively determine how the animal's capacities for feeling and doing will be exercised on any given occasion. The distinctive feature of the dispositions of a morally responsible agent is that they dispose the agent to act and react in a way that expresses her conception of happiness. I have been referring to each such disposition of a morally responsible agent as a "state of moral character". Courage, temperance and incontinence are examples of such states of moral character. In the following chapters, it will be useful to refer to the set of such dispositions, which collectively determine the moral agent's behavior, as her "moral character". We may think of the agent's moral character as the set of her virtues and vices of character – provided that we include among the virtues and vices the states that fall short of perfect virtue and vice.

It is sometimes remarked that virtues and vices do not exhaust a person's character, that to describe someone in terms of his virtues and vices is not to describe his individuality, but rather to categorize him very roughly as a "type" rather than an individual. For example, W. F. R. Hardie writes that:

> [T]he effective constituents of a personality, the moving forces, are not virtues and vices, but sentiments such as attachment to family or friends or to a society, and interests in, for example, a science or music or a game. It is not possible to describe a personality in terms of virtuous and vicious qualities and the lack of such qualities. This is a fact familiar to the writers of testimonials. To say of a man that he has courage and industry and sobriety is not to say anything very significant about him . . .
>
> If the "character" of a man is that in him which will enable us to understand his conduct, it should mean primarily a "system of sentiments" and interests not a system or collection of virtues and vices. [footnote omitted] We know that this is what matters about ourselves.[27]

We must distinguish, however, between the moral character a person has and the sorts of labels we have at our disposal to describe that character. An agent's moral character will be the set of dispositions that together determine the full range of an agent's sentiments and interests. The range of intentional objects the "passions" (*pathē*) can take reflects the whole range of possible human interest and attachment.[28] On Aristotle's account, a moral character is a fully determinate way in which an agent is disposed to feel interested, involved, or inclined to act in the complete range of situations in which he will find himself. To say that a person is virtuous or vicious is to classify his disposition according to whether it disposes him well or ill, and to identify the particular virtue or vice as, for example, temperance or intemperance is to indicate roughly the range of activity in which the agent's disposition falls short of or achieves the demands of right conduct. Thus the various labels we have for describing a moral character may fail to discriminate between the idiosyncratic ways in which different agents fail to hit the mean, ways which Aristotle himself acknowledges to be infinitely varied (1106b28–34). But this does not mean that the particular moral character that one labels intemperate or unjust or generous is not fully determinate and individual, and sufficient to determine the full range of the agent's behavior.

NOTES

1   I here follow the account in P. F. Strawson's classic paper (Strawson 1962).

2   Strawson 1962, p. 66.

3   Henceforth, unless indicated otherwise, I will be using 'virtue' and 'vice' to refer to the ethical and not the intellectual virtues, and similarly with the adjectives 'virtuous' and 'vicious'.

4   The virtuous person acts and reacts *hōs dei*, and the vicious person fails to do so: *EN* 1106b21–3, 1107a2–6; *EE* 1221a18–19, 1222a6–17; *MM* 1186a18–19. The virtuous person pursues the *kalon* and eschews the *aischron*: *EN* 1099a21–3, 1115b11–13, 1116a10–12, 27–9, 1117b9, 1121a1–2; *EE* 1229a4, 1229a8–9, 1230a26–33, 1248b19–23, 36–7; cf. *EN* 1179b7–16.

5   The *kalon* and the good of others: *Rhet.* 1366b4–7. Justice and the prohibition on *pleonektein*: Plato, *Gorgias* 483b–c. All of virtue and vice as instances of general justice: *EN* 1129b11–30. For a detailed discussion of the Aristotelian evidence, and an extended defence of the claim that the virtues and vices of character are moral qualities, see Irwin 1985b. For a detailed criticism of the view that Greek ethics in general does not concern the same subject matter as modern moral theory, see Annas 1992.

6 Bernard Williams claims that in addition to its orientation to an impersonal standard of conduct that takes the good of others into account, "morality" (as distinguished from what he proposes to label "ethics") is characteristically preoccupied with praise and blame of agents – attitudes which, he claims, presuppose that morally relevant alternatives are up to agents in a way that is incompatible with facts about the way we acquire our states of character. He claims that these distinctive features of "morality" are lacking from Aristotle's conception of virtue and vice of character (Williams 1985; and Williams 1986).

Aristotle, however, emphasizes that the virtues and vices of character are praiseworthy and blameworthy states of agents (*EN* 1106b26–7, 1108a14–16, 1109a24–30, b24, 1126b5–7; *EE* 1228b30–1, 1233b17; *MM* 1185b5–8, 1186a30–1, 1187a3–4); indeed, virtue and the virtuous person are his primary examples of praiseworthy things (*epaineta*) (*EN* 1101b14–16, 31–2; *EE* 1219b8). And he insists that an agent is praiseworthy and blameworthy only if his actions are up to him (*eph' hautō(i)*) to do and not to do (*EE* 1223a4–16; cf. *EN* 1109b30–1, 1113b3–14). One of the burdens of my argument will be to establish, in chapters 2 and 6, that this causal precondition of praiseworthiness is not inconsistent with the facts about how agents acquire their ethical dispositions, but that it is nonetheless strong enough to justify the discriminations we make between agents who are and agents who are not subject to the demands of morality. The attitudes characteristic of morality include not only praise and blame, but also the rest of the reactive attitudes, which Williams relegates to the category of the so-called ethical. All of these attitudes presuppose that the recipient agent is a fit subject of the demands of the impersonal standard of conduct central to Aristotle's notion of virtue and vice of character. To identify the features that subject agents to these demands is to accomplish what I have called the first task of a theory of moral responsibility. And I propose that Aristotle's conception of the features distinctive of the virtues and vices of character accomplishes such a task.

7 *EN* 1105b21–3; *EE* 1220b12–14; *MM* 1186a12–14; *Rhet.* 1378a19–22, 1388b32–3; cf. 1356a14–16. These lists of the *pathē* include but are not restricted to the two Platonic species of non-rational desire: appetite (*epithumia*) and spirit (*thumos*). At *Top.* 126a3–13 Aristotle appears to suggest that all the *pathē* can be classified into the Platonic categories of desire, but he nowhere carries out this project in detail.

8 He sometimes calls virtue or vice a condition (*diathesis*) of this aspect of the soul (e.g. *EE* 1218b38, 1220a29) but his usual label for it is "*hexis*" (*MM* 1185a38, 1186a28–32; *EN* 1103a9, b22, 23, 1104b4, 1106a10–12; *EE* 1218b38, 1222a6, b5, 12).

9 *EE* 1220a22–4, a39–b6; *MM* 1185b13–32, b38–1186a8; *EN* 1103b14–25, 1104a11–b3, b18–21.

10   This is why the *EN* emphasizes that virtue concerns both feeling and
     actions (1104b13–14, 1106b16–17, 23–7, 1107a4–5, 1109a22–4, b30).
     In the *EE*, by contrast, with the exception of 1220a31, which refers to
     erga and *pathē*, virtue of character is explicitly described only as being *peri
     pathē*. But the list at *EE* 1221a13–b9 includes both *pathē* and *praxeis*, even
     though the general heading is given as *pathos*; 1222a11 indicates that
     virtue concerns pleasures and pains and pleasant and painful things, the
     latter presumably being actions, the former feelings (cf. *EN* 1104b13–16).
     The *MM*, like the *EE*, mentions only *pathē* in its theoretical remarks,
     concluding that virtue is a mean of *pathē* (1186b33–4). However, the
     examples in all cases indicate that both feelings and actions are involved
     in the activity. Indeed the *MM* labels the action of adultery as a *pathos*.

11   The characteristic activity of animals is to live or act "according to feeling"
     (*kata pathos*) or "by desire" (*tē(i) orexei*) (*EN* 1116b31–1117a1; *EE*
     1224a26–7, 1230a23–5; *Pol.* 1287a30–2).

12   In *EN* vi 2, a book common to the *EE* and the *EN*, Aristotle denies *praxis*
     to non-human animals (1139a19–20). The context suggests that he denies
     them *praxis* because they lack *prohairesis*, for "*prohairesis* is the origin of
     praxis" (1139a31). This would also exclude children from *praxis*. Aristotle
     regularly attributes to immature human beings the distinctively animal
     mode of activity, living by desire or feeling (*EN* 1095a4–8, 1128b15–18,
     1156a31–3).

13   Aristotle goes on to mention a second reason why children are not happy:
     happiness is the property of a whole life (*EN* 1100a5–9). This is the reason
     he cites in *EE* ii 1, 1219b5–8. However, in the passage we are discussing
     from *EN* i 9, the requirement of a complete life (*biou teleiou*) is the second
     reason given for excluding children from happiness. The first reason,
     expounded in the passage quoted, is their lack of complete virtue (*aretēs
     teleias*).

14   *EE* 1234a26–7 implies that these dispositions are not states (*hexeis*) but
     feelings (*pathē*). The parallel passage in the *EN*, 1128b10–11, claims this
     explicitly. But *EN* 1144b8–9 explicitly allows that they are states. This
     wavering in Aristotle's description of these conditions simply reflects, I
     think, the fact that in the case of many of the "feelings" (*pathē*), the
     distinction between disposition and feeling can be drawn in different
     places. For example, shame (the feeling in question in *EN* 1128b10ff.) is
     a feeling of pain at the thought of being ill-thought of, but it is also a
     disposition to feel such pain at such intentional objects (cf. 1128b26–9).
     Similarly also for the examples in *EE* iii 7: *nemesis*, spite, etc.

15   Aristotle identifies a single rational desire: *DA* 414b2; *Top.* 126a8–13;
     EN 1111a24–b2, b11–18; *EE* 1223a26–7, 1223b25–7, 1225b25; *MM*
     1187b36–7; *Pol.* 1334b22–5; *Rhet.* 1369a1–4; *boulēsis* as the rational
     desire: *Top.* 126a13; *DA* 432b5, 433a23–5; *Rhet.* 1369a1–3; *prohairesis* as
     a rational desire: *MM* 1189a3–4; *prohairesis* as most important for virtue

and vice of character: *EN* 1105a31–3, 1117a5, 1135b25; *EE* 1228a2–3; but cf. *MM* 1187b33.

16   Plato: rational desire aims at the good: *Republic* 441c; *Laws* 864a–b. Aristotle: wish aims at the good: *Top.* 146b5–6; *EN* 1113a24; *Rhet.* 1369a2–4, b7–9; at the apparent good: *Top.* 146b36–147a5; *EN* 1113a15–24; *Rhet.* 1369b18–20. Decision aims at the good: *EN* 1094a1–2, 1112a7–8; *MM* 1189a25–6.

17   In 1113a12, instead of Bywater's *bouleusin*, I read *boulēsin* – a reading in one MS and an alternative reading according to Aspasius. If we have reason to prefer *bouleusin*, then this passage does not support the claim that *prohairesis* must derive from a *boulēsis*. However, 1113b3–5, which explicitly discusses actions done according to *prohairesis*, indicates that the goal is the object of wish (*boulētou men tou telous*, b3). Furthermore, the incontinent, who acts on his *epithumia* or *thumos*, may deliberate about how to satisfy these non-rational desires (*EN* 1142b18–20), but the resulting desire is not a *prohairesis* but rather is contrary to the agent's *prohairesis* (*EN* 1148a13–17). See Anscombe 1965, p. 143. Positive evidence that *boulēsis* is the desire setting the *telos* of a genuine *prohairesis* comes from the discussion of *prohairesis* in *EN* vi 2, 1139a31–b5, where Aristotle states that the goal of *prohairesis* is *eupraxia* (1139b3), which is the same thing as *eudaimonia* or happiness, the goal of *boulēsis*.

18   Following Anscombe 1965, contra Charles 1984.

19   Considerations such as these lead A. W. H. Adkins to deny that the subject matter of Greek ethics is anything we would recognize as morality (Adkins 1960, p. 253). H. A. Prichard expresses this criticism of Aristotle especially forcefully (Prichard 1935). See J. L. Austin's discussion of Prichard in Austin 1967.

20   For example, on Prichard's view, "a state, or rather a feeling, of happiness" (Prichard 1935, p. 52).

21   Following Ackrill 1980; the interpretation is contested in Kraut 1989.

22   Frankfurt 1971, p. 82. The ellipsis omits Frankfurt's "and problematical". Unlike Frankfurt, Aristotle does not suggest that the criterion of moral agency is something we regard as "problematical" in our lives, but like Frankfurt, he insists on its supreme importance.

23   Moreover, at *EN* 1104b3–9, when Aristotle explains how an agent's feelings of pleasure and pain are signs of his character, he applies the epithets 'temperate,' 'intemperate,' 'courageous,' and 'cowardly' to agents whom he has not shown to satisfy the strict criteria for perfect virtue, or its analogue in the case of vice.

24   The vagueness and incompleteness in Aristotle's exposition are presumably explained by his goal, in the ethical treatises, of describing the conditions of the best human life, which requires complete virtue of character.

25   He thinks they are states whose activity is properly described as "doing justice" (*dikaiopragein*) or "doing injustice" (*adikein*) (*EE* 1223a39, b11, 14–15). This is to make a specifically moral assessment of them (cf. *MM* 1188a18).

26   In *Catg.* 8, Aristotle denies that health is a *hexis*, on the grounds that it lacks the requisite stability. But in the ethical works he repeatedly compares states of character with states of health and sickness: *EN* 1104a11–19, 29–33, 1105b12–18, 1114a14–21; *EE* 1220a22–34, 1228b31, 1242a31; *MM* 1185b13–23, 1199b26–35; cf. *EN* 1137a9–17; *EE* 1222a28–36; *MM* 1207b33–6.

27   Hardie 1980, p. 121. A similar view is expressed by Christopher Pelling in the conclusion to Pelling 1990, and is part of the motivation for Christopher Gill's distinction between "character" and "personality" in Gill 1990. Similar views about Aristotle's notion of character are expressed in Halliwell 1986, p. 164 and Jones 1962, p. 32.

28   Indeed, the family of feelings that fall under the heading of *philia* (e.g. those prefaced by '*phil-*') seem to capture the sorts of sentiments Hardie here suggests are not part of a virtuous or vicious state of character. Granted, at *EE* 1227b10–11, Aristotle denies that having a sweet tooth (being *philoglukus*) and being fond of pungent food (*philopikros*) are qualities of one's character; but presumably this is because he is conceiving of them as dispositions of our faculty of taste that are not amenable to rational redirection, and for this reason not dispositions of the *pathē* that virtue and vice concern (cf. *EE* 1220a39–b7). At *EN* 1118a1–13 he claims that the disposition to take the proper pleasure in sights and sounds is not temperance; but this does not entail that they are not states of character.

It seems strange to call dispositions such as *oinophilia* (love of wine) or having a sweet tooth states of character because such dispositions do not normally dispose one to behavior that is morally significant. The oinophile's selection of good wine over bad seems no more within the scope of morality than the sweet-lover's choice of cake over fruit for dessert. However, the totality of one's dispositions regarding such objects of pursuit is nonetheless morally relevant. To the extent that one's disposition regarding wine or sweets is not just a tendency to take pleasure in tasting them, but a disposition to actively seek out such pleasures, it will determine in what circumstances, and at the expense of what other goods, one is prepared to pursue them. For example, the sweet-lover or wine-lover generally has the opportunity to kill or steal in order to satisfy his sweet tooth or his desire for fine wine, opportunities which it would be reprehensible for him to take. While it would be strange to say it is *kalon* of the oinophile not to rob the wine store, it would surely be *aischron* if he were to do so.

2

Voluntariness, Praiseworthiness, and Character

———————————— ◆ ————————————

Having examined Aristotle's general account of virtue and vice of character and seen that it is itself concerned with moral responsibility, we are now in a position to see that the discussions of voluntariness that Aristotle inserts into these general accounts are intended to be accounts of moral responsibility for action. Let us first establish that Aristotle intends his accounts of voluntariness to capture a causal relation between agent and action, and then establish that this causal relation is the one relevant to moral responsibility.

1 Voluntariness and Causal Responsibility

Aristotle clearly believes that a voluntary action is one to which the agent stands in a certain causal relation. He emphasizes this point in the *EE*, where he introduces the discussion of voluntariness and involuntariness with the claim that a human being is an "origin of actions" (*archē praxeōn*):

> Let us make a new beginning of our ongoing inquiry. All substances are naturally origins of a kind, which is why each is able to generate another of the same type – a man can generate men, an animal animals, and a plant plants. But in addition to these things, man alone of the animals is also an origin of certain actions. (*EE* 1222b15–20)

After describing in some detail the sort of origin (*archē*) a human being is (1222b20–1223a4), Aristotle indicates that the actions of which a human being is the origin are ones of which the agent is "responsible" (*aitios*)[1] (1223a4–9). He introduces the topic of voluntariness on the recommendation that voluntary actions are the ones for which the agent is responsible:

> We must identify the sort of actions of which he is the origin and responsible. Now we all agree that those that are voluntary and those that are according to his decision are ones he is responsible for, while he is not responsible for the involuntary ones. (*EE* 1223a15–18)

In interpreting Aristotle's claim that an agent is responsible (*aitios*) for his voluntary actions, it is important to keep in mind that he distinguishes four different ways in which one can be responsible (*aitios -a -on*) for something. These are his four kinds of "cause" (*aitia*) or "responsible thing" (*aition*):

> In one way a cause (*aition*) is that from which something comes to be but which remains – as for example the bronze is the cause of the statue and the silver of the cup, as well as the genera of these things.
>
> In another way, it is the form and paradigm; this is the definition of the essence and its genera (for example, the cause of the octave is the ratio two to one, and in general number) as well as the parts in the definition.
>
> Further, it is that from which the primary origin of change or of rest is. For example, the advisor is the cause, and the father is of the child and in general the maker of the thing made and the changer of the thing changed.
>
> Furthermore, it is the goal for the sake of which, as health is of walking. For why does he walk? In order to become healthy, we say, and in saying this we think we have given the cause (*to aition*). (*Ph.* 194b23–35; cf. 198a14–21; *Met.* 983a26–32, 1013a24–35)

This list indicates that Aristotle's notion of causal responsibility is considerably wider than the modern one. In his view, the premises of an argument are no less "responsible" for the conclusion[2] than the sculptor is "responsible" for the statue. Only the third cause on the list, which is traditionally labeled the "efficient cause", has the sort of "responsibility" for its effect that is recognizably causal in the modern sense.[3] But this is in fact the sort of cause Aristotle has in mind when he claims agents are responsible for their voluntary actions. He makes this clear when he continues his introductory remarks at the beginning of *EE* ii 6:

Those origins that are of this sort – from which primarily change is – are called "controlling" (*kuriai*).[4] Most properly so-called are those whose result cannot be otherwise, which presumably the god rules (*archei*). But as for unchanging origins (*akinētois archais*), for example mathematical ones, there is no control (*to kurion*), although they are so-called in virtue of similarity – since in these contexts too if the origin were to change, everything that is demonstrated from them would certainly be different. (*EE* 1222b20–6)

In calling human beings origins of actions, Aristotle is not talking about the sort of "responsibility" premises might have for a conclusion. He has in mind the sorts of origins that control change in the world. An origin of action is an "origin of change": "A human being is an origin of change (*archē kinēseōs*) of a certain kind, for action is a kind of change (*EE* 1222b28–9)." And the "origin of change" is simply one of Aristotle's ways of referring to the efficient cause.[5]

Unlike the *EE*, the *EN* and *MM* do not introduce the topic of voluntariness by emphasizing its efficient-causal nature; however, this difference is simply one of emphasis. In both works Aristotle indicates that the voluntary agent is the efficient cause of his action. In *EN* iii 1–5, Aristotle indicates that a voluntary action is one whose origin is in the agent[6] and makes it clear that the origin in question is, like the "controlling origin" described in *EE* ii 6, the sort of origin which makes it depend on the agent whether the action happens or not:

In such cases the agent's action is voluntary, for the origin of moving his bodily parts is in him, and that whose origin is in him is up to him to do and not to do. (*EN* 1110a15–17; cf. *EE* 1223a4–7)

In *EN* iii 5, his examples of the sort of origin he has in mind are the same as his examples of "controlling origins" in *EE* ii 6, and correspond to one of his favourite examples of efficient causation: the generation of offspring by a parent (*EN* 1113b17–19; cf. *EE* 1222b17; *Ph.* 194b30–1, 198a26–7; *GA* 716a5–8). So too in the *MM*, the voluntary agent is described as a "generator of actions" (*tōn praxeōn esti gennētikos*, 1187b9; cf. 1187a30–3), and the sort of causal responsibility he has for his actions is such that it is up to him (*ep' autō(i)*) whether they occur or not (1187a7–24). The relation of voluntariness is clearly that of Aristotelian efficient causation.

A modern reader, however, might still hesitate to call the relation "causal". This is because contemporary accounts of causation tend to take causation to be a relation between events,[7] while the Aristotelian efficient cause is not an event but a substance (e.g., the builder, the parent, or in the present case, the agent). Aristotle's claim that the agent is the cause of his action is sometimes taken to be an instance of a view that has come to be known as "agent-causation". According to this view, there are two irreducibly different types of causation: the ordinary sort in which events bring forth events, and an extraordinary sort (labeled "immanent causation") in which substances (in particular, agents) bring forth events in an exercise of causality that is not itself an event.[8] Clearly, if Aristotelian efficient causes are causes of the latter sort, then his conception of efficient causation is radically at odds with prevailing contemporary notions.[9] But Aristotle's efficient causes do not engage in "immanent causation", for they exercise their causality in events. For example, the builder who is the efficient cause of the house exercises his causality in an event (the exercise of his capacity for house building) which brings about another event (in which the building materials acquire the form of a house) (*Ph.* 195b16–21), and Aristotle clearly thinks this is true of efficient causes in general.[10]

Aristotle's view does differ from contemporary orthodoxy in identifying as the cause the substance whose capacities are exercised in the event, rather than the event itself. However, on both views, causality is a process in which substances exercising their causal powers in events cause other causal powers of substances to be exercised in other events. Given this substantial common ground between the two views, contemporary readers of Aristotle should not feel uncomfortable about interpreting at face value Aristotle's claim that the agent is the cause of his voluntary actions.

2 The Significance of Voluntariness

Having established that Aristotle investigates voluntariness in order to capture the conditions in which an agent is causally responsible for an action, we may now raise the question of why he is interested in this causal relation. In all three ethical treatises, he indicates that it is because he is interested in the conditions of praise and blame. We praise and blame people only for what they are responsible for (*EE* 1223a10–13); only voluntary actions are praised and blamed (*EN* 1109b30–2; *MM* 1187a19–21). Does this show that Aristotle's concern with voluntariness is a concern with moral responsibility? Not yet. If the praise and blame in question are retrospective moral evaluations of agents for what they have done or failed to do, then we have good reason to suppose moral responsibility is Aristotle's concern in these contexts. However, for all we have seen so far, the praise and blame for which Aristotle thinks voluntariness is necessary might simply be tools of behavioural control and character formation justified by purely prospective considerations.[11] If this is the case, then his concern with voluntariness is not a concern with moral responsibility.

In both the *EE* and the *EN* Aristotle indicates that the connection between voluntariness and praiseworthiness is what makes the study of voluntariness relevant to the study of character. Therefore, in order to determine the nature of the praise and blame for which Aristotle thinks voluntariness is necessary, it will be useful to consider his reasons for inserting the discussion of voluntariness into the middle of his general discussion of virtue and vice of character. The discussion in *EN* iii 1–5 begins:

> Since virtue concerns (*peri*) feelings and actions, and since praise and blame are given for (*epi* + dative) voluntary things, while forgiveness and sometimes even pity are given for involuntary things, it is presumably necessary for those inquiring into virtue to define the voluntary and the involuntary. This would also be useful to those who legislate about fines and punishments. (*EN* 1109b30–5)

Aristotle here claims that the study of voluntariness is relevant to the study of virtue and vice of character because voluntariness is a condition of praiseworthiness and blameworthiness. His unstated but clearly assumed premise is that virtue is praiseworthy and vice blameworthy (cf. *EN* 1108a14–16). Aristotle makes this premise explicit in the corresponding passage of his introduction to the account of voluntariness in the *EE*:

> Since virtue and vice and their products are praiseworthy and blameworthy respectively (for one is blamed and praised not because of what happens from necessity or from chance or from nature but ⟨sc. because of⟩ those things of which we are ourselves responsible – what someone else is responsible for, he has both the blame and the praise) it is clear that virtue and vice concern (*peri*) those actions for which one is oneself responsible (*aitios*) and the origin. So we must identify the sorts of actions of which he is himself responsible and the origin. Now we all agree that he is responsible for his voluntary actions . . . and that he is not responsible for his involuntary ones. (*EE* 1223a9–18)

As in *EN* iii 1, Aristotle here recommends the study of voluntariness to the student of moral character on the grounds that (a) voluntariness is a condition of praiseworthiness and blameworthiness, and (b) states of character are praiseworthy and blameworthy things. But exactly how does Aristotle think voluntariness is necessary for the praiseworthiness of virtue and the blameworthiness of vice? An answer that naturally suggests itself is that Aristotle thinks that virtue is praiseworthy and vice blameworthy only if these states of character are acquired voluntarily.[12]

This suggestion derives initial support from the remarks that introduce the discussion of voluntariness in the *MM*. That discussion begins with the question, whether "it is up to us (*eph' hēmin*) to be good or bad" (1187a5–8). Since *MM* i 9–11 uses 'up to us' interchangeably with 'voluntary,' the introductory question appears to ask whether our states of character are voluntary. After a series of arguments for the affirmative answer to this question (1187a13–b30), the introductory remarks conclude:

> Since being good is clearly up to us, we must next take up the topic of voluntariness and say what the voluntary is. For this, the voluntary, is the most important thing for virtue. (*MM* 1187b31–4)

These introductory remarks in the *MM*, when juxtaposed with those in the *EE* and *EN*, seem to confirm the suggestion that Aristotle thinks that virtue is praiseworthy and vice blameworthy only if these states of character are voluntary, and that this is why he includes a discussion of voluntariness in his general account of states of character. Indeed, the introductory remarks in the *MM* include an argument that appears to infer the voluntariness of virtue and vice from the fact of their praiseworthiness and blameworthiness:

> So it seems to be up to us to be good and bad. Further evidence of this comes from praise and blame; for praise is for virtue, and blame for vice, but praise and blame are not for involuntary things. So it is clear that it is up to us in the same way to do good things and bad things. (*MM* 1187a18–23)

So are Aristotle's discussions of voluntariness motivated by the thought that states of character must be voluntary if they are to be praiseworthy or blameworthy? If this is their motivation, then the connection he sees between voluntariness and praiseworthiness coincides in a very important respect with many modern accounts of moral responsibility. According to most modern views, all moral praiseworthiness and blameworthiness is ultimately praise or blame of agents for having the good or bad states of character that they do, and hence presupposes that the agents are responsible for their virtues and vices of character. Responsibility for character is, on these modern views, the most basic feature of moral responsibility.[13] And it is often assumed that Aristotle has an adequate account of moral responsibility only if he can show that we are responsible for the states of character from which we act.[14] On closer examination, however, the evidence of this alleged affinity between Aristotle and modern theorists of moral responsibility evaporates. While we will see that the conditions of praiseworthiness and blameworthiness that Aristotle intends his account of voluntariness to capture are in fact conditions of moral responsibility, it is important to recognize that Aristotle's conception of moral responsibility differs significantly from modern ones in that it does not assign this fundamental role to responsibility for character.

The apparently emphatic insistence in *MM* i 9–11 on the claim that it is up to us to be good or bad is what lends support to the suggestion that the voluntariness of states of character is Aristotle's prime concern in discussing voluntariness. On closer examination, however, the discussion in these chapters provides very weak support for that suggestion. For it does not distinguish between the theses:[15]

> It is up to us to be good or bad.
> It is up to us to do good or bad things.

A good example of this conflation is in the argument just quoted (*MM* 1187a18–23). The argument proceeds from two premises which entail that virtue and vice are voluntary (they are praised and blamed; and nothing involuntary is praised or blamed); however, it fails to draw the conclusion that virtue and vice are up to us, concluding instead that virtuous and vicious actions are up to us.[16] Aristotle's failure to distinguish between these two theses casts doubt on whether the former thesis really is a thesis about the voluntariness of good and bad character rather than an alternative way of stating the thesis that good and bad actions are voluntary.[17] But if the latter is the case, we have lost the original motivation for the suggestion.

The discussion of voluntariness in the *EE* casts further doubt on the suggestion, for the suggestion makes it reasonable to expect that Aristotle's point in discussing voluntariness is to establish that states of character are voluntary. Nowhere in the Eudemian discussion of voluntariness, however, does Aristotle show any concern to establish the voluntariness of states of character. The remarks about "controlling origins" (*kuriai archai*) that introduce the discussion of voluntariness in *EE* ii 6 clearly concern an agent's causal responsibility for particular actions. Except perhaps in the concluding line of that chapter (1223a19–20) Aristotle makes no reference in any of the *EE*'s discussion of voluntariness and related notions (*EE* ii 6–11) to the question of whether character is voluntary.[18]

Moreover, in the one place in the *EE* where we should expect him to claim that we are responsible for our states of character, Aristotle explicitly stops short of concluding this. This is where he explains why voluntariness is relevant to the study of character:

> Since virtue and vice and their products are praiseworthy and blameworthy respectively (for one is blamed and praised not because of what happens from necessity or from chance or from nature but ⟨sc. because of⟩ those things of which we are ourselves responsible – what someone else is responsible for, he has both the blame and the praise) it is clear that virtue and vice concern (*peri*) those actions for which one is oneself responsible (*aitios*) and the origin. (*EE* 1223a9–15)

Aristotle first claims here that virtue, vice, and their products are praiseworthy and blameworthy (a9–10). He then claims that we are praised and blamed only because of things for which we are responsible (a10–13). At this point, we should expect him to conclude that we are responsible for virtue, vice, and their products. Instead, however, he concludes only that virtue and vice "concern those things for which we are ourselves responsible" (a13–15). We have already seen that these remarks about the causal presuppositions of praise and blame explain why Aristotle includes the discussion of voluntariness in the discussion of moral character (cf. 1223a15–19, quoted above). If Aristotle's goal in discussing voluntariness is to establish the praiseworthiness of virtue (and the blameworthiness of vice) by establishing that we are responsible for our states of character, then surely we should expect him to say so in this passage.

In contrast to the *EE*, the discussion of voluntariness in the *EN* does include an argument, in *EN* iii 5, that we acquire our states of character voluntarily (1114a3–31).[19] This conclusion is presumably one of the things Aristotle intends to establish by introducing the discussion of voluntariness into the general account of states of character.[20] But the suggestion we are considering is not simply that Aristotle thinks virtue and vice are voluntary; nor is it that this is one of the things Aristotle intends to establish in discussing voluntariness. We are considering the suggestion that Aristotle discusses voluntariness because he thinks the praiseworthiness of virtue and the blameworthiness of vice requires that they be voluntary. This suggestion is not confirmed by the mere fact that one of the things Aristotle sets out to establish in his account of voluntariness in the *EN* is that states of character are voluntary.

3 Aristotle's Canonical Account of Praiseworthiness

Nowhere in any of his discussions of voluntariness does Aristotle indicate that he thinks the praiseworthiness and blameworthiness of states of character requires that they be voluntary. His general account of praiseworthiness (*to epaineton*), and the corresponding account of blameworthiness that it implies, also fails to support this conclusion. He presents this account in *EN* i 12, *EE* ii 1 (1219b8–16), and *MM* i 2 (1183b20–7). In these passages, Aristotle undertakes to distinguish praise from encomium, and gives an account of what it is to be praiseworthy (*epaineton*). While encomium is reserved for good achievements or success (*EN* 1101b32–4; *EE* 1219b9, 14–15), praiseworthy things (*epaineta*) are praised because they are productive of good things:

> Clearly, everything praiseworthy is praised for being of a certain sort and for being disposed toward something in a certain way. For we praise the just person and the brave person, and in general the good person, as well as virtue, because of the actions and products, and we praise the strong and the swift person and each of the others for being of a certain sort and for being disposed in a certain way toward something good and excellent. (*EN* 1101b12–18; cf. *EE* 1219b8–9)

It is no accident that virtue and the virtuous person are Aristotle's primary examples of praiseworthy things (cf. *MM* 1183b26). For the formula Aristotle uses to capture the grounds of praiseworthiness, "being of a certain sort (*poion ti einai*) and being disposed toward something in a certain way (*pros ti pōs echein*)" (1101b13), captures the salient features of his account of virtue and of states of character in general. A state of moral character is what makes an agent of a certain sort (*poios tis*).[21] Being a state (*hexis*), it disposes her toward (*echein pros*) acting or feeling in a particular way (*EE* 1220b9–10; *EN* 1105b25–8, 1106a1, 6). A virtuous state of character disposes the agent toward good actions and feelings (*EN* 1105b26). Aristotle here indicates that this causal fact about virtue is what makes it praiseworthy.[22] As he summarizes the view a little later in the chapter, "praise is of virtue, for it makes us productive of fine things" (1101b31–2).

Aristotle consistently abides by this analysis of the praiseworthiness of virtue throughout his accounts of praiseworthiness (*to epaineton*). In the corresponding discussion in the *EE*, he claims, "praises are of virtue, because of its products" (*EE* 1219b8; cf. 1220a7–8). In the *MM*, when explaining why virtues are praiseworthy goods, he claims that "praise comes from (*apo*) the actions according to them" (*MM* 1183b27). In the *Rhetoric*, he claims that virtue is praiseworthy because it is a "capacity for providing goods" (*dunamis poristikē agathōn*, *Rhet.* 1366a37).[23] Aristotle's account of the praiseworthiness of virtue makes it quite clear that virtue is praiseworthy because of its causal powers. He does not claim that virtue is praiseworthy because of its causal antecedents. *A fortiori*, he does not claim that virtue is praiseworthy because we are responsible for it.

Aristotle's detailed examination of the different virtues and vices of character, which follows the discussion of voluntariness in each of his ethical works, is in part an inductive argument for the thesis that a mean state is always praiseworthy and an extreme state blameworthy (*EN* 1108a14–16; cf. *EE* 1222a6–12, 1222b12–14). Throughout this examination, Aristotle adheres to the account of praiseworthiness we have just been examining. He invariably explains the praiseworthiness of a mean state (and the blameworthiness of an extreme state) by referring to its characteristic activity, never to its causal antecedents. For example, when he claims that mildness (*praotēs*), the mean state concerning anger, is praiseworthy, he explains this by saying that it is "that according to which (*kath' hēn*) we get angry as we ought" (*EN* 1126b5–7). Courage is praised, he explains, because the courageous person is disposed to act and feel appropriately in the face of fearful things (*EE* 1228b30–1). Magnanimity (*megalopsuchia*) is "most praiseworthy," because of the judgements the magnanimous person is the sort to make (*EE* 1233a4–8).[24]

In all these cases, Aristotle claims that virtue is praiseworthy because of the actions or feelings it produces, not because of the actions or feelings that produce it. Virtue is praiseworthy, and presumably also vice blameworthy, because of its causal powers rather than its causal antecedents. Aristotle's explicit account of praiseworthiness gives us no reason to suppose that he thinks the praiseworthiness and blameworthiness of states of character requires that their acquisition be voluntary.

4 The Causal Presuppositions of Praise and Blame

But still, one might wonder what relation that explicit account of praiseworthiness bears to Aristotle's equally explicit remark in *EE* ii 6 that praise and blame require efficient-causal responsibility:

> Since virtue and vice and their products are praiseworthy and blameworthy respectively (for one is blamed and praised not because (*dia*) of what happens from necessity or from chance or from nature but ⟨sc. because of⟩ those things of which we are ourselves responsible; what someone else is responsible for, he has both the blame and the praise) it is clear that virtue and vice concern (*peri*) those actions for which one is oneself responsible (*aitios*) and the origin. (*EE* 1223a9–15).

Is this requirement of efficient-causal responsibility an additional condition necessary for praiseworthiness intended to supplement Aristotle's official account? If so, then we might after all have evidence that Aristotle thinks the praiseworthiness of character requires that we be responsible for it. But this is not the correct way to interpret the requirement of causal responsibility. We can see that it is not if we pay careful attention to the way Aristotle states the requirement. He does not claim that anything praiseworthy is something for which the recipient of praise must be efficient-causally responsible. He claims rather that we must be responsible for the things because of which we are praised and blamed (1223a11).[25]

In Aristotle's account of praiseworthiness, the things because of (*dia*) which we are praised are the things that virtue produces – its products (*erga*):

> Praise is of virtue because of its products (*dia ta erga*). (*EE* 1219b8–9; cf. b12–13)

> We praise the just and brave person and in general the good person as well as virtue because of the actions and products (*dia tas praxeis kai ta erga*). (*EN* 1101b14–16)

These products, the account of virtue tells us, are feelings and actions. Aristotle sometimes refers to the actions and feelings "because of which" we are praised as the things "from which" (*apo, ek*) we are praised, and "for which" (*epi* + dative) we are praised. But he never in these contexts claims that we are praised or blamed because of, from, or for states of character.[26] Feelings and actions, Aristotle tells us, are the things that virtue and vice of character concern (*peri*).[27] And it is the things that virtue and vice concern (*peri*) that Aristotle explicitly concludes we must be responsible for if we are to be praiseworthy or blameworthy (1223a14). In requiring efficient-causal responsibility for praiseworthiness at *EE* 1223a9–15, Aristotle therefore requires only that if we are praised and blamed because of (*dia* + accusative), from (*ek, apo*) or for (*epi* + dative) an action or feeling, then we must be responsible for such action or feeling. He does not claim that character – which praise is of (objective genitive – *EN* 1101b31–2; *EE* 1219b8) or according to (*kata* + accusative – *EN* 1106a1–2; *MM* 1185b8–9) – is praiseworthy only if we are responsible for it. This is why, in his conclusion to the argument in this passage, he stops short of concluding that we are responsible for virtue, vice, and their products, and concludes instead simply that "virtue and vice concern (*peri*) those things for which one is oneself responsible (*aitios*) and the origin of action" (*EE* 1223a13–15).

Far from being a supplement to Aristotle's canonical account of praiseworthiness, Aristotle's claim that the products of virtue and vice (*tōn ap' autōn erga*, *EE* 1223a9) are praiseworthy and blameworthy only if we are efficient-causally responsible for them makes perfect sense within that canonical account. According to that account, agents and their states of character are praiseworthy because they are productive (*praktikoi*) of good things:

> Praise is of virtue, for it makes us productive (*praktikoi*) of fine things. (*EN* 1101b31–2; cf. *EE* 1219b8; *MM* 1183b27)

To claim that an agent is productive (*praktikos*) of good or fine things is to claim that the agent is the efficient cause of these good things, for the relation of producer (*poioun*) to product is the relation in which an efficient cause stands to its effect. Just as the builder is productive (*poiētikos*) of houses in virtue of the capacity of housebuilding (*oikodomikē*), and the statuary (*andriantopoios*) is productive of statues in virtue of the statuary skill (*andriantopoiikē*), the virtuous person is productive (*praktikos*) of good things in virtue of her states of character.[28]

The good things of which virtue is productive are feelings and actions. So Aristotle's account of praiseworthiness, in requiring that the praiseworthy agent be productive of goods, requires that the virtuous person be causally responsible for good actions and feelings – the things because of which she is praised. The efficient-causal relation necessary for the praiseworthiness of states of character is the causal relation between the agent (or her state of character)[29] and a good action or feeling. It is not an efficient-causal relation between the agent and the state of character. Hence the voluntariness that Aristotle thinks is necessary for the praiseworthiness and blameworthiness of states of character is not a feature of the acquisition of these states, but rather of their exercise.[30]

5 The Focal Nature of Praiseworthiness

Aristotle's account of praiseworthiness shows that he does not think the praiseworthiness (or blameworthiness) of our states of character amounts to our being praiseworthy (or blameworthy) for having them. He does not endorse the view that the praiseworthiness of virtue and the blameworthiness of vice require that we be responsible for acquiring them. His account of the praiseworthiness of character therefore differs significantly from modern accounts of moral responsibility, which take responsibility for character to be necessary for character's praiseworthiness and blameworthiness, and for moral responsibility in general. Such views take character and action to be praiseworthy in exactly the same way; in each case the agent is praised for bringing about the character or action, and so must be causally responsible for it. Aristotle, by contrast, supposes that states of character and actions are praiseworthy in different, although related, ways.

Aristotle's canonical account of praiseworthiness is satisfied by states of character and agents, not the actions or feelings they cause. However, outside his canonical definitions of praiseworthiness, he does not hesitate to label "praiseworthy" or "blameworthy" the actions and feelings produced by states of character.[31] But in calling these products of agents and states praiseworthy, Aristotle does not mean that they satisfy the definition of praiseworthiness that the praiseworthy states and agents satisfy. A passage in *EE* viii 3 makes this clear. In defining the sorts of goods that are noble (*kala*), Aristotle says:

> These are themselves praiseworthy and the actions from them are also praiseworthy: justice itself and the actions from it, as well as the tem-

perate person – for temperance too is praiseworthy. But health is not
something praiseworthy, for neither is its product. (*EE* 1248b19–24)

Praiseworthy things here include: states of character (justice and temperance), the possessors of such states (the temperate person), and the
actions from these states. In claiming that the product of the praiseworthy state must itself be praiseworthy, Aristotle clearly does not mean
that the product, like the praiseworthy state, must have a praiseworthy
product; otherwise an infinite regress would loom. He means rather that
the products of the praiseworthy state must be good. He denies here
that the products of some states, such as health and strength, are
praiseworthy because they are not necessarily good; they can be misused
(1248b23–34).

Aristotle requires us to be responsible for our praiseworthy actions
and feelings, but not for our praiseworthy states of character, because
he thinks these two sorts of items are praiseworthy in different ways.
The latter are praiseworthy because they produce good actions and
feelings, while the former are praiseworthy because they are the good
products produced by praiseworthy states. These two ways of being
praiseworthy are intimately related, for the criterion each praiseworthy
thing must satisfy, whether it is a state of character or an action or
feeling, is part of the single complex of conditions identified in Aristotle's canonical account of praiseworthiness: an agent, in virtue of her
state, producing a good product.

To apply terminology that Aristotle uses in another context, we may
say that in his view praiseworthiness is a "focal" (*pros hen*) notion. He
explains what a focal notion is in the *Metaphysics*:

> Being is said in many ways, but with reference to one thing (*pros hen*),
> some one nature, and not homonymously. Rather, just as everything that
> is healthy (*hugieinon*) is healthy with reference to health – some things
> by preserving it, others by producing it, others by being a sign of it,
> others by being receptive of it. (*Met.* 1003a33–b1)

For Aristotle, praiseworthiness (*to epaineton*) is a focal (*pros hen*) notion
because it is with reference to his canonical definition of praiseworthiness that all praiseworthy things (agents, their states, and their actions
and feelings) are praiseworthy. States are praiseworthy if they produce
good actions and feelings; agents are praiseworthy if their states produce good actions and feelings; and the feelings and actions produced
by a state are praiseworthy if they are good. While many different things

are praiseworthy, they are all praiseworthy because of their relation to the one fundamentally and non-derivatively praiseworthy thing: a praiseworthy state of character. This is why Aristotle repeatedly insists that all praise is given "according to virtue" or "according to the state (*hexis*)".[32]

The focal nature of praise and blame reflects the obvious fact that when an agent's actions or feelings are praised or blamed, the agent is the ultimate object or recipient of the praise or blame. Praise and blame are attitudes toward agents. Although agents are praised or blamed for their actions or feelings, the recipient of the praise is the agent, not the action or feeling, and it is the recipient of praise who must satisfy the conditions for praiseworthiness.[33] The fact that states of character are not things for which (*epi* + dative) agents are praised, but are rather respects in which they are praised, reflects an equally salient feature of Aristotelian efficient causation. To praise an agent, in Aristotle's view, is to take him to be the efficient cause of a good outcome. And efficient causes, in his view, are identified in terms of their causal powers. Just as the builder (*oikodomos*), who is the efficient cause of the house, is identified in terms of the capacity of building (*hē oikodomikē*) (*Ph.* 195b21–5), the voluntary agent who is the efficient cause of the good action or feeling is identified in terms of her moral character. In contrast with contemporary accounts of moral responsibility, which suppose that an agent cannot be respons-ible for an action unless she is responsible for the state of character from which she acts, Aristotle no more requires that the agent be responsible for her character in order to be responsible for the action or feeling produced by that character than he requires that the statuary be responsible for his statuary skill in order to be responsible for the statue he produces using that skill, or requires that a man be responsible for his reproductive powers in order to be called the "origin and generator" of his children (*EN* 1113b18; cf. *EE* 1222b16–18; *MM* 1187a30–4).[34] In an important even if hard to articulate sense, the causal power (the character) is what the agent *is*. Hence the question of whether the agent is responsible for it does not arise when we are considering what she is responsible for.

6 Voluntariness and Moral Responsibility

We have been investigating the nature of the praiseworthiness for which Aristotle thinks voluntariness is necessary because our goal is to determine whether Aristotle's inquiry into voluntariness might properly be construed as an inquiry into the conditions of moral responsibility for action. We have seen that the praiseworthiness Aristotle is concerned with – both of character and of action – in no way depends on an agent's being responsible for her states of character. Aristotle's conception of praiseworthiness fails to endorse an assumption that is common to most modern accounts of moral responsibility. But it would be a mistake to conclude from this that Aristotle's concern with voluntariness is not a concern with moral responsibility. This would be a valid inference to make only if the thesis that responsibility for character is the basis of all moral responsibility were constitutive of the notion of moral responsibility, instead of a view about moral responsibility that one might hold or reject. Such a claim is far from obviously true.

Moreover, the account of praiseworthiness that Aristotle offers gives us very good reason to suppose that his concern with voluntariness is a concern with moral responsibility. Aristotle intends his account of voluntariness to capture the conditions in which an agent's states of character are praiseworthy and blameworthy. And these conditions, we have seen, are those in which the agent is causally responsible for particular good and bad actions or feelings. The sort of praise and blame the agent deserves for (*epi* + dative) these actions and feelings is therefore based on a retrospective evaluation – for the question is whether the agent's character produced them. Furthermore, they are moral attitudes – for they are essentially evaluative of the agent's states of character, which, as we saw in chapter 1, are recognizably moral properties of agents. Aristotle intends his general account of the virtues and vices of character to (among other things) identify the capacities which properly subject agents to moral evaluations and expectations – to explain, for example, why children and beasts are neither courageous nor cowardly, temperate nor intemperate, nor just or unjust, but most adult humans are. We are now in a position to conclude that he introduces a discussion of voluntariness into that general account of virtue and vice in order to identify the causal conditions in which an agent's action may properly be taken to manifest a particular virtue or vice of character – to give a criterion for deciding when, for example, an agent's action is a case of acting the coward (*deilainein*), or acting intemperately (*akolastainein*), or in general acting justly (*dikaiopragein*) or doing injustice (*adikein*). When an agent acts the coward or acts intemperately, he is properly reproached as cowardly or intemperate, and when he does justice he is properly praised as just. These evaluations are recognizably moral evaluations. Since

Aristotle intends his account of voluntariness to capture the conditions in which they are appropriate, we may conclude that he investigates voluntariness in order to capture the conditions of moral responsibility for action.

This is not, of course, to say that Aristotle thinks every voluntary agent is morally responsible for his voluntary action. He clearly does not, for he ascribes voluntariness to animals and children (*EN* 1111b8–9), but denies that their behavior is properly classified in moral terms, as for example, temperate, brave, cowardly or just (*EN* 1145a25–7, 1149b31–5). Voluntariness, in his view, is a necessary but not a sufficient condition for moral responsibility. In addition to voluntariness, a morally responsible agent must have dispositions that satisfy the conditions for being genuinely temperate, brave, cowardly, just, etc. In his view, only agents who have a moral character are morally responsible for their voluntary actions.[35]

Of course, a proponent of a modern view of moral responsibility might worry that without assigning a fundamental role to responsibility for character, whatever account of moral responsibility Aristotle develops in his account of voluntariness will be too weak to support the crucial thesis that the moral agent is the genuine origin of the action for which he is held responsible, and that it is up to him both to do it and not to do it. This worry, however, is not about whether Aristotle is offering an account of moral responsibility, but about whether the account he offers succeeds. We will not be in a position to address it fully until we have understood more about the causal notions Aristotle presupposes in discussing voluntariness. Chapter 6 will consider Aristotle's resources for responding to it.

In the meantime, we have much to explore in Aristotle's discussions of voluntariness. Our consideration of the motivation Aristotle offers for discussing voluntariness has given us reason to believe that he has a positive theoretical project to accomplish in giving an account of voluntariness: he wants to capture the conditions in which an agent's action is produced by, or a genuine expression of, his states of character. In the next chapter we will see that, in developing his various definitions of voluntariness, he executes this project in his typical dialectical fashion. In chapter 4, which considers his treatment of compulsion, we will see that carrying out this project is far from straightforward, and requires him to draw deeply on the resources of his account of causation. It is on these resources that we will rely in chapter 6 when we return to consider whether Aristotle's claim, that the voluntary agent is an "origin of action", is sufficiently strong to support an adequate account of moral responsibility.

NOTES

1 By "responsible", I mean simply "causally responsible". Sometimes 're-sponsible' is used with specifically moral connotations, indicating moral responsibility or blameworthiness; at other times, however, it simply indicates a causal connection – as when heavy rain is said to be responsible for flooding. It is in this merely causal sense of 'responsible' that I will use it to translate *aitios*. An alternative translation of *aitios* would be "the cause." The adjective is cognate with the noun *hē aitia*, whose semantic field ranges from "cause" to "accusation" and "blame" but in these contexts means "cause"; Aristotle regularly indicates that *to aition* or *hē aitia* of something is what that something is "because of" (*dia* + accusative: *Ph.* 194b19, 198a14–16; *Met.* 983a28).

2 As "that from which" (*to ex hou*), *Ph.* 195a16–20.

3 See Annas 1982, and Fine 1987. Michael Frede denies that even this Aristotelian "cause" is recognizably causal on the ground that Aristotle "in more theoretical contexts will tell us that it is not the sculptor . . . who is the moving cause, but the art of sculpture" (Frede 1980, p. 218). But we will see that Aristotle does not intend the latter claim to under-mine the claim that the sculptor is the cause.

4 I follow Michael Woods's translation of *kuriai* (Woods 1982). An alterna-tive rendering preferred by Solomon (Solomon 1915) and Dirlmeier (Dirl-meier 1962) is 'proper'. On this interpretation, Aristotle is claiming that only origins of change are origins properly speaking. But this interpreta-tion conflicts with Aristotle's claim at *Met.* 1013a17 that all four causes are origins. Furthermore, Aristotle's subsequent uses of *kurios* in *EE* ii 6, for example at 1223a5, show that he thinks *kurios* describes the relation between the man and his actions, not the relation between the man and the epithet 'origin.'

5 Aristotle's canonical description of the so-called efficient cause is not "origin of change" (*archē kinēseōs*) but rather "that from which the origin of change or rest is" (*hothen hē archē tēs metabolēs . . . ē tēs ēremeseōs*, *Ph.* 194b29–30, *Met.* 1013a29–30; *hothen he archē tēs metabolēs ē staseōs*, *Ph.* 195a22–3). However, he does not always refer to the efficient cause by means of this canonical description. He sometimes refers to it as the "origin of change" (*Ph.* 195a8–12) or as "that from which the change" (*hothen hē kinēsis*, *Ph.* 195a3–8, *EN* 1139a31–2). This is how he describes the "controlling origins" (*kuriai archai*) in *EE* 1222b20–2. At any rate, Aristotle does in one passage use the canonical description of the efficient

cause to refer to the voluntary agent. At *EN* v 9, 1136b25–9, he indicates
that the voluntary agent (*hō(i) to hekonta touto poiein*, b27, the antecedent
of *touto* in b28) is "that from which the origin of the action is" (*hothen hē
archē tēs praxeōs*). This is exactly how we should expect Aristotle to state
the claim that the agent is the efficient cause of action if he stated the
claim in its canonical form.

6   *EN* 1110a15–17, 1110b4, 1111a23, 1113b17–19; cf. *MM* 1187b14–16.
In *EN* iii 1–5 (as in *MM* i 9–16) Aristotle typically claims that the origin
of action is *in* the voluntary agent, while in *EE* ii 6 he claims that the
voluntary agent *is* the origin of the action. But he clearly takes these two
locutions to be equivalent. For example: in *EN* iii 3, he describes deliberation as a process of seeking something to do whose "origin is in us"
(1112b28), and a few lines later he says, "so it seems, as has been said,
that a human being is an origin of actions" (1112b31–2). Nowhere previously has he said that a human being is an origin of actions, only that
the origin of voluntary actions is in an agent. In *EN* iii 5, he asks
rhetorically whether we should "deny that a man is the origin and generator of actions just as he is of his children" (1113b17–19) – using the
locution "origin of action" characteristic of the *EE*. But when he replies
that the proposition in question is evident (*phainetai*, b19), he restates it
using the locution characteristic of *EN* iii 1: "If we are unable to refer
things whose origins are in fact in us to origins beyond those in us, then
they are up to us and voluntary" (1113b19–21). In the course of his
account of voluntariness in *EE* ii 6–10, Aristotle refers to the origin of a
voluntary action as internal to the agent (*esothen hē archē*, 1224b15). And
in *EN* v 9, a book common to the *EE* and *EN*, he indicates that the origin
of action is in the agent whom he describes as "that from which the origin"
(1136b28–9). In *EN* vi 2, another common book, Aristotle refers to
something in the agent (*prohairesis*) as the "origin of action" (1139a31),
but after analyzing the nature of *prohairesis*, concludes that "man is such
an origin" (1139b5).

7   One of the most influential articulations of the view that causes are events
is in Davidson 1967.

8   The classic contemporary articulation of this view is in Chisholm 1964,
which explicitly cites (n. 1) Aristotle's account of voluntariness as an
instance of the view.

9   See, for example, Davidson's criticisms of Chisholm in Davidson 1973.

10 Indeed, in some passages, he even cites events (such as a raid, *Ph.* 198a19–20;
cf. *APst.* 94a36–b2) as efficient causes. The evidence is fully discussed in
Annas 1982, pp. 319–21. Gail Fine goes further and takes it to show that
the true efficient cause is an event, not a substance (Fine 1987). In order
to defuse the challenge we are considering, however, it is sufficient to note
that the exercise of efficient causality is an event. I offer a fuller discussion
of agent-causation as an interpretation of Aristotle in Meyer (1994).

11 As Jean Roberts claims (Roberts 1989).
12 So Bondeson concludes (Bondeson 1974, p. 59). Broadie finds the view expressed in *EE* 1223a9–18 (Broadie 1991, pp. 128, 162).
13 The presupposition is especially clear in Williams 1985 and Wolf 1990.
14 For example, Hardie 1980; Furley 1967; Adkins 1960; Engberg-Pedersen 1983; and Urmson 1988.
15 Respectively: *eph' hēmin to spoudaiois einai* and *eph' hēmin ta spoudaia prattein*.
16 In another example, the argument immediately preceding infers that it is up to us to be good and bad from evidence that it is up to us to do good and bad actions. No indication is given as to how the former follows from the latter. One might be tempted to suppose that Aristotle is presupposing an argument similar to the one in *EN* iii 5, 1114a4–21, where he argues that our voluntary actions form our states of character. However, the ensuing argument (*MM* 1187a18–23, quoted and discussed in the text above) suggests the alternative hypothesis that Aristotle here recognizes no distinction between the two claims.
17 In *EN* iii 5, 1113b11–14, Aristotle claims that being good and bad are nothing other than doing good and bad things. A charitable interpretation of this claim treats 'being good' and 'being bad' as claims about action rather than character. (I argue for this interpretation in detail in chapter 5.) Given the strong similarities between *MM* i 9 and *EN* iii 5, I would be inclined to interpret the corresponding claims in *MM* i 9 in the same way. In fact, the Socratic claim against which Aristotle is arguing in these passages (*MM* 1187a6–8; cf. *EN* 1113b14–17) is not obviously a thesis about good and bad character as opposed to good and bad action. At *Protagoras* 345d–e the "Socratic" thesis is that no one does bad things voluntarily. At *Laws* ix, 860d, the thesis is first stated as *ho kakos akōn toioutos* (d5) (the bad person is bad involuntarily), but on elaboration, the thesis is stated as a thesis about actions: *akontas adikein pantas* (d9) (everyone does wrong involuntarily). There is a use of 'being good' (*spoudaios einai*) that means nothing different from acting well on an occasion. In English, we can say of someone who did something bad (or good) on an occasion that he was bad (or good) on that occasion. So too in Greek, as for example in Sophocles *Tyr.* fr. 582: *akōn hamartōn outis anthrōpōn kakos* ("no man is bad who errs involuntarily").
18 *EE* 1228a7–11 may appear to be a counterexample. But this passage, like *MM* i 12 appears to use 'virtue' (*aretē*) and 'vice' (*kakia*) for actions.
19 I discuss this argument in detail in chapter 5.
20 As his concluding remarks indicate (*EN* 1114b26–30). However, this intention is not announced at the beginning of the discussion of voluntariness.
21 *EE* 1222a17, 1227b9–11, 1228a1–2, 1233a3; *EN* 1114a32–b1, 1127a27; cf. *Rhet.* 1366a26.

22 One might worry that since Aristotle includes strength and speed among his examples of praiseworthy things, the praiseworthiness he here attributes to states of moral character is not specifically moral. But in *EE* viii 3, Aristotle restricts the account of praiseworthiness to exclude such states, on the grounds that the goods they produce are not good without qualification (*EE* 1248b19–34). He restricts praiseworthiness to the virtues of character because only their products cannot be misused. Praiseworthiness in this restricted sense is a specifically moral assessment. Aristotle in *EN* i 12 includes examples of non-moral praiseworthiness because he is concerned in part to illustrate the difference between praise and encomium, and both non-moral and moral examples of praiseworthiness support the distinction.

23 A phrase reminiscent of Meno's proposed definition of virtue at *Meno* 77b.

24 The enumeration of the individual virtues and vices in the *MM* is less detailed than those of the *EE* and *EN*, but there too the praiseworthiness or blameworthiness of a state is invariably explained by reference to the activities to which it gives rise, not its causal antecedents. For example, states concerning appetite (1191b2), and states concerning anger (1191b34–8; cf. 1192a1–7, b2, 20, 36–7; 1193a21–4).

25 Fritzsche suggests deleting *dia* ("because"), a recommendation with which Woods concurs (Woods 1982), and which is executed by Rackham in the Loeb text of the *EE* (Rackham 1935). The exclusion removes the awkwardness of *hosōn* in 1223a12, but the whole passage is severely anacolouthic, and it is easy to suppose that *hosōn* represents the accusative object of *dia* attracted into the genitive of the relative clause. All the MSS read *dia*, and it is clearly the *lectio difficilior*. Furthermore, as I will argue, the difficulty disappears once we understand the claim in the context of Aristotle's account of praiseworthiness.

26 Praise is from (*apo* or *ek*) feelings or actions: "praise comes from the actions according to the virtues" (*apo gar tōn kat' autas praxeōn*) *MM* 1183b27; "praise is from the actions" (*ek tōn praxeōn*) *Rhet.* 1387b22; cf. *EE* 1219b10–11. We are praised and blamed for (*epi* + dative) actions and feelings (*EN* 1109b30–1, 1110a23, 1127b18; *MM* 1188a19). At *MM* 1187a20–21, praise and blame are said to be for (*epi* + dative) virtue and vice; however, this context is one in which terms like 'virtue' and 'vice' are used interchangeably with locutions for good and bad actions. So this use does not count as a credible counterexample to the claim that the things because of which (*dia*), from which (*ek*, *apo*), and for which (*epi* + dative) we are praised and blamed are not states of character but their products, feelings and actions.

27 *EN* 1104b13–14, 1106b16–17, 23–7, 1107a4–5, 1109a22–4, b30; *EE* 1220b35–1221a15; cf. *MM* 1186b33–4.

28 *EN* 1099b31–2; cf. *Met.* 1026b4–10. *Met.* 1026b5 indicates that the difference between *praktikos* and *poiētikos* is not significant for the efficient-

causal nature of the relation. Aristotle alternates between calling the agent and the agent's state of character productive of good things in exactly the same way that he alternates between referring to an ordinary efficient cause (e.g. the sculptor) either as the sculptor, or as the capacity that makes him a sculptor. That capacity makes him productive of sculpture, and also is itself productive of sculpture; the sculptor produces sculpture according to (*kata*) that capacity (cf. *Met.* 1027a4; *Ph.* 195b24).

29 Aristotle appears to recognize no difference between saying that the virtuous person is productive of good things, and that her state of character is. This too is typical of his treatment of efficient causes, which he generally identifies in terms of their causal powers (as, for example, when he insists that properly speaking the cause of the house is not the man, but the builder – *Ph.* 195b21–5), but sometimes refers to the causal power itself as the efficient cause (195a5–11).

30 Hence *MM* i 9, in a characteristic overstatement, claims that "voluntariness consists in being according to virtue or vice" (*eoiken oun en tō(i) kat' aretēn kai kakian einai to hekousion*, 1187a28–9). The remark belies the initial impression of *MM* i 9–11 that voluntariness is relevant to virtue and vice because they are acquired voluntarily; it indicates that voluntariness is a feature of the exercise of character. It is an overstatement because it leaves no room for voluntary activity by agents (e.g. children and animals) without states of character.

31 *Epainetos* (or *psektos*) applied to actions: *EN* 1109a29, 1169a31–5; *EE* 1232a33, 1248b19–25. *Epainetos* (or *psektos*) applied to feelings: *EN* 1175b29; cf. 1178b16.

32 *EN* 1103a8–10, 1105b31–1106a2; 1185b8–9; cf. *MM* 1187a3–4, *EE* 1219b8–17. Aristotle's non-technical discussion of virtue in *Rhet.* i 9 also emphasizes the centrality of virtue to praiseworthiness. There he claims that "virtue and vice are the targets (*skopoi*) of the one praising and blaming" (1366a23–4) and that the activity of praise "displays the magnitude of virtue" (1367b28).

33 Aristotle emphasizes this aspect of praising and blaming in the *Rhet.*, when he remarks that deeds (*erga*) are signs of the agent's state, and that we might praise someone even if he has not performed the deed in question if we think he is the sort to do so (1367b32–4). The remark is clearly motivated by the thought that when praising someone's actions, one is really praising the person whose actions they are on the ground that his state is of a praiseworthy sort.

34 Randall Curren makes a similar point in his discussion of Aristotle's views on responsibility for character in *EN* iii 5 (Curren 1989). I discuss that chapter of the *EN* in chapter 5.

35 For this reason, we need not choose between the positions of Roberts, who concludes from Aristotle's ascription of voluntariness to non-moral agents

that his concern with voluntariness is not a concern with moral responsibility (Roberts 1989), and Irwin, who explores the possibility that the ascription is not Aristotle's considered view, because he thinks Aristotle's account of voluntariness is concerned with moral responsibility (Irwin 1980b, pp. 124–6).

3

The Dialectical Inquiry into Voluntariness

◆

The argument of the preceding chapter gives us reason to suppose that Aristotle has a positive theoretical project to pursue in his inquiries into the nature of voluntariness, and that this project amounts to an inquiry into the conditions in which agents are morally responsible for their actions. That is, he intends his account of voluntariness to capture those actions for which agents are praiseworthy and blameworthy, and his account of praiseworthiness, with its connection to the account of virtue and vice of character, shows that the praiseworthiness and blameworthiness in question are the sort relevant to moral responsibility.

This diagnosis of Aristotle's goals in discussing voluntariness arises from considering the reasons he himself gives for including such a discussion in his general discussion of the virtues and vices of character. It is, however, at odds with an influential assessment of Aristotle's account of voluntariness. According to this view, the "account" simply reproduces contemporary criteria for imputability, and displays no concern to provide a theoretical account of moral responsibility, or indeed of anything else.[1] My project in the present chapter is to contest this view, and to support the diagnosis by examining the discussions of voluntariness themselves. I shall be concerned less with the actual definitions of voluntariness that Aristotle offers[2] than with the arguments on the basis of which he arrives at these definitions. I will argue that Aristotle arrives at these definitions using his characteristic argumentative and heuristic method, dialectical argument, and that the nature of the dialectical argument he offers shows his concerns to be exactly what the previous chapter leads us to expect.

1   Dialectic and the Inquiry into Voluntariness

A dialectical argument proceeds by appeal to the reputable opinions (*endoxa*) about the subject under consideration.[3] These preliminary considerations are the views "of the many and the wise", which appear to have at least some initial plausibility, and in the light of which any philosophical account of the matter must be evaluated. The first stage of dialectical argument is critical: it examines the preliminary considerations and exposes conflicts or puzzles that arise from their combination. The second stage of dialectical argument is constructive; it solves the conflicts by revising the preliminary considerations that give rise to them. The account that emerges from this revision is supposed to be justified to the extent that it preserves the "most and the most important" of the preliminary considerations. We will see that the preliminary considerations from which Aristotle begins his dialectical inquiry into voluntariness, the sorts of difficulties he finds in them, and the solutions he proposes, show that his goal is to find an account of voluntariness that counts as voluntary those actions for which agents are praiseworthy and blameworthy, and that the praise and blame in question are of the sort relevant to moral responsibility.

The "reputable opinions" (*endoxa*) from which Aristotle develops his account of voluntariness include: ordinary pre-philosophical criteria for and paradigms of voluntariness and involuntariness available to any Greek speaker competent in the use of '*hekōn*' and '*akōn*'; ordinary assumptions about the significance of voluntariness, including the assumption that praiseworthy and blameworthy activity must be voluntary; independently plausible examples of praiseworthy and blameworthy activity; and a rival philosophical account of voluntariness. In the "aporetic" stage of the dialectical argument, Aristotle shows that these preliminary considerations conflict. In particular, he shows that both the ordinary criteria for voluntariness and involuntariness and the rival philosophical account of voluntariness fail to count as voluntary a significant range of activity that is clearly praiseworthy and blameworthy. In the constructive stage of the argument, Aristotle revises the ordinary criteria so as to accommodate this activity as voluntary, and rejects the rival philosophical account because it fails to count it as voluntary. His various accounts of voluntariness are products of this dialectical inquiry, and the conception of praiseworthiness and blameworthiness that plays such an important regulative role in its constructive stages turns out to be the same account of praiseworthiness that we saw, in chapter 2, Aristotle intends his account of voluntariness to capture.

The view that Aristotle's concern with voluntariness is not theoretical arises from paying disproportionate attention to *EN* iii 1, where he appears to arrive at his definition of voluntariness by means of a simple negative contrast with two apparently well-understood categories of involuntary activity:

> Since the involuntary is what happens by force and what happens because of ignorance, the voluntary would seem to be that whose origin is in the agent who knows the particulars in which the action occurs. (*EN* 1111a22–4)

If his definition of voluntariness emerges from such a simple "negative" procedure, then it is not the product of the sort of dialectical inquiry I have described above. If, however, we examine the discussions that yield the definition of voluntariness in the *EE* (and the very similar argument in the *MM*),[4] the account of voluntariness in the *EN* takes on an entirely different appearance. In the *EE*, Aristotle arrives at his proposed definitions of voluntariness from considerations that are more clearly dialectical, aporetic, and theoretical, and his discussion does conform to the dialectical strategy I have sketched. This dialectical discussion leaves unresolved a major difficulty, which the account of voluntariness in *EN* iii 1 solves. Far from employing a simple negative procedure, it marks the final stage of the dialectical argument begun in the *EE*. Indeed, once we are acquainted with the nature of that dialectical argument, we will see that the two conceptions of involuntariness with which Aristotle contrasts voluntariness in *EN* iii 1 are not simply pre-theoretical givens, well-understood and uncontroversial examples of involuntary activity. They, no less than the definition of voluntariness with which Aristotle contrasts them, are to a significant degree achievements of the dialectical argument begun in the *EE*.

So let us turn to consider the discussion, in *EE* ii 7–9, from which Aristotle adduces the definition of voluntariness articulated in *EE* ii 9. As with *EN* iii 1, the initial appearance of the discussion is misleading. When considered at a certain level of abstraction it does not appear to be dialectical. Rather, it appears to be a simple deductive argument by elimination which proceeds from an assumption articulated at the beginning of *EE* ii 7:

Let us first inquire into the voluntary and the involuntary. Now it would appear to be one of these three things – either according to (*kata*) desire or according to decision or according to thought – the voluntary being according to (*kata*) one of these, the involuntary contrary to (*para*) one of these. (*EE* 1223a23–6)

The assumption can be stated as the following two premises:

1   For some X, voluntariness consists in being according to X, and involuntariness consists in being contrary to X (1223a25–6).[5]
2   X is either desire, decision, or thought (1223a23–4).

After stating this assumption, Aristotle proceeds to argue that:

3   X is not desire (1223a29–b38).
4   X is not decision (1223b38–1224a4).
5   Therefore, X is thought (1224a5–8).

Aristotle recapitulates this argument at the beginning of *EE* ii 9 (1225a36–b1), and offers his definitions of voluntariness and involuntariness in interpretation of the argument's conclusion (1225b1–10). Considered at this level of abstraction, the argument that generates the Eudemian definition of voluntariness is perfectly straightforward and deductive rather than dialectical. While the premises from which it proceeds may well be dialectical, the argument lacks the aporetic and revisionary features characteristic of dialectical argument.

However, if we examine the considerations Aristotle adduces in support of premise (3) in this argument – a set of considerations whose length and detail is all out of proportion to the subordinate role it plays in this simple deductive argument – the aporetic features of Aristotle's argument will become apparent. And if we understand the relation between these aporetic considerations and the extended discussion of force (*bia*) in *EE* ii 8, which Aristotle inserts immediately following the conclusion of the argument at 1224a7 but before the interpretation of that conclusion at *EE* ii 9, 1225a36, we will see the revisionary and constructive aspects of Aristotle's argument.[6] These discussions of desire (1223a29–b38) and force (1224a7–1225a36) comprise the bulk of Aristotle's discussion of voluntariness and involuntariness in *EE* ii 7–9. They comprise the extended dialectical inquiry into voluntariness that I have sketched. Let us first examine the considerations Aristotle adduces in the argument against defining voluntariness and involuntariness in terms of desire. For simplicity, I will sometimes refer to this discussion as "the argument against desire".

2 The Aporetic Discussion of Desire (*EE* 1223a29–b38)

Aristotle's argument for step (3) in the deductive argument by elimination appears quite out of place in that argument. It appeals to premises that are obviously mutually inconsistent and not all of which Aristotle endorses.[7] Viewed as a piece of deductive argument in support of Aristotle's definition of voluntariness, these features of his discussion render it unsound. However, these features are quite compatible with good dialectical argument, for a dialectical inquiry explores different initially plausible considerations which may have conflicting consequences. The premises of a dialectical inquiry therefore need not be mutually consistent. Furthermore, in cases where the initial considerations conflict, the dialectical conclusion is reached by revising the initial considerations to avoid the conflict. Therefore, the premises of a dialectical argument may be inconsistent with its conclusion. The initial inconsistencies are the puzzles (*aporiai*) that one raises in the initial, critical stage of a dialectical inquiry. Aristotle's argument against defining voluntariness and involuntariness in terms of desire gives every indication of being such an aporetic discussion. Indeed, the corresponding argument in the *MM* (1187b37–1188a37) explicitly proclaims itself to be aporetic (1188a25–6; cf. a36–7).[8]

When Aristotle considers the proposal that voluntariness is to be defined as what is according to desire and involuntariness as what is contrary to desire, he first divides desire (*orexis*) into its three subspecies: appetite (*epithumia*), spirit (*thumos*), and wish (*boulēsis*) (1223a26–8). He then argues against the proposed definition by taking up each of these three kinds of desire in turn: appetite at 1223a29–b17, spirit at 1223b18–24, and wish at 1223b24–36. He discusses each of these by appeal to three sets of dialectical considerations. These considerations, and the use to which Aristotle puts them, are spelled out most fully in the discussion of appetite (1223a29–b17), which begins by introducing a set of considerations about the relation between force, pain, voluntariness and involuntariness:

I

It seems that everything according to appetite is voluntary. For it seems that everything involuntary is forced (*biaion*), and what is forced is painful. . . . So if something is painful, it is forced, and if forced, painful. What is contrary to appetite is painful (for appetite is of what is pleasant), so it is forced and involuntary. So what is according to appetite is voluntary, for these are opposites. (1223a29–36)

He next introduces a set of considerations about the injustice of incontinent and the justice of continent activity:[9]

II
Furthermore, every vice (*mochthēria*) makes its possessor worse; incontinence seems to be vice; and the incontinent person (of the sort who acts contrary to his reason and according to his appetite) acts incontinently whenever he acts according to appetite. But doing injustice (*adikein*) is voluntary . . . , so he will act voluntarily and what is according to appetite is voluntary. Indeed, it would be strange if becoming incontinent were to make one more just. (1223a36–b3)

From each of these sets of considerations Aristotle draws the consequence that incontinent action is voluntary. He next introduces a third set of considerations, which entails the contradictory verdict. These are considerations about the relation between voluntariness and wish:

III
From the former considerations, it would appear that what is according to appetite is voluntary, but from the following considerations, we get the opposite result. For whatever someone does voluntarily, he wishes to do, and whatever he wishes to do he does voluntarily. No one wishes to do what he thinks is bad; yet, the incontinent person does what he does not wish to do – for acting contrary to what one thinks best but because of appetite is acting incontinently. So it follows that the same person acts voluntarily and involuntarily. But this is impossible. (1223b3–10)

Having shown that the first and second sets of considerations conflict with the third, Aristotle proceeds to show that the first set conflicts with the second. While the first set entails that continent action is involuntary, the second entails that it is voluntary:[10]

But still, the continent person will do justice (*dikaiopragēsei*) (that is, he rather than the incontinent person will do so). For continence is virtue (*aretē*), and virtue makes people more just. One acts continently when one acts contrary to appetite and according to reason. So if doing justice, like doing injustice (*adikein*), is voluntary (and it appears that both are voluntary, and if one of them is voluntary, so is the other), but what is contrary to appetite is involuntary, then the same person at the same time will perform the same action both voluntarily and involuntarily. (1223b10–17)

This concludes the discussion of appetite. The discussion of spirit, which follows immediately (1223b18–24), explicitly invokes only considerations of the first set (those concerning force and pain). But Aristotle indicates that *mutatis mutandis* the arguments used in the discussion of appetite yield contradictory verdicts about the voluntariness of the variety of continent and incontinent activity in which spirit, rather than appetite, opposes rational desire (1223b18–19, 24–6). Therefore, these arguments must also appeal to considerations of the second set (about the justice and injustice of continence and incontinence) and third set (about the relation of voluntariness and wish).

The discussion of wish (1223b28–36), which concludes Aristotle's discussion of desire, is considerably less elaborate than his discussions of appetite and spirit. But, as he does in those discussions, here too he indicates that considerations of the second set conflict with those of the third about the voluntariness of incontinent action. He appeals to the considerations about the injustice of incontinence (II) to draw the conclusion that such action is voluntary, and to the considerations about wish and voluntariness (III) to draw the conclusion that it is involuntary:

We assume, and it appears to be the case, that vice (*mochthēria*) makes one more unjust, and incontinence is clearly a vice. But the opposite turns out to be the case. For certainly no one wishes for what they think is bad, but one does do such things when one becomes incontinent. But if doing injustice (*adikein*) is voluntary, and the voluntary is what is according to wish, then someone who becomes incontinent no longer does injustice, and is on the contrary more just than before he became incontinent. But this is impossible. (1223b30–6)

Having taken up each of the three types of desire, Aristotle immediately concludes that "the voluntary is not what is according to desire, and the involuntary is not what is contrary to desire" (1223b36–8). That is, he asserts premise (3) of the deductive argument. The discussion on the basis of which Aristotle has established this conclusion conforms exactly to the critical or "aporetic" stage of a dialectical argument. He appeals to three sets of views about voluntariness and involuntariness that appear initially plausible,[11] and shows that they conflict with each other.

One might well wonder why Aristotle chooses to appeal to these conflicting considerations in order to argue against the proposal that the voluntary and the involuntary are to be defined as, respectively, what is according to and what is contrary to desire.[12] For the contradictory verdicts about the voluntariness of continent and incontinent actions are straightforward consequences of the proposal itself. The proposal entails that any action according to desire is voluntary, and that any action contrary to desire is involuntary. But continent (or incontinent) action is contrary to one desire and according to another. So the proposed definition entails the contradictory claim that continent (or incontinent) action is both voluntary and involuntary. Anything that entails a contradiction is false, so Aristotle would have a valid and considerably more streamlined argument against the proposal if he inferred the contradictory verdicts directly from it, and then concluded that it is false. In order to appreciate why Aristotle chooses instead to proceed aporetically, let us examine the three sets of dialectical considerations from which he raises the contradictory verdicts, and identify the relation of these considerations to the proposed definition. Once we identify the roles they play in Aristotle's discussion of the proposed definition, and the ways they are revised in the light of the conflicting results they produce, we will be able to appreciate the constructive aspects of Aristotle's argument, and we will see that in it he has succeeded not only in eliminating the proposed definition. He has indicated why he thinks the proposal is initially plausible, what he thinks is correct about it, and where he thinks it goes wrong.

3 The Dialectical Premises

The first set of considerations[13] that Aristotle introduces into the discussion of desire may be stated as follows:

I
(a) All involuntary actions are forced (*biaion*).
(b) All painful actions are forced.
(c) Voluntary and involuntary are contraries (*enantia*).

These claims take forced action to be the paradigm for all involuntariness, and take the contrast between forced and unforced action to provide a model for the general distinction between involuntary and voluntary. A central feature of forced action, Aristotle indicates in the next chapter in a definition he also presents as intuitive and uncontroversial, is that it is contrary to one's inclination or impulse (*hormē*) (1224a15–23). This is why forced movement is painful in sentient beings. Given these assumptions, voluntary and involuntary turn out to be contrary properties, not merely contradictories (1224a14–15); force involves contrariety to the impulse that unforced activity is in accord with.

These considerations betray the assumption that motivates and makes plausible the proposal that is under consideration in this aporetic discussion: the thesis that voluntariness consists in acting according to desire, and involuntariness in acting contrary to desire. Indeed, they motivate the general assumption with which Aristotle begins his search for a definition of voluntariness in *EE* ii 7: the assumption that voluntariness is according to, and involuntariness contrary to, some faculty of the soul.[14] Aristotle acknowledges this explicitly immediately after concluding the deductive argument:

> The preceding discussion concerned doing things by force and not by force, since we say that what is forced is involuntary and everything involuntary is forced. (1224a9–11)

He here indicates that the first set of dialectical considerations invoked in the discussion of desire – the considerations that take forced movement to be a paradigm for all involuntariness – provides the original premise (1) from which the deductive argument by elimination begins. This feature of the strategy is especially clear in the *MM*'s version of the argument, which begins with the proposal that "roughly speaking, the voluntary is what we do when we are not compelled" (1187b34–5) and whose subsequent discussion clearly assumes compulsion (*anankē*)[15] to be a feature of all involuntary activity (cf. 1188a1–2).

Clearly, Aristotle does not ultimately endorse the assumption (I(a)) that all involuntary actions are forced (*EE* 1223a29–30, 1224a11; *MM* 1188a1–2) – since his definition of involuntariness in *EE* ii 9 captures actions that are due to ignorance but do not involve force. Nor does he endorse the assumption (I(b)) that painfulness (or contrariety to impulse) is sufficient to render an action involuntary.[16] He rejects this principle while discussing incontinence in *EE* ii 8. However, as dialectical premises, these assumptions need not be ones Aristotle embraces without reservation or qualification; they need only state principles that have some core of plausibility. Even though Aristotle does not ultimately endorse the dialectical proposal that only forced or compelled actions are involuntary, his discussion of voluntariness begins from considerations that express the thought that some feature distinctive of forced action is common to all involuntary activity. Our examination of the later stages of the dialectical argument will indicate what feature Aristotle takes this to be.[17] But for the present, let us continue our examination of the dialectical considerations from which that argument begins.

The second set of dialectical considerations to which Aristotle appeals in the dialectical discussion of desire concerns the justice of continence and the injustice of incontinence.[18] These considerations can be stated roughly as follows:

II

(a) Continence is a virtue (*aretē*) and incontinence a vice (*mochthēria*).

(b) To act continently is to "do justice" (*dikaiopragein*), and to act incontinently is to "do injustice" (*adikein*).

(c) "Doing justice" (*dikaiopragein*) and "doing injustice" (*adikein*) are voluntary.

Unlike the first set of considerations, this second set does not express views about what makes an action voluntary. It presents continent and incontinent activity as examples of actions that express virtue and vice of character, and insists that such actions must be voluntary.

The claim (II(a)) that incontinence is a vice and continence a virtue should not be interpreted to mean that continence satisfies Aristotle's criteria for complete and perfect virtue of character, and incontinence the criteria for complete and perfect vice.[19] Although Aristotle does sometimes distinguish incontinence from full vice, and continence from full virtue (*EN* 1128b33–4, 1150b32), he also allows that incontinence is a kind of vice (1148a2–4, 1151a6). He endorses the view that, like full virtue, continence is an excellent and praiseworthy disposition; and that, like full vice, incontinence is a base and blameworthy disposition.[20] In calling continence a virtue and incontinence a vice, Aristotle means that they are more and less good states of character which, although they fall short of perfect virtue and vice, nonetheless make the agents who possess them praiseworthy and blameworthy.[21] Aristotle sometimes uses 'doing-justice' (*dikaiopragein*) and 'doing-injustice' (*adikein*) to capture the full range of virtuous and vicious activity.[22] This is how he uses the terms in II(b); to count continent activity as "doing justice" and incontinent activity as "doing injustice" is to count them as expressions of, respectively, virtue and vice of character.

Once we recognize that "doing justice" and "doing injustice" in II(b) encompass all activity for which agents are praiseworthy and blameworthy, the third claim (II(c)) – that all such activity is voluntary – is unsurprising. It simply repeats the view to which Aristotle appeals when he introduces the discussion of voluntariness into the discussion of character in the first place: the view that we are praiseworthy and blameworthy only for our voluntary activity (*EE* 1223a10–18; *EN* 1109b31). The *MM*'s version of these considerations makes it explicit that Aristotle is appealing to the view that praiseworthy and blameworthy activity is voluntary. In explaining why continent action is voluntary, it says: "The continent person does the continent action voluntarily, for he is praised, and praise is for voluntary things" (*MM* 1188a17–19). And in explaining why the incontinent action is voluntary, it says: "If he is not voluntary, then he is not blameworthy. But the incontinent *is* blameworthy, so he is voluntary" (1188a34–5).

In general, we can say that this second set of dialectical considerations presents what are supposed to be uncontroversial examples of praiseworthy and blameworthy activity – cases of doing justice and doing injustice, respectively – and expresses the requirement that such activity be voluntary. Later on, we will see that these considerations play an important regulative role in the constructive stage of Aristotle's dialectical inquiry into voluntariness. For the present, let us turn to examine the third and final set of dialectical considerations from which that inquiry begins.

These considerations are briefly stated and require only brief discussion at this point. Aristotle states these considerations in the *EE* as: "Whatever one does voluntarily one wishes (*bouletai*) to do, and whatever one wishes to do one does voluntarily" (1223b5–6; cf. *MM* 1188a6–9). These remarks express the Platonic view that:

III
   (a) All and only actions performed on rational desire are voluntary.

This Platonic view would certainly be familiar to the audience to whom Aristotle presents the dialectical argument of *EE* ii 7–9, and it is a rival to the account of voluntariness that he eventually develops.[23] His dialectical method requires him to take such a rival view into account because the class of the "reputable opinions" (*endoxa*) from which dialectical inquiry begins includes not only the views of "the many" – views whose wide acceptance is some evidence for their plausibility – but also those of "the wise" (*hoi sophoi*): the views of those who have thought carefully and competently about the subject and for that reason deserve to have their opinions taken seriously.[24] Just as Aristotle considers Socrates' account of incontinence in the course of his own dialectical inquiry into incontinence (*EN* 1145b22–7), he discusses Plato's account of voluntariness in the course of his dialectical inquiry into voluntariness. If Aristotle opts for an account of voluntariness other than the Platonic one, he needs to show what is wrong with the Platonic view, and also to acknowledge what makes it appear plausible.

We may now return to the question of why Aristotle, when he sets out to establish that voluntariness cannot be defined as what is according to desire and involuntariness as what is contrary to desire (1223a29–b37), fails to give the simple and valid deductive argument that is available to him but instead chooses to show that these three sets of dialectical considerations conflict. These considerations, we have seen, have a much wider significance than their subordinate place in the deductive argument would indicate. Considerations of the first set show why the proposed definitions of voluntariness and involuntariness are worthy of consideration in the first place. Considerations of the second set propose a test that these definitions must pass if they are to be acceptable. And considerations of the third set identify a rival view that must be defeated if they are to stand. Teasing out the conflicts between these sets of considerations is therefore not irrelevant to evaluating the proposed definitions.

I suggest that Aristotle chooses to raise these dialectical puzzles, rather than show in a more straightforward way that the proposed definitions are false, because he thinks the definitions are basically correct, and he has a view about how they can be revised to avoid the difficulties that the puzzles expose. Such revision of initially plausible premises is the constructive stage of dialectical argument. So far, we have seen only the aporetic stage of Aristotle's argument. But if we proceed to consider the rest of his discussion in *EE* ii 7–9 we will see that Aristotle proposes solutions to the puzzles he has raised, and that these solutions yield the account of voluntariness and involuntariness that he offers in *EE* ii 9. The next two stages of the discussion are the brief discussion of decision (*prohairesis*) at 1223b38–1224a4, and the extended discussion of force (*bia*) at 1224a8–1225a33. In the former passage, Aristotle indicates that he resolves the conflict between the judgments of praiseworthiness (II) and the Platonic account of voluntariness (III) in favour of the former set of considerations (II). In the latter passage, he indicates that he resolves the conflict between the ordinary criteria for involuntariness (I) and the judgements of praiseworthiness (II) in favour of the latter set (II). That is, we will see that the judgments of praiseworthiness play an important regulative role in Aristotle's dialectical discussion of voluntariness. By the end of *EE* ii 8, Aristotle has criticized and revised the ordinary criteria for voluntariness (I), in order to fit the criteria for praiseworthiness (II), and has appealed to these same criteria for praiseworthiness (II) in order to dispose of the Platonic definition of voluntariness (III). Let us first examine the discussion of decision (1223b38–1224a4), which functions as the argument for step (4) in the deductive argument by elimination. We will see that it also marks the first step in the constructive stage of Aristotle's dialectical inquiry into voluntariness.

4 Solving the Puzzles: The Discussion of Decision (*EE* 1223b38–1224a4)

After concluding that voluntariness is not to be defined in terms of desire, Aristotle next considers the proposal that it can be defined in terms of decision (*prohairesis*):

> It is now clear that the voluntary is not what is according to desire and the involuntary what is contrary to desire. That it is also not according to decision is clear from the following considerations. *It has been established that what is according to wish is not involuntary, but rather that everything that is wished is voluntary. (No, it has only been shown that one can do voluntarily even what one does not wish to do.)* And we do many things, wishing to do them, but suddenly, and no one decides on anything suddenly. (1223b38–1224a4; emphasis added)

His argument against the proposal is quite straightforward. He simply points out that the proposed definition fails to state a necessary condition for voluntariness (1224a3–4). For our purposes, the most significant feature of this brief argument is that Aristotle here indicates that the preceding dialectical discussion of desire has not been merely aporetic. The crucial remarks are at 1223b39–1224a3 (emphasized in the quotation above), where Aristotle maintains that two theses have been established. First of all, he claims that it was established (*apedeichthē*, 1224a1) that:

(i) all action according to wish is voluntary (1223b39–1224a2).

Next, in the parenthesis at 1224a2–3, he anticipates an objection to the effect that (i) has not in fact been established. The objector presumably claims that it has been shown (*dedeiktai*, 1224a3) that:

(ii) action not according to wish (*mē boulomenon*) can be voluntary.

In the parenthesis Aristotle agrees that thesis (ii) has been established (*dedeiktai*), but points out that thesis (ii) does not conflict with thesis (i). Thesis (ii) only (*monon*) establishes, he says, "that one can also do voluntarily what one does not wish to do" (1224a2–3) – i.e., that being according to wish is not necessary for voluntariness.[25]

In affirming that (i) and (ii) have been established, Aristotle in effect announces that he has rejected and revised the third set of dialectical considerations appealed to in the preceding dialectical discussion of desire: the Platonic proposal that all and only actions according to wish are voluntary (1223b5–6, 34). In claiming that thesis (i) has been established, Aristotle indicates that one half of the Platonic proposal has been confirmed: *all* actions according to wish are voluntary. In claiming to have established thesis (ii), he indicates that the other half of the Platonic proposal has been disproved: not *only* actions according to wish are voluntary. The only discussion in which Aristotle can think he has established theses (i) and (ii) is the preceding dialectical discussion of desire (1223a29–b37). Therefore, he must think that that dialectical discussion advances beyond the aporetic stage. In effect, Aristotle's brief remarks about decision indicate that the preceding dialectical discussion of desire has established the falsity of, and revised, one of its dialectical premises.[26] The premise that has been rejected and reformulated is the Platonic definition of voluntariness.

If we return to re-examine the dialectical discussion of desire, and identify the places in that discussion where Aristotle must think theses (i) and (ii) have been established, we will see that Aristotle has rejected the Platonic definition of voluntariness (the third set of dialectical considerations) because it conflicts with the second set of dialectical considerations (the judgements about praiseworthiness and blameworthiness). We will also see that he has revised the Platonic proposal by appeal to those same considerations. Let us first of all find out where Aristotle thinks he has established thesis (ii), and after that determine where he thinks he has established thesis (i).

Aristotle's articulation of thesis (ii) in the parenthesis at 1224a1–3 indicates that it has been established in response to the contradictory proposal that "what is contrary to wish is involuntary." Such a principle is appealed to at two places in the dialectical discussion of desire – in both cases as a consequence of the Platonic definition of voluntariness. The first is where Aristotle introduces the Platonic account as the third set of dialectical considerations, and draws from it the consequence that the incontinent agent, who acts contrary to his wish, acts involuntarily:

> From the former considerations, it would appear that what is according to appetite is voluntary, but from the following considerations, we get the opposite result. For whatever someone does voluntarily, he wishes to do, and whatever he wishes to do he does voluntarily. No one wishes to do what he thinks is bad; yet, the incontinent person does what he does not wish to do – for acting contrary to what one thinks best but because of appetite is acting incontinently. So it follows that the same person acts voluntarily and involuntarily. But this is impossible. (1223b3–10)

Aristotle points outs that this conclusion conflicts with the second set of dialectical considerations ("the former considerations" referred to at b3), which entails that the incontinent action is voluntary, since it is blameworthy (1223a36–b3). He does not here indicate how he proposes to resolve the conflict. But the second passage in which he considers the claim that action contrary to wish is involuntary shows that he proposes to resolve the conflict in favour of the second set of dialectical considerations.

This second passage is his brief consideration of wish, where he again shows that the considerations of the second set (the considerations about praiseworthiness and voluntariness) conflict with the Platonic definition of voluntariness:

> We assume, and it appears to be the case, that vice (*mochthēria*) makes one more unjust, and incontinence is clearly a vice. But the opposite turns out to be the case. For certainly no one wishes for what they think is bad, but one does do such things when one becomes incontinent. But if doing injustice (*adikein*) is voluntary, and the voluntary is what is

according to wish, then someone who becomes incontinent no longer does injustice, and is on the contrary more just than before he became incontinent. But this is impossible. (1223b30–6)

As in the first passage (1223b3–10), the aspect of the Platonic definition that generates the conflicting verdict is the principle rejected by (ii): the principle that action contrary to wish is involuntary. But unlike the first passage, Aristotle here makes it quite clear how he proposes to resolve the conflict. For he takes the considerations of the second set (the considerations about praiseworthiness and voluntariness) to be a fixed point in the argument. He presents them as considerations that hold a special status in the argument.[27] When the Platonic proposal yields a conclusion that conflicts with these considerations, he calls "impossible" not the conjunction of the conflicting claims (as he does at 1223b10), but the consequence of the Platonic proposal. Aristotle without hesitation resolves the conflict between the second and third sets of dialectical considerations in favour of the second set. He establishes thesis (ii) in the dialectical discussion of desire by showing that its contradictory conflicts with the second set of dialectical considerations.

Let us now consider where in the dialectical discussion Aristotle can have established the truth of thesis (i). We will see that he thinks he has done so by resolving another of the dialectical puzzles in favour of the second set of dialectical considerations. As in the case of thesis (ii), Aristotle's introduction of thesis (i) indicates that he has established it in opposition to the contradictory proposal that an action according to wish is involuntary:

It has been established (*apedeichthē*) that what is according to wish is not involuntary, but rather that everything that is wished is voluntary. (*EE* 1223b39–1224a2)

The only place in the discussion of desire where Aristotle considers such a proposal is at the end of his discussion of appetite, where he considers the proposal that the continent agent, who acts according to wish,[28] acts involuntarily.

But still, the continent person will do justice (*dikaiopragēsei*) (that is, he rather than the incontinent person will do so). For continence is virtue (*aretē*), and virtue makes people more just. One acts continently when one acts contrary to appetite and according to reason. So if doing justice, like doing injustice (*adikein*), is voluntary (and it appears that both are voluntary, and if one of them is voluntary, so is the other), but what is contrary to appetite is involuntary, then the same person at the same time will perform the same action both voluntarily and involuntarily. (1223b10–17)

He infers the proposal from the principle that "what is contrary to appetite is involuntary" (b16–17), which is itself a consequence of the first set of dialectical considerations. But first he points out that the proposal conflicts with the second set of considerations (b10–16). Aristotle does not explicitly indicate here how he proposes to resolve the conflict. However, since this is the only context in which he considers the proposal, and hence the only place in which he can have shown it to be false (and thesis (ii) to be true), he must resolve the conflict in favour of the second set of dialectical considerations.

We have now seen how the third set of dialectical considerations has fared in the constructive stage of Aristotle's dialectical argument in *EE* ii 7–9. Aristotle has rejected and revised the Platonic definition of voluntariness, and has done so by consistently resolving dialectical puzzles in favour of the second set of dialectical considerations. Let us now consider how the first set of considerations fares in that stage of the argument. These are the considerations that take force to be the paradigm for all involuntariness. Here too we will see that Aristotle rejects and revises these considerations by appeal to the second set of dialectical considerations.

Our examination of the constructive stage of the argument has already shown that Aristotle is committed to rejecting this first set of considerations. For we have just seen that he establishes thesis (i) at 1223b10–17 by resolving a conflict between considerations I and II in favour of II. But, as in the case of the third set of considerations, he thinks the first set contains a core of plausibility, and he revises it accordingly. The dialectical discussion of desire shows that Aristotle thinks the plausible view motivated by the first set of considerations is the proposal that voluntariness consists in acting according to desire. For in discussing each of the three types of desire, he appeals to considerations of set II to endorse the consequence of set I that activity according to that kind of desire is voluntary: he first introduces the considerations of set II (1223a36–b4) in support of the verdict of set I that action according to appetite is voluntary; he indicates that the same argument shows that activity according to spirit is voluntary (1223b18), and we have already seen that at 1223b10–17 Aristotle establishes that all activity according to wish is voluntary (thesis (i)) by appeal to considerations of set II.

While the dialectical discussion of desire supports the account of voluntariness promoted by the first set of dialectical considerations (that voluntariness consists in being according to desire), it shows to be problematic the account of *in*voluntariness supported by these considerations (the view that involuntariness consists in being contrary to desire). This conception of involuntariness entails that both continent and incontinent activity are involuntary, a result that conflicts with the second set of dialectical considerations, in whose favour we have so far seen Aristotle consistently revises dialectical conflicts. If we turn to examine the extended discussion of force, we will see that in this instance too, Aristotle resolves the conflict in the same direction. He revises the conception of force (*bia*) assumed by the first set of dialectical considerations in such a way that these considerations no longer entail the unacceptable consequence that continent and incontinent action is involuntary.

5   Force and Involuntariness in *EE* ii 8

When introducing the discussion of force, Aristotle makes it clear that the first set of dialectical considerations is now up for reconsideration:

> Let us advance the discussion a little further and complete the definition of the voluntary and involuntary. It seems that the preceding discussion concerned doing something by force and not by force. For we say that what is forced is involuntary and everything involuntary is forced. For this reason, we should inquire first into what happens by force (*bia(i)*) – what it is and its relation to the voluntary and the involuntary. Indeed, it appears that the forced and the compelled (as well as force and compulsion) are contrary to the voluntary and to persuasion in the case of actions. (1224a8–15)

The discussion of force will "complete" the definition of voluntary and involuntary because it will address the remaining puzzle left over from the aporetic discussion of desire: continent and incontinent actions appear to satisfy the conditions for force, and hence (according to I) for involuntariness, but they also satisfy the conditions for praiseworthiness, and hence (according to II) for voluntariness. In the dialectical argument, it was assumed that mere contrariety to desire is sufficient for force, and hence for involuntariness. Aristotle here targets this assumption for re-examination.

When considering force as it applies to the motions of the simplest bodies, Aristotle indicates that contrariety to impulse is sufficient for force:

> Quite generally, force and compulsion apply even to inanimate entities. For we say that a stone travels upward and fire downward by force and under compulsion. When these things travel according to their nature and intrinsic impulse, they are not forced (although not voluntary either, for the contrary has no name). But when they travel contrary to this, we say they are forced. (1224a15–20)

But when he considers the more complex case of animals, whose forced motions are also properly described as involuntary, he explicitly identifies external causation as an additional requirement for force:

> In the same way too, in the case of living things and animals, we see them undergoing and doing many things by force – whenever something from the outside moves them against their internal impulse. (1224a20–3)

Aristotle correctly claims he is applying the same conception of force to both the inanimate and animate cases (a20), even though he does not explicitly state the requirement of external causation in the former case. Since the simple bodies have only a single source of local movement, motion contrary to this internal impulse must be externally caused.[29] External causation is therefore a feature of the forced movements of the simple bodies. But in making this feature an explicit requirement for force, Aristotle makes an important theoretical decision. For not all entities whose activity admits of being forced have only a single internal impulse. As Aristotle himself proceeds to point out:

> In inanimate things, there is only one origin, while in animate creatures there is more than one – for in their case desire and reason do not always agree. So in the case of the other animals, just as in the case of inanimate things, what is forced is simple (*haploun*) (for they do not have opposing reason and desire, but live by desire). But in a human being, there are both ⟨sc. reason and desire⟩ – that is, at a certain age, the one at which we attribute action. (1224a23–8)

In beings with more than one internal impulse, activity contrary to impulse need not be externally caused, since it can be caused by another internal impulse. In order to decide which activities of these more complex entities count as forced, Aristotle must decide whether external causation is an incidental or an essential feature of force in the simple case.

In opting for the latter alternative, Aristotle dissolves the puzzle about continent and incontinent actions. Such actions appear to be forced, Aristotle acknowledges, because they are contrary to impulse, and so have features (e.g. painfulness, reluctance) typically associated with forced movement (1224a31–b2; cf. b15–21). But they fail to be genuinely forced, he insists, because they are not externally caused:

> These agents appear to be forced because of a certain similarity to being forced, a feature which in fact makes the motions of inanimate things forced. However, if one also considers the additional part of the defini-tion, the difficulty is resolved. For whenever something from the outside moves or impedes something contrary to its internal impulse, we say it is forced, but when this is not the case, it is not. But an intrinsic internal impulse drives the incontinent person and the continent person (since they have both kinds ⟨sc. of impulse, reason and desire⟩). Hence neither is forced or compelled, but rather each acts voluntarily. (1224b3–11)

In revising the conception of force assumed by the first set of dialectical considerations, Aristotle resolves the final dialectical puzzle in the same direction as he has resolved all the previous ones; he decides the conflict in favour of the second set of dialectical considerations.

Once he has isolated external causation as necessary for force, Aristotle concludes his discussion of force by considering cases in which it is controversial whether an action has been externally caused and is there-by not up to the agent in the way voluntariness requires (1225a2–33). These controversial cases are ones in which an agent appears to be "forced" by the structure of choices facing him to do something he does not want to do. In the next chapter I will discuss Aristotle's treatment of these difficult cases. For our present purposes, it is more important to note that Aristotle has at this point proposed solutions to all the puzzles raised in the aporetic stage of the dialectical argument. We should ask what that argument has achieved.

6 The Dialectical and Deductive Definitions

With his revised conception of force in hand, Aristotle is in a position to reformulate the account of involuntariness promoted by the first set of dialectical considerations. Given the guiding assumption that force provides a paradigm for all involuntariness, the revised conception of force entails the proposal that involuntary action is both contrary to desire and externally caused. The account of voluntariness and involuntariness that would seem to emerge from the constructive stage of the dialectical argument is therefore:

The dialectical definition
(a) Voluntary action is according to desire;
(b) Involuntary action is both contrary to desire and externally caused.

However, Aristotle does not conclude his discussion of voluntariness in *EE* ii 7–9 with this pair of definitions. Indeed, he never explicitly articulates such a conception of involuntariness. He concludes instead with the following definitions:

> Whatever one does that is up to one not to do, and one does it not in ignorance and because of oneself, must be voluntary. And what one does in ignorance and because of ignorance one does involuntarily. (*EE* 1225b8–10)

He asserts this pair of definitions on the strength of the deductive argument in *EE* ii 7–8 (1224a4–7, 1225a36–b1). It can be formulated as follows:

The deductive definition
(a) Voluntary action is action that is (i) up to one not to do; and that (ii) one performs knowingly and because of oneself.
(b) Involuntary action is action one performs in ignorance and because of being ignorant.

Since Aristotle articulates and endorses the deductive rather than the dialectical definition, it is clear that the deductive definition is the one he thinks the discussion in *EE* ii 7–9 supports. However, the deductive argument by elimination, on which Aristotle appears to be basing it, is effectively undermined by the dialectical argument. As we have seen, that deductive argument proceeds as follows:

The deductive argument by elimination
(1) For some X, voluntariness consists in being according to X, and involuntariness consists in being contrary to X (1223a25–6).

(2)   X is either desire, decision, or thought (1223a23–4).
(3)   X is not desire (1223a29–b38).
(4)   X is not decision (1223b38–1224a4).
(5)   Therefore, X is thought (1224a5–8; 1225a36–b1).

While step (3) of the deductive argument is supposed to eliminate desire from the list of candidates for X, the dialectical considerations Aristotle actually adduces in support of (3) only raise preliminary objections to desire, and in the constructive stage of the dialectical argument (the discussion of force in *EE* ii 8), it is effectively rehabilitated as a candidate for X. That same discussion of force gives us reason to reject (1) in favour of the pair of "dialectical definitions" articulated above. So the dialectical inquiry that runs alongside of the deductive argument shows that argument to be unsound. While the deductive argument by elimination ostensibly yields the definition of voluntariness and involuntariness that Aristotle explicitly endorses in the Eudemian inquiry into voluntariness, the dialectical argument yields the conclusion to which he is there entitled. So why does he assert the deductive rather than the dialectical definition?

I propose that in preferring the deductive to the dialectical definition, Aristotle is extending the dialectical argument begun in *EE* ii 7 by introducing and responding to a new set of considerations not explicitly considered so far. In raising and resolving puzzles involving the three sets of considerations we have examined, Aristotle has succeeded in generating accounts of voluntariness and involuntariness (the dialectical definitions) which conform to the principle that forced action provides a paradigm for all involuntary action. But these definitions succeed too well in satisfying the principle. For according to the dialectical definition of involuntariness only forced actions will count as involuntary. The definition does not count as involuntary actions due to ignorance, since these originate from within the unknowing agent and hence fail to be externally caused. The deductive definition of involuntariness, by contrast, entails that such actions are voluntary. In substituting the deductive for the dialectical definitions, Aristotle is in effect appealing to a fourth set of dialectical considerations:

IV
Actions due to ignorance are involuntary.

Reflecting on this consideration would show that the dialectical definition of involuntariness is unsatisfactory. Thus a new puzzle emerges from the dialectical discussion, and I propose that the so-called "deductive" definition is intended by Aristotle to solve it.

The puzzle, which is generated by dialectical considerations I and IV, might easily be solved by rejecting I. However, Aristotle makes it quite clear when introducing the "deductive" definitions in *EE* ii 9 that he has not abandoned I:

> Since the voluntary is defined neither in terms of desire nor in terms of decision, the remaining possibility is that it is defined as what is according to thought (*to kata tēn dianoian*).
>
> [1] Now it seems that the voluntary is contrary to the involuntary. And [2] to act knowing either to whom or how or with what result one acts (. . .) is contrary to acting in ignorance both of to whom and how and what one does, because of ignorance, not accidentally. [3] What is because of ignorance – of what and how and to whom – is involuntary. [4] So the contrary is voluntary.
>
> So whatever one does that is up to one not to do, and one does it not in ignorance and because of oneself, must be voluntary. And what one does in ignorance and because of ignorance one does involuntarily. (*EE* 1225b1–10).

The "deductive" definition is offered as an interpretation of the conclusion, implicit at 1225a37–b1 (cf. 1224a4–7), that voluntary activity is according to thought and involuntary activity contrary to thought. Thus the definition articulated at 1225b8–10 is here presented as satisfying I(a), the constraint motivated by the first set of dialectical considerations that voluntary activity be according to the faculty to which involuntary activity is contrary. I(a) entails that voluntary and involuntary are contraries, and Aristotle here insists (1225b1–8) that the definition satisfies this constraint. Rather than solving the puzzle by rejecting I(a), Aristotle reaffirms I(a) and proposes to solve the puzzle by casting thought (*dianoia*) in the role of the relevant faculty.

Of course the deductive definition succeeds no better than the dialectical definition at capturing both recognized varieties of involuntary activity. It entails of involuntary action in general that it is due to ignorance; actions due to force, however, need not involve ignorance of any kind. The definition fails because the deductive argument has mistakenly cast thought (*dianoia*) in the role of the impulse (*hormē*) to which voluntary action must be according and involuntary activity contrary. Thought is an inappropriate candidate for this impulse because it is not an impulse at all. Thought on its own moves nothing, Aristotle readily admits (*EN* 1139a35–36; *DA* 432b26–7). Since thought provides no impetus toward action, action cannot be "contrary to thought" in the way that it can be "contrary to desire." Therefore, when Aristotle articulates the "deductive" definition of involuntariness at 1225b9–10 in interpretation of the conclusion that involuntary action is "contrary to thought," he inevitably does so in a way which fails to capture the contrariety to impulse that is essential to forced action.[30]

The failure of the "deductive" definition to solve the problem it addresses is, for our purposes, less important than its goal. For in identifying the problem that Aristotle intends the definition to address, we have seen that it too is a product of the dialectical inquiry into voluntariness in *EE* ii 7–9. The deductive argument that ostensibly generates it is awkwardly imposed on that dialectical discussion in order to address a problem generated by the discussion's preliminary constructive results. We are now in a position to see that the discussion of voluntariness and involuntariness in *EN* iii 1 addresses and solves that remaining problem, and therefore that it too is a product of that same dialectical inquiry.

7 The Nicomachean Discussion of Voluntariness Reconsidered

While the dialectical discussion of *EE* ii 7–9 tries but fails to accommodate both of the recognized classes of involuntary activity, the discussion Aristotle offers in *EN* iii 1 succeeds in doing so. Of course, this feature of the Nicomachean discussion does not of itself establish that Aristotle's concerns there are the same as those that motivate his discussion in *EE* ii 7–9. But it is worth noting that if Aristotle's theoretical concerns in the *EN* are continuous with those of the *EE*, then the emphasis he places in *EN* iii 1 on the two different types of involuntariness is explicable by the fact that he has succeeded in achieving the goal unsuccessfully pursued in the *EE*. We can see the continuity between his concerns in the *EN* and the *EE* by focussing on one of the more puzzling details of his conception of involuntariness in *EN* iii 1.

At the beginning of his discussion of the class of involuntary actions that are not forced but due to ignorance, in a set of remarks that has proved troubling to many commentators, Aristotle insists that being due to ignorance is insufficient to render an action involuntary. An action due to ignorance is involuntary only if it is also painful or regretted:[31]

> Everything that is because of ignorance is not voluntary, but what is involuntary is ⟨also⟩ followed by pain and regretted. For someone who has done something because of ignorance but is not at all pained at the action has not acted voluntarily – since he didn't know what it was – but not involuntarily either, since he is not pained. Of those who act because of ignorance, the one who regrets ⟨acts⟩ involuntarily, but the one who does not regret, since he is different, let ⟨us say he acts⟩ "not-voluntarily." Since he is different, it is better that he have his own name. (*EN* 1110b18–24)

The requirement that involuntary actions be painful or regretted (1110b18–24) is not an isolated remark. Aristotle repeats it at 1111a20–1 after he identifies the kind of ignorance that counts toward involuntariness. Nor does he restrict it to cases of involuntariness due to ignorance, for he requires pain of involuntary actions in general at 1111a32. And he explicitly claims that forced actions are painful:[32]

> Those who act because of force and involuntarily do so with pain, while those who act because of the pleasant and the fine do so with pleasure. (1110b11–13)

We can therefore identify two distinct conditions required of involuntariness in the *EN*:

> Involuntariness in *EN* iii 1:
> (i) Involuntary action is either externally caused or due to ignorance of particular facts.
> (ii) The involuntary agent feels pain at or regret for the action.

The requirement (ii) of pain or regret becomes intelligible when it is viewed in the light of the dialectical argument in *EE* ii 7–9. There we saw that Aristotle takes forced movement to be his paradigm for all involuntary activity, and takes the salient feature of force to be contrariety to impulse. When he revises the criteria for force in *EE* ii 8, he does not abandon the requirement of contrariety to impulse; he simply adds the requirement of external causation. In the *EE*'s discussion, pain is considered necessary for involuntariness because it is a sign (or consequence) of that essential contrariety to impulse, the relevant impulse in the case of involuntary actions being desire. It is therefore reasonable to interpret the *EN*'s requirement of pain for involuntariness in the same way. Aristotle requires pain for involuntariness because he takes contrariety to desire to be necessary for involuntariness and takes pain to be a sign of that contrariety.

The *EN*, like the *EE*, takes the view that involuntary actions must be contrary to the impulse that voluntary actions are according to. But the *EN*, unlike the *EE*, appears to be successful in incorporating this view into the account of involuntariness involving ignorance. It recognizes that, of the two conditions for force identified in *EE* ii 8 (external causation and contrariety to impulse) the agent's knowledge or ignorance of what she is doing is relevant to the satisfaction of the first, not the second.[33] Having located the "place" of the cognitive criterion for involuntariness, Aristotle recognizes that an additional requirement must secure the relevant contrariety to impulse. In requiring that involuntary actions due to ignorance be painful, Aristotle proposes an account of involuntariness due to ignorance that makes this type of involuntariness similar to force both in terms of its causation, and in terms of its contrariety to desire. While involuntary actions due to ignorance are not externally caused in the way forced actions are, they still do not originate in the agent in the way voluntary actions must.[34] And like forced actions, involuntary actions due to ignorance are contrary to the agent's desire. The discussion of involuntariness in *EN* iii 1 achieves what the dialectical discussion in the *EE* aims to do but fails to achieve: to give an account of voluntariness and involuntariness that makes both types of involuntariness contrary to the impulse that voluntary actions are according to.

The account of involuntariness expressed in *EN* iii 1 is in effect the dialectical definition that emerges from *EE* ii 7–8, revised to accommodate the consideration (IV) that actions due to ignorance can also be involuntary. It is therefore a mistake to suppose that the two types of involuntariness with which Aristotle contrasts his account of voluntariness in *EN* iii 1 are uncontroversial pre-theoretical givens. On the contrary, they are achievements of the dialectical argument begun in *EE* ii 7. One might well suspect that they mark a rather dubious achievement.[35] This concern is best addressed in the context of a general assessment of the goals and achievements of the dialectical argument as a whole.

8 Goals and Achievements of the Dialectical Inquiry

The dialectical inquiry into voluntariness and involuntariness that begins in *EE* ii 7 and concludes in *EN* iii 1 raises puzzles by appealing to four sets of "reputable opinions" (*endoxa*). The first and fourth of these appeal to the two commonly recognized types of involuntary action – forced action (I) and action due to ignorance (IV) – and the third appeals to the Platonic conception of voluntariness (III). The second set (II) proposes that all actions for which agents are praiseworthy and blameworthy – those that express the virtues and vices of character – must turn out to be voluntary. In effect, it captures the reasons Aristotle initially offers for including the discussion of voluntariness in his general account of virtue and vice of character, reasons which, as we saw in chapter 2, show his concern to be with moral responsibility. In the constructive stage of the dialectical argument, during which Aristotle develops his own account of voluntariness and involuntariness by solving the puzzles, considerations in this second set play an important regulative role. All conflicts are resolved in their favour. This feature of Aristotle's argument indicates that the goal of his inquiry into voluntariness is to capture the conditions in which agents are praiseworthy and blameworthy for their actions, and that the praise and blame in question are of the retrospective sort relevant to moral responsibility.

But considerations in set II are not the only ones to play an important regulative role. Those in set I, which take force to be a paradigm for all involuntariness, also put constraints on an acceptable account. Although the account of force they presuppose is revised in the course of the constructive argument, the revised account continues to function as a paradigm for all involuntariness. All involuntary action, Aristotle presupposes, must be contrary to the agent's desire. The account of involuntariness in *EN* iii 1 completes the dialectical argument because it finally succeeds in satisfying this desideratum.

One might well wonder what theoretical function is served by this constraint on the account of voluntariness. The requirement would clearly be ill-motivated if Aristotle intended his account of involuntariness simply to capture the conditions in which agents are not praiseworthy and blameworthy for their actions. Since he thinks agents are praiseworthy and blameworthy only for actions for which they are causally responsible (*EE* 1223a10–13), we would then expect the account of involuntariness to capture the conditions in which an agent is not causally responsible for an action. But while Aristotle's account of involuntariness entails that we are not responsible for our involuntary actions, the requirement of contrariety ensures that some actions for which agents are not causally responsible (since they do not originate in agents who know what they are doing) are nonetheless not involuntary (since they are not contrary to the agent's desire). Aristotle's interest in identifying the conditions in which praise and blame are appropriate therefore cannot explain why he thinks involuntary actions must be contrary to desire.

Praise and blame, however, are not the only moral attitudes to which Aristotle claims voluntariness and involuntariness are relevant. While praise and blame figure most prominently in the remarks that serve to motivate the discussion of voluntariness and involuntariness (and are the only attitudes mentioned in the *EE* and *MM*), the *EN* adds two additional attitudes to the list:

> Praise and blame are given for voluntary things, while forgiveness (*sungnōmē*) and sometimes even pity (*eleos*) are given for involuntary things. (*EN* 1109b31–2)

The additional attitudes, *sungnōmē* (forgiveness or excuse)[36] and pity, are explicitly identified as attitudes appropriate to involuntary actions. If we investigate the nature of these attitudes, we will be able to see why the requirement of contrariety for involuntariness is well motivated. The case of *sungnōmē* will illustrate the point.[37]

Sungnōmē is an attitude one takes to the apparent perpetrator of an injustice. A third party may take this attitude to the alleged offender, in which case to have *sungnōmē* is to judge that he should not be blamed or receive legal sanction for the injustice (*Rhet.* 1374b4–22, 1374a21–5; cf. *MM* 1201a4–5). But the renunciation of blame is not the only, or even the most important feature of *sungnōmē*. For it is also a first-person attitude which the injured party may have to the apparent offender. In such cases, not only praise and blame but also such attitudes as goodwill, gratitude, and friendliness are at issue (*Rhet.* 1374a21–5). These favourable attitudes are withdrawn from a person at whom one is angry or resentful. To have *sungnōmē* toward someone is to renounce anger or resentment toward him (*EN* 1126a1–3).

Anger may still be appropriate in cases in which blame is not. This is because anger is an attitude that focusses on the attitudes of the person with whom one is angry. The victim is angry because he thinks the apparent wrongdoer considers him and his concerns to be of little importance, or unworthy of regard or consideration:

> People get angry at those who take pleasure at their misfortunes or stay cheerful in them, for this is a sign of hatred or contempt. And they get angry with those who don't care if they cause them pain. (*Rhet.* 1379b17–19; cf. *EN* 1135b28–9)

Initially, the injured party is aggrieved because he thinks the injury is caused by such reprehensible attitudes on the part of the alleged perpetrator. Should he discover that this is not the case (for example, that the agent acted in ignorance of the relevant particulars), he has lost his grounds for blaming him for the injury. But if at the same time he learns that the agent is not at all displeased at the outcome, he has not lost his reason for being angry. As long as the outcome fails to be contrary to the desires of the agent, the victim may still be justifiably angry at the agent, and hence the agent does not deserve *sungnōmē*.

Aristotle's insistence that all involuntary action must be contrary to impulse is well motivated because there are moral attitudes other than praise and blame – anger, friendliness, goodwill, gratitude, etc. – whose appropriateness depends on whether a given action is contrary to an agent's desire. While the account of voluntariness that emerges from Aristotle's dialectical inquiry articulates conditions in which praise and blame are appropriate, the account of involuntariness articulates a criterion for deciding when these other attitudes are appropriate. To recognize that the inquiry into voluntariness and involuntariness has this wider scope is not, of course, to concede that moral responsibility is not Aristotle's concern here. For these other attitudes, no less than the praise and blame in question, are appropriate only toward agents whom it is appropriate to subject to the demands and evaluations of morality.[38]

NOTES

1 For example, Austin 1956–7. The view is echoed in Robert Sharples's introduction to Sharples 1982.

2 At *EN* 1111a22–4; *EE* 1225b8–10; *MM* 1188b25–6. Aristotle also offers a definition of voluntariness in *EN* v 8 (1135a23–8), a book common to the *EE* and *EN*, but he presents this definition without argument, claiming it to be the result of previous discussion. Since my present concern is with the basis on which Aristotle arrives at his definitions of voluntariness, I will not discuss that definition.

3 Aristotle describes the method in *Met.* 995a24–b4; *Top.* 100b21–101a17, b1–4, 104a4–b17; and *EN* 1145b2–7. For discussion see Owen 1961; Barnes 1980; Irwin 1981; and Nussbaum 1982.

4 The discussion in *MM* i 12–16, which generates the definition of voluntariness articulated in *MM* i 16, is strikingly similar to *EE* ii 7–9 both in structure and in the detail of its argument.

5 Aristotle's formulation of the assumption at 1223a23–6 leaves open the interpretation that the voluntary might be according to one thing, and

the involuntary contrary to another. However, as the preliminary conclusion at 1223b36–8 indicates explicitly, Aristotle's argument proceeds by taking up each of the candidate faculties individually and considering whether the voluntary is according to it, and the involuntary contrary to it.

6   The discussion of force (1224a7–1225a33) begins with the announcement that it treats the same subject matter as the preceding argument (1224a9–10). Since it has no role to play in that deductive argument, its inclusion appears completely unmotivated and the claim that it treats the same subject matter is quite surprising.

7   Kenny 1979, pp. 14–22; Woods 1982, pp. 131–7.

8   As Kenny points out (Kenny 1979, p. 21). The discussion in *MM* i 12–16 differs from that of *EE* ii 7–9 in that the assumption corresponding to premises (1) and (2) is not explicitly articulated, although the inference at the beginning of *MM* i 16, that "since the voluntary consists in no impulse, the remaining possibility is that it is what happens from thought" (1188b25–6) indicates that something very much like (1) is implicit, and that instead of (2), it is assumed that (2'): the faculty in question is either impulse or thought. The discussion begins with an elaborate discussion of desire that corresponds quite closely to the argument for (3) in *EE* 1223a29–b37, and presumably rules out impulse as the faculty in question. This entitles Aristotle to make the inference that begins *MM* i 16. But before he does so, he inserts a discussion of force and compulsion (*MM* i 14–15). The argument proceeds, and is interrupted, in almost exactly the same way as the argument in *EE* ii 7–9.

9   Aristotle here mentions only incontinence, but at 1223b10–17 he indicates that the same considerations apply to continence.

10 In this passage (1223b10–17), Aristotle appeals explicitly only to considerations of the second set. But the conflict is generated by combining these considerations with the claim that "what is contrary to appetite is involuntary" (1223b16–17), and this claim is a consequence of the first set of considerations (cf. 1223a33–5).

11 He indicates of each set that they appear or seem (*dokein*) to be true: 1223a29, 37, b4, 15, 30.

12 Aristotle's remarks at 1223b26–30 (cf. b34) suggest that his argument against the proposed definition follows the following invalid strategy:

(i)   Voluntariness and involuntariness cannot be defined in terms of appetite;
(ii) they cannot be defined in terms of spirit;
(iii) they cannot be defined in terms of wish;
(iv) therefore, they cannot be defined in terms of desire.

So Woods (Woods 1982, ad loc.) and Irwin (Irwin 1980b) construe the argument. This argument is invalid because it does not follow from the proposal that X can be defined in terms of desire that X can be defined in terms of some one kind of desire. However, nowhere in the discussion does Aristotle ever draw an inference that depends on the assumption that being according (or contrary) to a given type of desire is *necessary* for voluntariness (or involuntariness). Rather, each of the contradictory conclusions he infers requires at most that this constitutes a *sufficient* condition for voluntariness (or involuntariness). Indeed, Aristotle's discussion of appetite and spirit make it clear that he is considering the claim that being according to the type of desire in question is sufficient for voluntariness, and being contrary to it is sufficient for involuntariness (cf. 1233a29–35; b19–21). These claims are valid consequences of the proposed definition.

Only in the discussion of wish does Aristotle state a condition for voluntariness or involuntariness that does not follow from the proposed definition – the claim that (A) "what is wished ⟨*i.e.*, what is according to wish⟩ is the same thing as the voluntary" (1223b29; cf. b34). However, even in this discussion, the damaging consequence he infers from the claim is that the incontinent action is involuntary (1223b32–6). This consequence follows equally well from the claim that (B) what is contrary to wish is involuntary, a claim that does follow from the proposed definition.

Aristotle might be led to substitute (A) for (B) for two reasons. First of all, he might be conflating the consequences of the proposed definition that concern wish with the third set of dialectical considerations. These considerations take being according to wish to be both necessary and sufficient for voluntariness (1223b5–6). Second, he might be conflating the claim (B) with the claim (C): what one does not wish is not voluntary. (C) states a necessary condition for voluntariness, while (B) states a sufficient condition for involuntariness. It is easy to conflate (C) with (B) because the natural scope of the negative in "what one does not wish" (*ho mē bouletai*) is within the scope of the verb "wish" (*bouletai*). Hence (as in English) what one does not want to do (*ho mē bouletai*) is naturally construed as what one wants not to do, which is what is contrary to what one wants (*par' ho bouletai*).

13 *EE* 1223a29–36, 1223b18–24. The corresponding considerations appear in the *MM*'s aporetic discussion at 1188a1–5, 10–13, 19–21.

14 The faculties in question in *EE* ii 7 – desire, decision, and thought – are all instances of the faculties involved in the impulse (*hormē*) with which an animal moves itself. In the *MM*'s version of the argument, the three faculties of desire discussed are subsumed under the general category of impulse (1188b25). And in *EE* ii 8, the "impulse" or "origin" connected with voluntary movement is clearly understood to be "desire and reason" (1224a20–7).

15 The *MM* uses "compulsion" (*anankē*), while the *EE* uses "force" (*bia*), to mark the common feature of involuntariness (*MM* 1188a1–2; *EE*

1223a29–30, 1224a11). But this does not indicate a substantive difference. For *MM* i 14–15 indicates that the category to which it refers initially as "compulsion" includes both force and compulsion. And in *EE* ii 8 Aristotle indicates that the category, which he initially introduced in *EE* ii 7 with the label "force", can equally well be referred to as "compelled" (1224b11–15, 1225a2, 6). For a discussion of the difference between force and compulsion, see chapter 4.

16 As Kenny (Kenny 1979) and Woods (Woods 1982) point out.

17 He takes contrariety to impulse to be essential to involuntariness – a misguided view, according to Broadie 1991, p. 134.

18 *EE* 1223a36–b3, 1223b10–16, and 1223b30–6. The corresponding considerations are invoked in the *MM* at 1188a13–19 and 1188a33–5.

19 As Woods 1982, p. 134 interprets the claim, and for that reason finds it problematical.

20 Continence is excellent and praiseworthy: *EN* 1145b8–10, 1151a27. Incontinence is base and blameworthy: *EN* 1146a4, 1148b5–6, 1151b29; cf. 1146a16, 1151a24–5.

21 Just as animals and small children cannot be virtuous or vicious, and for that reason are excluded from moral evaluation and expectation, they are also excluded from incontinence (*EN* 1147b3–5) and presumably also from continence.

22 *EN* 1129b25–1130a13.

23 The view underlies the refusal by the Athenian in *Laws* ix to count as voluntary actions due to anger (866d–867b, 878b–d). Together with the thesis of *Gorgias* 467c–468e (cf. *Meno* 77b–78b), that what one really wants (*bouletai*) in acting is the good one expects to achieve, this view explains why the "Socratic" paradox, that no one does wrong voluntarily, turns up in *Laws* ix, 860d–e.

24 *Top.* 100b21–3; for further discussion, see Barnes 1980, pp. 500–1.

25 Understanding the proposed objection in this way makes sense of *monon* in *touto dedeiktai monon* (1224a2–3), which Susemihl, Solomon, and Dirlmeier find troubling.

26 Scepticism that the discussion of desire has yielded any positive conclusions leads Woods (Woods 1982), following Rassow (Rassow 1861), to read *to men kata boulēsin ouch hōs akousion apedeichthē* ("what is according to wish has not been shown to be involuntary") at 1223b39–1224a1, for the MSS' *to men kata boulēsin hōs ouk akousion apedeichthē* ("what is according to wish has been shown not to be involuntary"). I follow Dirlmeier and Walzer and Mingay in retaining the MSS reading. If we understand the dialectical nature of the preceding argument, we will see why Aristotle can claim to have established these claims.

27 He introduces them with the preface: "We assume, and it appears to be the case . . ." (*hupokeitai gar hēmin kai dokei*, 1223b30). As Kenny notes,

this introduction accords to these considerations more than the simple *prima facie* plausibility of an *endoxon* (Kenny 1979, p. 23).

28 1223b13–14 claims that the continent agent acts according to reasoning (*logismon*), not that he acts according to wish (*boulēsis*). But Aristotle often uses the former to stand for the latter.

29 *Ph.* 254b20–7; cf. 254b13.

30 Aristotle tacitly acknowledges that thought does not properly fill the role in the definition when he draws the conclusion that thought is the faculty in question. While the deductive argument entitles him to conclude that voluntariness consists in acting according to thought, and involuntariness in acting contrary to thought, he concludes quite simply: that "the voluntariness consists in acting with thought in some way" (*en tō(i) dianooumenon pōs prattein to hekousion*) (1224a7). When he reiterates the conclusion at the beginning of *EE* ii 9, he states the definitive feature of voluntariness as "according to thought", but wisely shies away from stating the corresponding claim about involuntariness (1225b1).

31 Those who reject the pain requirement include Nussbaum 1983, pp. 149–50; Charles 1984, pp. 260–1; and Siegler 1968, p. 275. Those who suppose the requirement results from a conflation or confusion on Aristotle's part include Hardie 1980, pp. 153, 156; and Gauthier and Jolif 1970, vol. 2.1, p. 170. As a result, these critics decline to take seriously the tripartition of actions into the voluntary, the non-voluntary, and the involuntary, a view shared by W. D. Ross (Ross 1923, p. 198). Those who take seriously the tripartition include Aquinas, iii lect. 3:C406–8; and Irwin 1980a, p. 347 (but cf. his note on the text of 1110b18 in Irwin 1985a, p. 317).

32 Aristotle's claim that forced actions must be painful makes it tempting to interpret the remark that the forced subject must "contribute nothing" to the forced action (1110a2, b2–3, b16) as expressing a similar requirement. On this interpretation, someone who feels no pain at an action thereby contributes to it in such a way that the action fails to be forced. Such an interpretation of the requirement of non-contribution may be found in Kenny 1979, p. 29; Irwin 1985a, ad 1110a2; Aquinas, iii lect. 1:C387; and Aspasius 59.14–17.

I am inclined to resist this interpretation, on the grounds that (a) the requirement of non-contribution states a condition necessary for the origin of the action to be external to the forced subject (for the antecedent of *toiautē* in 1110a1–2 must be *hē archē* in 1110a1, and the only qualification given of the *archē* is that it be external). And (b) the origin of an agent's bodily movement can be completely external to that agent even if the subject of that movement feels no pain at its occurrence. Since Aristotle does not take the agent's regret at an action to be a necessary condition for the action's being due to particular ignorance (1110b18–24), there is no reason to suppose that he takes the agent's pain at an action to be necessary for the action's being externally caused. The requirement of non-contribution explains that the motive power productive of the forced action must come from completely outside the agent, as in the case of the examples given at 1110a3–4. Even in cases in which there are many external factors influencing the agent (e.g. in cases of duress or coercion), the "origin of moving the bodily parts ⟨sc. involved in the action⟩" (*ta organika merē*) is in the agent (1110a15–17).

To resist this interpretation of the non-contribution requirement is not, however, to deny that Aristotle thinks forced actions must be painful, for Aristotle makes the latter requirement abundantly clear independently of his expression of the former requirement.

33   The problem with the *EE*'s definition, we saw, is that it takes knowledge and ignorance to be relevant to the second.

34   In the next chapter we will see that both types of involuntary action fail to originate from within the agent non-accidentally.

35   For example, many readers worry that the resulting account of involuntariness commits Aristotle to holding that agents may be praiseworthy and blameworthy for actions that they are in no way causally responsible for, as long as the actions are not contrary to desire.

36   Since the semantic range of *sungnōmē* includes such attitudes as forgiveness, pardon, and excuse, it has no exact English equivalent, and I prefer to leave it untranlsated. See Kenny 1979, p. 28.

37   I discuss the cases of *sungnōmē* and pity in greater detail in Sauvé 1988.

38   As Strawson points out (Strawson 1962).

4

Force, Compulsion, and the
Internal Origin of Action

◆

Let us now consider Aristotle's treatment of a class of actions to which
I will refer under the general heading of "compulsion" (*anankē*). Examples of such actions include: the farmer who hurries to his fields
because otherwise his crops will be destroyed (*MM* 1188b22–3); the
agent who performs a shameful action at the command of a tyrant who
holds his family hostage (*EN* 1110a4–7); the captain who throws the
ship's cargo overboard in a storm in order to avoid capsizing (1110a8–
11); the person who divulges a secret under unbearable torture (*EE*
1225a9–27). Compelled action is similar to forced (*biaion*) action in that
the compelled agent, like the forced agent, is made to do something she
does not want to do. But unlike cases of genuinely forced action, which
is due to forces external to the agent (*EE* 1224b7–8), compelled action
is due, in an obvious way, to motive forces internal to the agent. The
compelled agent, unlike the forced agent, moves her own bodily parts.

Although Aristotle does not always observe the terminological distinction between "force" (*bia*) and "compulsion" (*anankē*), he does consistently distinguish between forced and compelled actions. He tells us
that it is disputed whether the latter sort of actions are voluntary (*EE*
1225a6–9; *EN* 1110a7–8), and in the different ethical works he defends
different answers to this question. In the *EE* and *MM* he claims that
compelled actions are involuntary, but in the *EN* he insists that they
are voluntary. We will see that his different verdicts about the voluntariness of these actions reflects a changing assessment of whether they
are internally caused in the way that voluntary actions must be. If we

explore the grounds for this differing assessment, we will appreciate better what it takes, in his view, for an action to have its origin (*archē*) in the agent. We will see that he is appealing to features of the theory of causation developed in his physical writings. The application of this theory to his account of human action is not straightforward – hence the differing verdicts. But once we understand the causal notions on which Aristotle relies, we will be able to see how the verdict he opts for in the *EN* is able to solve the problem that these sorts of actions pose for a theory of moral responsibility.

The problem is basically this. An agent who is compelled to perform a bad action seems no more blameworthy for performing the action than an agent who performs a good action under compulsion deserves credit or praise for it. It is natural to explain these intuitions by supposing that compelled agents are not morally responsible for what they do, and that this is why they are not praised or blamed for it. But this explanation cannot be correct, for it is simply false that agents are not praised or blamed for what they do under compulsion. An agent who is compelled to perform a bad action may very well be praised for doing so, if, for example, she has thereby averted a more terrible consequence. Furthermore, agents who choose wrongly in such circumstances are not immune from blame. These considerations support the conclusion that compelled agents are morally responsible for what they do. But this conclusion needs further qualification, for it leaves unexplained the fact peculiar to compelled actions that one may be responsible for a bad action, yet be praiseworthy rather than blameworthy, and that one may be responsible for a good action, yet merit no praise for it. A theory of moral responsibility should be able to provide an adequate account of such actions.

Let us examine Aristotle's account of these actions, beginning with a survey of the differing verdicts he offers about their voluntariness.

1   Force and Compulsion in the *MM*, *EE*, and *EN*

As we have seen, the discussion of voluntariness in the *MM* begins from the proposal that involuntary actions are compelled (*anankazomenos*, 1187b35). Within this general category of compulsion, Aristotle distinguishes actions due to force (*bia*) from actions due to compulsion (*anankē*) proper (*MM* i 14–15). In *MM* i 14, as in *EE* ii 8, he defines forced (*biaion*) action as not merely contrary to impulse but also exter-

nally caused (*MM* 1188b6–9). In *MM* i 15 he makes the same requirement of compelled (*anankaion*) action:

> Compulsion (*to anankaion*) does not obtain in just any situation, but must
> be in the externals – for example, whoever incurs something bad as the
> price of avoiding some greater ⟨sc. evil⟩ is compelled (*anankazomenos*) by
> the situation. For example, he is compelled to hurry to the fields because
> otherwise his crops would be destroyed. So in cases of this sort there is
> compulsion (*to anankaion*). (*MM* 1188b19–24)

Aristotle's example of a compelled action in this passage indicates that
compelled actions are not cases of physical force. The reluctant farmer
is not kidnapped and carried to his fields by external forces. The compelling feature appears to be the structure of alternatives the agent faces.
Yet Aristotle insists that in such cases, the compelling factor is "in the
externals" (*en tois ektos*, 1188b20). Despite their difference from physically forced actions, Aristotle here insists that compelled actions are,
like physically forced actions, externally caused. As in the case of physical force, the entity by which (*huph' hēs*) the compelled agent is made to
act contrary to desire is something external to him (1188b12–14, 21).

Aristotle's position in the *EE* is, in these respects, quite similar to
that of the *MM*. Although he appears not to honour any terminological
difference between force (*bia*) and compulsion proper (*anankē*) in the *EE*,
the structure of his discussion in *EE* ii 8 is the same as in *MM* i 14–15.
He first discusses physically forced actions, and insists that such actions
must have their origins external to the agent (*EE* 1224b7–15). He next
considers the class of actions which *MM* i 15 labels "compelled" – cases
in which the agent claims to be compelled not by an external physical
force but by the structure of choices he faces:

> There is another way in which people are said to be forced and compelled
> to act (*bia(i) kai anankasthentes praxai*), even if reason and desire do not
> disagree. This is when people do things they consider painful and base
> but if they do not do them they will be beaten or imprisoned or killed.
> They say they are compelled to do these things. (*EE* 1225a2–6)

He first considers an objection to the claim that such actions are "forced
and compelled":

> But don't these people all do what they do voluntarily? For it is possible
> for them not to do it and to undergo the suffering instead (*ekeino hupo-
> meinai to pathos*). (*EE* 1225a6–8)

Aristotle's response (1225a8–12) indicates that he takes the objection to claim that it is up to the agent (*ep' autō(i)*) whether to perform these actions:

> Presumably this ⟨charge⟩ is true of some such cases, but not of others. For if it is not up to him whether they obtain or not, it must be (*dei*)[1] that he does voluntarily what he does not want to do, and not by force. But if they are not up to him, he is in a way forced to do them, although not forced without qualification. For he does not decide upon the very thing he does, but he does decide upon what he does it for (*hou heneka*). After all, there is a difference between these. (*EE* 1225a8–14)

Since he has already made it clear that an action is up to the agent if and only if its origin is in the agent (1223a1–9), he must think it is controversial whether compelled actions are voluntary because it is controversial whether their origins are internal to the agent.[2] In conceding here that no action of this type is forced without qualification (1225a12), Aristotle recognizes in effect the distinction between compelled actions and physically forced actions. But in insisting that some such actions are not up to the agent, and are for that reason forced in a qualified way (*bia(i) pōs*, 1225a12), he denies that they are internally caused in the way that voluntary actions must be.

In *EN* iii 1, by contrast, Aristotle insists that the respect in which merely compelled actions fall short of being physically forced is sufficient to make them voluntary: they are up to the agent and internally caused. As in the *EE* and *MM*, Aristotle first defines physical force:

> Something is forced if its origin is external – such an origin being one in which the agent, or rather patient, contributes nothing, as if, for example, the wind or men who have control of you were to carry you somewhere. (*EN* 1110a1–4)

He then immediately raises the question of whether actions performed under duress or constraint are involuntary:

> Actions that are performed because of fear of greater evils or on account of something noble – for example if a tyrant were to command you to do something shameful when he has control of your parents and children and will kill them if you do not comply but will release them if you do – concerning these actions there is a dispute about whether

they are involuntary or voluntary. There is a similar dispute about cases
in which cargo is thrown overboard in a storm. (1110a4–9)

The question of whether such actions are involuntary presumably turns
on whether they are forced. Although Aristotle allows that such actions
are involuntary when considered without qualification (*haplōs*) (1110a9,
18), he insists that they are, in the final analysis, voluntary. They are
voluntary, he insists, because they are internally caused:

> And he acts voluntarily, for in such cases the origin of moving his bodily
> parts is in the agent, and whatever has its origin in him is up to him
> both to do and not to do. (1110a15–17)

The agent, in moving his own bodily parts (e.g. in carrying out the
tyrant's orders or in throwing overboard the ship's cargo), contributes
to the action in such a way that its origin is internal to him, and its
performance up to him. Aristotle proceeds to demonstrate that some
such agents can be properly labelled "compelled" (*anankazomenos*), and
he indicates that the fact of compulsion should make a difference to
whether the agent is praised, blamed, or forgiven for the action
(1110a16–b1). But he insists, contrary to the *EE* and *MM*, that the
features that make an action compelled are compatible with the action's
being up to the agent, and do not keep it from being internally caused
in the way voluntariness requires. Indeed, the respect in which such
actions differ from forced actions is precisely what makes them voluntary: the agent moves his own bodily parts (1110a15–16).

We may conclude that Aristotle's differing views about the voluntariness of compelled actions does not stem from any uncertainty or dis-
agreement about the criteria for voluntariness. All three of his discussions of voluntariness agree that if such actions are internally caused
and up to the agent then they are voluntary, and that they must be
internally caused and up to the agent if they are voluntary. These
discussions differ, rather, on whether compelled actions satisfy this
requirement for voluntariness. Aristotle is clearly of two minds, in the
different ethical works, about how to interpret the requirement in the
case of human action. If we investigate the reasons behind his different
views, we will understand better what he thinks it takes for the origin
of action to be in the agent.

Before we proceed to do so, however, we should take note of a feature
that complicates Aristotle's discussions of compulsion.

2   Criteria for Compulsion: Psychological and Rational

There are two very different kinds of compulsion. There is first of all what I will call *rational compulsion*, where an agent performs the action he does because it is the lesser of two evils facing him. The compelled action is the rationally preferable alternative. Second, there is what I will call *psychological compulsion*, where the alternative to the compelled action is so painful or otherwise insupportable that the agent is quite literally unable not to perform the action he does. The person who divulges a secret under unbearably painful torture would satisfy this criterion for compulsion.

An action that satisfies the criterion for rational compulsion need not satisfy the criterion for psychological compulsion, and vice versa. In the case of the agent subjected to unbearable torture, the consequence of divulging the secret might be so bad that it would be better to suffer the most extreme torture than to divulge the secret – in which case the agent cannot claim to have been rationally compelled to divulge the secret. But the torture might still be physically unbearable by the agent. Conversely, the secret might be of comparatively little importance, so that it would be reasonable for the agent to divulge it rather than submit to torture, even if the torture would be physically bearable.[3]

Aristotle, however, does not appear to distinguish adequately these two different types of compulsion in his discussions. In the *EE*, which contains his most extensive discussion of compulsion (*EE* ii 8, 1225a2–36), he begins by describing the conditions for genuine compulsion as follows:

> For if someone were to kill in order not to be caught in a game of tag, it would be ridiculous if he said he was forced and compelled. It is necessary that what he will suffer if he fails to perform the action be a greater evil and more painful. In this way he will act under compulsion and by force, or not by nature – when he does something bad for the sake of something good, or in order to avoid a greater evil. He will at any rate act involuntarily, for these things are not up to him. (*EE* 1225a14–19)

In claiming that the alternative to the action in the example must be "a greater evil and more painful" (a16), Aristotle appears to invoke the criteria for both rational and psychological compulsion. But in stating the general requirement two lines later, that the agent do "something

bad for the sake of something good, or in order to avoid a greater evil"
(1225a18–19), he invokes the criterion for rational compulsion alone.
Immediately afterwards, however, he makes a comparison that suggests
that he has psychological compulsion in mind:

> For this reason too sexual desire (*erōs*) is supposed by many people to be
> involuntary, as well as certain instances of anger and the natural ⟨sc. pas-
> sions⟩, on the grounds that they are strong and overpower nature. And
> we do excuse on the grounds that these passions force one's nature
> (*biazesthai tēn phusin*). And one would seem to be forced and to act
> involuntarily when one acts to avoid a strong pain rather than a light
> one, and in general when one acts in order to avoid pain rather than to
> gain pleasure. For what is up to one, on which all this depends, is what
> one's nature is able to bear. What one's nature cannot bear, and is not
> within the scope of one's natural desire or reasoning, is not up to one.
> (*EE* 1225a19–27)

To require that the alternative to the compelled action be too painful
to bear is to invoke the criterion of psychological compulsion.[4] In the
concluding lines of this passage (a25–7), Aristotle applies this criterion
to the disputed cases quite generally. But this contradicts his earlier
explanation (a18–19), that satisfaction of the criterion for rational compulsion will suffice to make an action not up to the agent. A worse
alternative need not be physically unbearable. Aristotle here does not
appear to be distinguishing psychological from rational compulsion.

Aristotle's discussion in *EN* iii 1 suffers from a similar conflation. His
preliminary discussion of the disputed cases suggests that they are cases
of rational compulsion, since they are actions that "any sensible person
would perform" (*EN* 1110a11). After claiming that agents receive
praise, blame, or forgiveness for what they do in such situations depending on whether their actions count as compelled (1110a29–b1), his
explanatory remarks clearly allow both rational and psychological compulsion to count as compulsion:

> Some such actions are even praised – whenever someone submits to
> something shameful or painful as the price of greater and noble things.
> And whenever the opposite is true, they are blamed – for to put up with
> something exceedingly shameful in exchange for nothing fine or com-
> mensurate is the mark of a base person. And in some cases there is not
> praise but forgiveness, whenever someone does what one ought not to
> (*ha mē dei*) because of things that overstrain human nature and that no
> one could endure (*mēdeis an hupomeinai*). (1110a23–6)

If one's action satisfies the criterion for rational compulsion, by avoiding a greater evil, then one can be praised for what one does. But if one selected the alternative that is rationally less preferable, then one can be blamed. However, if in a case of the latter sort, one acted because of things that overstrain human nature (and thereby satisfy the criteria for psychological compulsion), one can be forgiven for what one has done. These remarks suggest that either rational or psychological compulsion can make an action compelled. However, the immediately following remarks indicate that Aristotle does not clearly distinguish these two types of compulsion:

> There are presumably some things which one cannot be compelled to do (*ouk estin anankasthēnai*), but which one ought to die suffering the greatest torment rather than do – for indeed the things that "compelled" Euripides' Alkmaeon to kill his mother are truly ridiculous. (1110a26–9)

Aristotle here appeals to criteria for rational compulsion, denying that one can be compelled to do anything that one ought to avoid, even if one can avoid it only at the price of the most extreme suffering. But clearly such suffering might overstrain human nature, and so even if it does not make the alternative rationally compelling, it still might be psychologically compelling. Aristotle here does not appear to recognize that the criteria for rational and for psychological compulsion diverge – that an action may fail to be rationally compelled but still satisfy the criteria for psychological compulsion. In *EN* iii 1, as in *EE* ii 8, Aristotle does not seem clearly to distinguish the different grounds for the plea of compulsion.[5]

In spite of Aristotle's conflation of psychological and rational compulsion, I think it is nonetheless safe to conclude that Aristotle is inclined to consider both psychologically and rationally compelled actions to be cases of compulsion. In the *MM* and *EE*, he thinks such actions fail to originate in the agent in the way voluntariness requires. In the *EN* he thinks they do originate in the agent in the appropriate way. We may now return to consider why Aristotle changes his mind about whether these actions originate in the agent.

3 Voluntariness and the Non-accidental Origin of Action

It might appear that Aristotle's verdict in *EN* iii 1 is obviously correct; that of course the compelled action's origin is in the agent, since the agent moves her own bodily parts. What else could it be for the origin of an action to be in the agent? Certain remarks Aristotle makes in *EN* v 8, however, suggest that it is not this easy to determine whether the origin of an action is in the agent. At the beginning of *EN* v 8, Aristotle invokes the notion of voluntariness in the course of his discussion of justice and injustice. He indicates there that if I do something voluntarily, then I bring it about non-accidentally; and that if I do something involuntarily, then I bring it about only accidentally:

> Just and unjust things being as we have said, someone does injustice and does justice whenever he does them voluntarily. Someone who does them involuntarily does not do injustice or do justice – except accidentally (*kata sumbebēkos*), for he does things to which being just or being unjust is accidental. (*EN* 1135a15–19)

In elucidation of these remarks, Aristotle proceeds to offer a definition of voluntariness that explicitly includes the requirement of non-accidental production:

> I mean by voluntary, as I said earlier, whatever, of the things that are up to him, someone does knowingly and not in ignorance either of to whom or how or for what result (for example, whom one hits and with what and for what result), and each of these things neither accidentally nor by force. (*EN* 1135a23–7)

The examples he proceeds to offer of doing something accidentally are all examples of compelled actions: someone who returns a deposit, but because of threats, does justice only accidentally; and someone who fails to return a deposit, but because of threats, does injustice only accidentally (*EN* 1135b4–8).

The definition of voluntariness that Aristotle presents here (in a book common to the *EE* and *EN*) as something he has stated previously (1135a23) is more like that of *EE* ii 9 (1225b8–10) than that of *EN* iii 1 (1111a22–4).[6] He here agrees with *EE* ii 8 that compelled actions fail to satisfy the criteria for voluntariness. So it is reasonable to suppose that the reasons he gives here for thinking compelled actions are involuntary should explain why he holds this view in *EE* ii 8. That is, his claim in *EN* v 8 that compelled actions are performed only accidentally promises to explain his denial in *EE* ii 8 that they are voluntary.

In appealing to the distinction between doing something accidentally and doing it non-accidentally, Aristotle invokes a causal distinction familiar from his natural philosophy, where he regularly distinguishes between two ways in which one thing can be the cause (*aition*) of another. On the one hand, it can be the cause "without qualification" (*haplōs*), or "in virtue of itself" or "intrinsically" (*kath' hauto*). On the other hand it can be the cause merely "accidentally" (*kata sumbebēkos*) or "in virtue of something else" (*kath' heteron*).[7] It is natural for Aristotle to appeal to this distinction in a context where he addresses the question of whether the origin of an action is in an agent. For, as we saw in chapter 2, an action whose origin is in the agent is one for which the agent is responsible, or "the cause" (*aitios*). While he maintains that a cause is "that because of which",[8] Aristotle regularly denies that anything is because of (*dia*) its accidental cause.[9] So it is natural of him to require that an agent be the non-accidental cause of her voluntary actions.

This requirement, although rarely explicit in his discussions of voluntariness, is tacitly presupposed throughout them. We have seen that Aristotle intends his account of voluntariness to capture all actions produced by an agent's moral character. In *EE* ii 3, he indicates that this relation of production must be non-accidental:

> There is no point to saying in the definition (*periergon diorizein*) that they are inclined non-accidentally toward each of these things (*to de pros hekaston mē kata sumbebēkos houtōs echein*). For no science whether theoretical or practical adds this to the definition either in word or in deed. (*EE* 1221b4–6)

The qualification "non-accidental" goes without saying, Aristotle explains, because it is a general presupposition of scientific practice.[10] His discussion of voluntariness in the *EE* makes the requirement explicit at one point, when Aristotle explains that the continent or incontinent agent's action is voluntary because "his own intrinsic internal impulse (*hē kath' hauton enousa hormē*) drives him" (*EE* 1224b9). The *EN*'s discussion of voluntariness fails to state the requirement explicitly; however, the remarks that conclude the discussion of virtue and vice of character in the *EN* confirm that the requirement of non-accidental production has been tacitly assumed in the account of voluntariness:

> We have given their genus in outline – that they are means and states; that they are productive of the same [activities] as they are produced by, and productive of them in themselves (*kath' hautas*). (*EN* 1114b27–8)

The significance of the distinction between accidental and non-accidental production for the question of whether compelled actions are internally caused will become apparent if we consider some of Aristotle's examples of it. First of all, consider the sculptor Polycleitus, who sculpts a statue. Aristotle claims that the sculptor is the non-accidental cause of the statue, while Polycleitus is only its accidental cause (*Ph.* 195a32–5). Second, consider the chef who exercises his culinary craft to produce tasty food, which in addition to being tasty also happens to be healthy for someone. Aristotle claims that the chef is the non-accidental cause of the tasty food, but only the accidental cause of the healthy food (*Met.* 1027a3–5). These examples show that for an agent to produce a result non-accidentally, it is not enough that the result originate from spatially within the agent, or that the agent move his bodily parts in the production of that result. Polycleitus certainly moves his own bodily parts in sculpting the statue, but is still only its accidental cause. The chef is only the accidental cause of the healthy food, although he produces it by moving his own bodily parts.

The cases of the chef and the sculptor who, like the voluntary agent, are efficient causes (*Ph.* 194b29–33, 195a8; *Met.* 1027a3–5), show that Aristotle individuates these causes and their effects very finely. He distinguishes Polycleitus from the sculptor and the tasty food from the healthy food. This fine-grained approach to individuating non-accidental causes and effects entails that it is not as easy as one might expect to tell whether an action originates in the agent non-accidentally. Observation might well indicate whether the action originates from spatially within the agent, but an origin's being in an agent non-accidentally is not simply a matter of its spatial location within the agent's body. Hence the verdict of *EN* iii 1, that the compelled action has its origin in the agent because the agent moves his own bodily parts, is not obviously correct. In moving his own bodily parts, the agent might still be only the accidental cause of the action.

Since Aristotle's presupposition that a voluntary action must originate in the agent non-accidentally promises to illuminate his reasons for classifying compelled actions as involuntary in the *EE* and *MM*, we should investigate his account of the difference between accidental and non-accidental production.

4 Accidental and Non-accidental Production

In order to understand the distinction between accidental and intrinsic efficient-causal relations, we must first understand Aristotle's distinction between accidental and instrinsic properties. An intrinsic property of something, in Aristotle's view, is a property that belongs to it either in its essence or because of its essence.[11] For example, a human being is intrinsically animal, because part of what it is to be a human being is to be animal. But a human being is only accidentally pale or musical, for pallor or music are not essential to being human, nor are they consequences of anything essential to being human (*Met.* 1026b35–7).

The relation between an efficient cause and its non-accidental or intrinsic effect is analogous to that between a substance and its intrinsic properties. An efficient cause, on Aristotle's view, is identified in terms of its efficient causal powers. For example, the housebuilder (*oikodomos*) is the possessor of the skill of housebuilding (*oikodomikē*), and the chef (*opsopoios*) is the possessor of culinary skill (*opsopoiētikē*).[12] The intrinsic effect of an efficient cause is a result of the type that the causal power is productive of (*poiētikē*) or that it naturally produces (*pephuke poiein*). This is what the causal power produces reliably or "always or for the most part."[13] The housebuilder is the non-accidental cause of the house because what it is to be a housebuilder (*oikodomos*) is to possess the skill of housebuilding (*oikodomikē*), and what it is to possess this skill is to be productive (*poiētikos*) of houses (*oikiai*). While the intrinsic effect (e.g. the house) of an efficient cause (e.g. the housebuilder) is not an intrinsic property of that cause, it is something mentioned in the definition of the intrinsic property of the efficient cause.

If we combine the distinction between accidental and intrinsic properties with the preceding account of the intrinsic efficient-causal relation, we will identify the two basic ways in which one can be the accidental efficient cause of a result (Table 4.1).[14] First of all, A can be the accidental efficient cause of B if the property in terms of which A is identified is accidental to the efficient-causal power that is "naturally productive" of B. For example, Polycleitus is only accidentally the cause of the statue because the statue is naturally produced by a statuary (*andriantopoios*), while the property of being Polycleitus is only accidental to the property of being a statuary (*Ph.* 195a32–5). In another example, a housebuilder who happens also to be a doctor cures a patient by exercising his medical skill. The housebuilder is only accidentally the cause of the cure because the cure is the intrinsic effect of the doctor's causal power and it is purely accidental that a doctor should also be a housebuilder:

> And it is accidental that the housebuilder cures, since it is not the housebuilder but the doctor who naturally produces this (*pephuke touto*

poiein). Rather, it is an accident that the builder is a doctor. (*Met.* 1026b37–1027a2; cf. *Ph.* 196b26–7)

The second way in which A can be merely the accidental efficient cause of B is if B is identified in terms of properties that are merely accidental properties of the result of which A is naturally productive (*pephuke poiein*). For example, the chef is naturally productive of tasty food, but there is no intrinsic connection between being tasty and being healthy.[15] This is why the chef produces healthy food only accidentally (*Met.* 1027a3–5).

Table 4.1 Two scenarios for "A produces B accidentally"

(I)   A ← – – – – – – – – – – – → C ————————————→B
       (is accidental to)   (naturally produces)

Example: Polycleitus (A) produces the statue (B) only accidentally; C = the statuary.

(II)   A ————————————————→C ← – – – – – – – – – – →B
       (naturally produces)   (is accidental to)

Example: The chef (A) produces the healthy food (B) only accidentally; C = the tasty food.

Aristotle's general accounts of the distinction between accidental and non-accidental efficient causes show that he identifies the non-accidental efficient cause of a result in terms of the causal powers "naturally productive" of that result. For example, he claims that the doctor and not the builder is the cause of the cure because the doctor's, rather than the builder's, skill is naturally productive of the cure (*Met.* 1026b37–1027a2). He identifies the doctor in terms of his medical skill, and the housebuilder in terms of his housebuilding skill. In claiming that an agent is the intrinsic efficient cause of his voluntary actions, Aristotle must therefore have some conception of the causal power in terms of which he identifies the agent. And he must think that the actions that the agent performs voluntarily are the actions that this causal power "naturally produces" (*pephuke poiein*). Chapters 2 and 3 have established that Aristotle intends his account of voluntariness to capture the conditions in which an agent's moral character is productive of his actions. So it is reasonable to suppose that the agent's moral character is the

causal power in terms of which Aristotle identifies the agent, and that
he thinks the agent's voluntary actions are the ones of which his moral
character is "naturally productive."

Aristotle must therefore have one of the following two scenarios in
mind when he claims, in *EN* v 8, that compelled actions are ones of
which the agent is only accidentally the efficient cause. Each scenario
is an instance of one of the two types of accidental efficient-causal
relation identified above:

(I) Compelled actions (B) are naturally produced by causal powers
     (C) that are spatially within the agent, but are only
     accidentally related to his moral character (A).

This scenario satisfies the first model of accidental efficient causation
sketched above. According to this model, the agent performs the compelled action only accidentally in the way that Polycleitus produces the
statue only accidentally or the builder effects a cure only accidentally.
The second scenario satisfies the second model sketched above:

(II) The action the agent is compelled to do (B) is only acciden-
      tally related to the action (C) that his or her character (A)
      "naturally produces".

According to this second scenario, the compelled agent brings about
accidentally the action he is compelled to do in the way that the chef
produces the healthy food only accidentally.

5 Compelled Actions as Accidentally Caused

When Aristotle claims, in *EN* v 8, that an agent who is compelled to
perform an unjust action brings it about only accidentally, he clearly
has in mind this second schema for accidental production.[16] For he
explicitly says of such cases that the agent does something "to which
being just or being unjust is accidental" (1135a18–19). Just as the chef
produces non-accidentally something pleasant-tasting, to which being
healthy is accidental, the agent who is compelled to not return the
deposit does something (presumably, avoiding the threatened consequence) to which being unjust is only accidental. These remarks,
which promise to explain the Eudemian position on compulsion, do not

identify the agent's moral character as the causal power in terms of which he is identified as efficient cause. However, we will see that this is indeed Aristotle's view if we turn to consider the explanation he offers in *EE* ii 8, for claiming that compelled actions are "forced in a way but not without qualification" (1225a11–12), and the remarks he makes in *EN* vii (a book common to *EE* and *EN*) about objects of choice and pursuit.

In *EE* ii 8, when Aristotle first claims that some actions performed under constraint or duress are "forced in a way (*bia(i) pōs*), but not without qualification" (1225a12), he explains this verdict by making a distinction about the agent's decision (*prohairesis*):

> For he does not decide upon the very thing he does, but rather on what he does it for (*ouk auto touto prohaireitai ho prattei, all' hou heneka*). (1225a12–13)

The claim that the agent "does not decide upon the very thing he does" presumably explains why the action is forced, while the admission that he does decide on "what he does it for" explains why the action is not forced without qualification. Aristotle's denial here, that the agent decides on (*prohaireitai*) the action he is compelled to do, is striking, and appears to be in tension with his general account of decision.[17] However, the denial is not an isolated occurrence, for he repeats it in his discussion of decision in *EE* ii 11:

> We always praise and blame people looking to their decision (*prohairesis*) rather than to their actions, even though the activity of virtue is more choiceworthy ⟨sc. than its mere possession⟩. We do so because people also do base things when they are compelled (*prattousi men phaula kai anankazomenoi*), but no one decides upon them ⟨sc. when they are compelled⟩. (1228a11–15)

Until the last clause of this passage, Aristotle's remarks leave open the possibility that one performs on decision (*prohairesis*) the action one is compelled to do, but that it depends on what the goal of that *prohairesis* is, on what one does the action for, whether one will be praised, blamed, or excused. The last clause, however, makes the stronger claim: that the action one is compelled to do is not something that one decides upon (*prohaireitai*).[18]

Aristotle here denies that the compelled action is the object of decision (*prohairesis*) in a context in which he elaborates on the moral significance of the agent's decision (1227b35–1228a19). He indicates that the goal of the agent's decision, which is what the agent does the action for (*hou heneka*), indicates whether the agent is virtuous or vicious (1227b36–1228a4). But he also claims that:

> If it is up to someone to do noble things and to refrain from doing base things, but he does the opposite, he is clearly not a good person (*ou spoudaios*). (1228a5–7)

So even though he distinguishes between what the agent's decision is of (*tinos*, an action) and what it is for (*hou heneka*, a goal) (1227b36–7), Aristotle here implies that the goal (*telos*) of the agent's action can be read off the action itself as long as the action is up to him in the way that voluntariness requires. An agent who voluntarily does noble (*kala*) things thereby shows himself to be good, while an agent who voluntarily does base things (*phaula*) thereby shows himself to be bad. He proceeds to deny, at 1228a11–15, that an action is done on decision if the agent is compelled to do it, precisely because these are cases in which "what the action is for" (*hou heneka*) cannot be read off the action performed. In such cases, we must look to the agent's decision, rather than simply to his action, to see whether the goal of his action is characteristic of virtue or vice.

These remarks, which explain why Aristotle denies that the compelled action is performed on decision, show that the denial is motivated by the thought that actions one is compelled to do are not indicative of one's character. Aristotle invokes this denial in *EE* ii 8 in order to explain why compelled actions are "forced in a way" and for that reason involuntary (1225a10–13). So his view in the *EE* that compelled actions are involuntary is motivated by the view that they do not reflect the goals of the agent's character. What the agent does the compelled action for reflects his character, but this goal (*telos*) of his action is quite different from the action itself, which Aristotle here denies reflects the agent's character.[19]

These remarks in *EE* ii 11 support the proposal that Aristotle thinks the agent performs non-accidentally, and therefore voluntarily, the actions produced by her character in the appropriate way. In the *EE*, Aristotle thinks compelled actions do not stand in this appropriate causal relation to one's character, and so are performed only accidentally. Since Aristotle claims here that the goal of the compelled action does stand in the appropriate relation to her character, we should expect that he thinks that the goal is something the agent brings about non-accidentally. This expectation is confirmed by remarks Aristotle makes about objects of pursuit in *EN* vii (another book common to the *EE* and *EN*):

> If someone chooses or pursues one thing because of another, then he pursues and chooses the latter intrinsically (*kath' hauto*), and the former accidentally. (*EN* 1151a35–b2)

Aristotle here indicates that only something whose pursuit constitutes a reason or goal for one's action is performed non-accidentally, while something that is performed as a means to achieving that goal is done only accidentally. In general, Aristotle here indicates that the description of an action under which it is performed non-accidentally mentions the features that make it desirable to the agent, while the description of the action under which it is performed merely accidentally does not. The features of the compelled action that make the action desirable are intrinsic not to it, but to its results – in the *EE*'s terminology, what the agent does the action for. Hence, only what the agent does the action for is brought about non-accidentally. In the examples of *EN* v 8, the agent who keeps the deposit instead of returning it at the appointed time, but does so in order to avoid some greater evil and not because she wants to keep the deposit, does non-accidentally what will avoid the greater evil (e.g. keeps the depositor from injuring himself) but does the unjust action (failing to return the deposit) only accidentally.

We therefore have reason to believe that in *EN* v 8, when Aristotle claims that the compelled agent performs the unjust action only accidentally, he bases this claim on the fact that the agent does not perform the unjust action because it is unjust, or because of the features that make it unjust, but rather for some other reason. For example, suppose the agent withholds the deposit in order to save the life of a hostage. The agent's desire to save the hostage's life is the desire that leads her to bring about the unjust state of affairs. What she does non-accidentally is "save the life of the hostage", because this is the reason for which she performs the unjust action (withholding the deposit). But saving the life of a hostage does not intrinsically involve bringing about injustice, for there is nothing in the nature of this goal (saving the life of a hostage) that involves or requires injustice. Saving the hostage and bringing about an injustice are only accidentally the same action, and so the compelled agent performs the former non-accidentally and the latter only accidentally. Since these remarks in *EN* v 8 promise to explain the Eudemian (and presumably also the *MM*'s) view that compelled actions are not voluntary, we may conclude that such an assumption about the conditions of non-accidental production explains that view.

6   Problems with the Eudemian Conditions

Having identified Aristotle's reasons for claiming, in the *EE* and *MM*, that compelled actions are not voluntary, let us now consider what reasons he might have to be dissatisfied with that verdict, and so change his mind in the *EN* account of voluntariness. We will see that Aristotle in *EN* iii 1 rejects the *EE*'s view of compulsion because the conditions for non-accidental production it presupposes are too high to require of voluntariness; they would entail the unacceptable consequence that many uncontroversial examples of praiseworthy and blameworthy activity are not voluntary.

The account of non-accidental production that underlies the Eudemian view that compelled actions do not originate in the agent in the way that voluntariness requires captures the intuitively reasonable plea of such an agent: that he performed the action *only because* of the alternative its performance avoided, and for this reason is not blameworthy for doing what he did. However, the conditions for non-accidental production implicit in such a plea turn out to be far too strong if Aristotle intends them to capture a causal relation that is necessary for praiseworthiness and blameworthiness. According to the view presupposed by *EN* v 8, an agent performs an injustice non-accidentally, and hence voluntarily, only if she is motivated to perform the action because of the features that make it unjust. And an agent does justice (*dikaiopragein*) only if she brings about a just outcome because of the features that make it just. If the agent is motivated to bring about the just (or unjust) outcome because of features that are only accidentally just (or unjust), then she does justice (or injustice) only accidentally. According to these criteria, however, many ordinary cases of uncompelled action, actions for which the agent is uncontroversially blameworthy or praiseworthy, turn out to be performed only accidentally, and hence fail the conditions for voluntariness.

Consider, for example, the case of Roger who steals money from widows and orphans in order to finance his trip around the world. He clearly does an injustice, since he injures those whom he ought not to injure. But he does not commit this injustice because he wants to act unjustly, or because he enjoys harming vulnerable people. He is simply indifferent to considerations of justice, and to the interests of others. The motivation on which he acts is aimed at traveling around the world, or more generally, his own pleasure. But this goal of his action is only accidentally unjust (there is nothing intrinsically unjust about round-the-world travel or about one's own pleasure); hence, according to the conditions for acting non-accidentally presupposed by the *EE*'s position on compulsion, Roger does injustice only accidentally, and so does not voluntarily bring about the unjust state of affairs involved in his action.

According to the presupposition of the *EE*, Roger voluntarily performs the unjust action only if he thinks it is desirable because of the very features that make it unjust. What makes his action unjust is, roughly speaking, that it causes harm to those who do not deserve it. But only a person who thought injustice worth pursuing for its own sake would perform an action like Roger's for this sort of reason. It is a consequence of the Eudemian view that only those agents who shared the motivations, even if not the cognitive competence, of the fully and perfectly unjust person would count as performing unjust actions non-accidentally and hence voluntarily. (By the same argument, only actions performed with the motivation of the perfectly virtuous person would count as non-accidentally performed acts of justice.) This is clearly an unacceptable result, for Aristotle as well as for anyone else who thinks only voluntary actions are praiseworthy and blameworthy. We have already seen, in chapter 1, that Aristotle thinks agents who fall short of perfect virtue and vice are nonetheless subject to moral expectation and evaluations. And in *Rhet.* i 13, he gives explicit examples of the sorts of motivations with which an agent might bring about an unjust (*adikon*) action, and properly be said to act unjustly (*adikein*), and hence be blameworthy. Someone who steals in order to enrich himself, and someone who hits another for his own pleasure are properly described as acting unjustly (*adikein*) (1374a9–17); yet enriching oneself is only accidentally unjust, as is serving one's pleasure. Since Aristotle's inquiry into the nature of voluntariness is motivated by the guiding assumption that actions for which agents are praiseworthy and blameworthy must turn out to be voluntary, he has reason to be dissatisfied with the Eudemian analysis of what it takes for an action to originate in an agent non-accidentally.

7   Non-accidental Production and the Nicomachean View

In his Nicomachean discussion of voluntariness, Aristotle concedes to the intuitions motivating the Eudemian view that if we take the agent's action to be identified simply by the description under which the agent would say it was compelled – for example "doing something shameful" (*EN* 1110a5) or "throwing the cargo overboard" (a9–10) – we must conclude that the action is involuntary. This is what he means when he claims that "in themselves" (*kath' hauta*) or "taken without qualification" (*haplōs*), such actions are involuntary (*EN* 1110a9, 18, b3, 5). But he denies that this is the relevant description for determining whether the agent acted voluntarily. The proper characterization of what the agent actually does will cite both the features of the action considered without qualification (throwing the cargo overboard), and the goal for the sake of which the action is performed (to save the lives of those aboard ship):

> Those things that are in themselves (*kath' hauta*) involuntary, but are chosen (*haireta*) now and in exchange for these, and the origin is in the agent, these are in themselves (*kath' hauta*) involuntary, but now and in exchange for these voluntary. (*EN* 1110b3–5)

As in the *EE*, Aristotle in the *EN* considers that we must take the action's goal (*telos*) into account in order to tell whether it reflects the agent's character. But in contrast to his position there, he here insists that the goal is not the only thing we must consider. We must consider both what the agent does and what he does it for, because so characterized, the action does reflect the agent's character:

> And some such actions are even praised – whenever someone submits to something shameful or painful as the price of greater and noble things. And whenever the opposite is true, they are blamed – for to put up with something exceedingly shameful in exchange for nothing fine or commensurate is the mark of a base person. (*EN* 1110a19–23)

The Nicomachean view therefore shares with the Eudemian view the assumption that actions that display the agent's character, and so count as doing justice (*dikaiopragein*) and doing injustice (*adikein*), must turn out to be voluntary. The differing views of compulsion in these two works reflect differing assessments of whether compelled actions display the agent's character. The Eudemian view considers only the goal of the

action in considering whether it proceeds from character in the appropriate way, and so concludes that the action does not reflect the character. The Nicomachean view considers both what the agent does and
what she does it for, and so concludes that the agent's action does reflect
his character.

The Nicomachean way of characterizing the action is clearly preferable
to the Eudemian, which entails the unsatisfactory result that Roger's
action is not voluntary. The Nicomachean approach considers not only
the goal of Roger's action, which is in itself unobjectionable, but also
what he is willing to do to promote that goal. While agents such as
Roger are not aiming at injustice in their actions, they are indifferent to
the injustice (or the unjust features) of their actions, or if not indifferent,
care less about the justice of their actions than about the pursuit of their
own projects. They are blameworthy for these actions precisely because
these actions reflect their indifference or low level of concern. The bad
actions of these agents stem from bad features of their moral character.

One might wonder at this point whether in the *EN* Aristotle has also
abandoned the view that voluntary actions must be performed non-
accidentally. The Eudemian view, in taking the agent's goal to be what
she produces non-accidentally, identifies the non-accidental product of
the agent's moral character in the same way that Aristotle identifies
the non-accidental product of the chef's culinary skill. In each case, the
non-accidental product is what the agent aims at in exercising the causal
power in question. Pleasure is the goal of the chef's causal activity (*Met.*
1027a3–5), and injustice the goal of the blameworthy agent's causal
activity. Since the *EN* rightly points out that even cases where injustice
is not the agent's goal in acting can be genuine cases of acting unjustly
(*adikein*), is Aristotle there committed to abandoning the claim that
voluntary actions must be produced by the agent non-accidentally?
Does the concept of causation that he develops in his writings on physical
nature not, after all, fit the case of human action? Aristotle himself gives
no indication that he has abandoned, in the *EN*, the requirement that
voluntary actions be produced non-accidentally; indeed, his remarks at
1114b26–30 (discussed above) indicate that it is a tacit assumption of
the Nicomachean account. It is therefore incumbent on us to consider
whether there are alternatives to the *EE*'s construal of the conditions for
bringing about an injustice non-accidentally that will explain how even
injustices like Roger's are produced non-accidentally.

We know from Aristotle's account of non-accidental production that
an agent who non-accidentally produces an injustice must be exercising

a causal power that naturally produces (*pephuke poiein*) or reliably (*hōs epi to polu*) produces injustice. The problem with cases like Roger's is that the relevant causal power, Roger's moral character, does not appear to be reliably productive of injustice. It does not incline Roger to perform acts of injustice whenever these are available; rather, it disposes him to perform acts of injustice only on some occasions. How then could it be correct to claim that Roger brings about injustice non-accidentally? It is intuitively plausible to claim that it is not an accident that something unjust is brought about by Roger, since a defect in his moral character explains why the injustice occurs. But how are we to construe this explanatory relation in terms of non-accidental production as Aristotle understands it?

I propose that Roger's situation is analogous to that of someone who knows how to call for help in French, but is otherwise unable to speak French. Suppose this person yells "au secours" when in danger and intending to call for aid from French-speaking persons. It is not an accident that she speaks the French words that convey the demand for help, for she is able to do precisely this and will succeed if unimpeded whenever she tries. She cannot, however, speak French, for she does not have the ability to express her thoughts in French in circumstances other than this one. She does not have the capacity for speaking French, but nonetheless this particular case of her speaking French is not an accident. The Eudemian construal of the conditions for non-accidentally doing injustice assumes that the causal power that is naturally productive (*pephuke poiein*) of injustice must be relevantly similar to the ability to speak French — that it must be a disposition to bring about injustice no matter what the occasion. I suggest, on the other hand, that the kind of causal power whose exercise makes an agent like Roger a non-accidental cause of injustice is more like the ability to say one thing in French — a disposition to bring about only a particular sort of injustice.

What is the particular sort of injustice that Roger is disposed to bring about non-accidentally? Is it robbing widows and orphans? Although "robbing widows and orphans" does specify a particular sort of injustice, the description is still too general to specify an outcome that Roger is reliably disposed to bring about whenever the opportunity presents itself. He would not rob widows and orphans unless doing so furthered some project of his (as in the present case, his trip around the world). And even if doing so on a particular occasion would promote some project of his, he might still refrain from doing so — if, for example, the widows and orphans are relatives of his, or if he is likely to be caught and punished. But we can appeal to these features of Roger's motivation to specify a type of injustice even more specific than robbing widows and orphans:

A specific type of injustice
(Robbing widows and orphans ⟨when this will finance his vacation, and the widows and orphans are not related to him, and he is not likely to be caught and punished.⟩)

If we have adequately captured in the angle brackets the features of the situation relevant to Roger's motivation in robbing the widows and orphans, then we have specified in the parenthesis a type of outcome that (a) Roger is reliably disposed to bring about when the opportunity presents itself, and (b) is intrinsically unjust. Although the qualifications in the angle brackets are irrelevant to the injustice of the outcome, their addition to the description "robbing widows and orphans" does not make the outcome specified any less unjust, for robbing widows and orphans is (we are assuming) intrinsically unjust. If, on the other hand, the description in the angle brackets does not adequately capture the features of the situation relevant to Roger's motivation, then the description in the parenthesis will not specify a type of injustice Roger is reliably disposed to bring about unless it is supplemented by additional qualifications. But once these qualifications are added, we have still specified an outcome that is intrinsically unjust:

An even more specific type of injustice
(Robbing widows and orphans ⟨when this will finance his vacation, and the widows and orphans are not related to him, and he is not likely to be caught and punished, and P, and Q, and R, and . . .⟩)

Even though the additional qualifications "and P, and Q, and R, and . . ." are irrelevant to the injustice of the outcome, their addition to the description does not make the outcome specified any less intrinsically unjust. It simply serves to specify an even more particular type of injustice. Hence we have still identified a particular sort of injustice of which Roger is reliably, and hence non-accidentally, productive. Aristotle therefore need not abandon the presupposition that voluntary actions originate in the agent non-accidentally in order to count as voluntary actions such as Roger's.

8 Mixed Actions and Accidental Production

The preceding account of bringing about an injustice non-accidentally can be invoked to explain how all the actions that *EN* iii 1 counts as voluntary are performed non-accidentally. Since we have no reason to suppose that Aristotle has abandoned in the *EN* the presupposition that the voluntary agent is the origin of the action non-accidentally, we must understand his Nicomachean position on compulsion to entail that the person who is compelled to do something shameful, unjust, or otherwise undesirable brings about such an outcome non-accidentally. So on the Nicomachean view, in contrast to the Eudemian view, the person who is compelled to withhold the deposit brings about an injustice (*adikon ti*) non-accidentally. The Eudemian verdict, that such actions are involuntary, has the advantage of explaining easily why agents are not blamed for such actions, since praise and blame are only for voluntary things (*EE* 1223a9–20). Aristotle, in *EN* iii 1, agrees that the agent who has truly been compelled to perform a bad action is not blameworthy for it (*EN* 1110a19–b1). But given that he claims here that the agent brings about the result voluntarily, and by implication non-accidentally, how can he explain the fact that the agent should be forgiven, or sometimes even praised, rather than blamed?

In maintaining in the *EN* that compelled actions, although voluntary, contain a significant admixture of involuntariness – in his phrase, that they are "mixed" (1110a11) – Aristotle presumably means to indicate the features of compelled action that explain why the compelled agent does not deserve to be blamed for bringing about the bad outcome he voluntarily produces. These voluntary actions are involuntary when considered "in themselves" (*kath' hauta*), that is, unqualified (*haplōs*) by the various particular features of the situation that make them choiceworthy by the agent (for example, their contingent alternatives and consequences, 1110a9–14, 18–19, b3–5). Aristotle must therefore think that compelled actions, considered under this very general but morally significant description, satisfy the conditions for being forced (*bia(i)*). That is, so specified, they must be (a) contrary to the desire of the agent, and (b) externally caused.

It is relatively unproblematic to see that the actions, so considered, are contrary to the agent's desire.[20] As Aristotle says in the *EE*: the agent does "what he does not want to do" (1225a10–11). In the *EN*'s examples, the agent who is compelled by the tyrant to perform the shameful deed as the price of saving the lives of his parents and children does not want to perform a shameful deed (that is, he wants not to do so). The captain does not want to throw the ship's cargo overboard, since the point of his sea voyage is to bring the cargo safely to port. In the storm that requires him to choose between keeping the cargo on board and endangering the lives of passengers and crew, he is compelled to act contrary to the desire that motivates his whole journey.

It is less straightforward to see how such actions, so considered, are externally caused. But we must understand how this could be if we are to understand why the agent is typically not blamed for the bad thing she does under compulsion. If we are to identify this bad thing, we cannot be considering "what she does" under all the relevant particulars that make it choiceworthy, since, so considered, it is not a bad action at all. It is the right action to perform and the expression of a praiseworthy state of character (*EN* 1110a20–2). If we are to find the bad action for which the compelled agent is not blamed, we need to consider what the agent does without these particular qualifications – as some particular bad or shameful thing. That is, we must consider the action "in itself" or "without qualification." In what sense, if any, can it be true to claim that the origin of this outcome is not in the agent, but rather, as the *MM* claims, "in the externals" (1188b19)?

In ordinary cases in which an agent voluntarily brings about a bad outcome, the agent is blameworthy for that bad outcome because it is caused non-accidentally by his character. The fine-grained distinctions involved in Aristotle's conception of non-accidental causation allows him to distinguish between two different things for which such an agent is responsible: (a) she is responsible for the fact that this particular bad outcome occurs; (b) she is responsible for the fact that a bad rather than a good outcome occurs. When someone is compelled to perform a bad action (because in the situation it is the lesser of two evils), (a) is true but (b) is false. The situation in which the agent finds herself guarantees that regardless of what the agent does something bad will occur, either the bad thing the agent selects, or its worse alternative. In the *MM*'s terminology, "the externals" rather than the agent are responsible for the fact that something bad occurs. The agent's contribution to the situation, although it produced a bad outcome, made the outcome less bad than it would otherwise have been; therefore there is no level of badness causally attributable to the agent rather than to the externals. So it is inappropriate to blame the agent. And to the extent that the agent made the outcome better than it would otherwise have been it may even be appropriate to praise her, since, as we saw in chapter 2, praise is for being productive of good things (cf. *EN* 1101b15–18).

We can offer a similar explanation of why, in such a situation, the agent who fails to be truly compelled, because he chooses the worse of the two threatened evils, is less blameworthy than an agent who chooses the same action (*haplōs*) but in a situation in which no compelling circumstances exist. The former agent is responsible for making the worst of a bad situation. However, since the outcome is going to be bad regardless of what he does, the level of badness that is chargeable to him is only the difference between the evil of the alternative he should have chosen and the evil of the alternative he did in fact choose. The latter agent, by contrast, has all the evil of his action chargeable to him, since the situation does not guarantee that something bad will occur. Therefore he is more blameworthy than the former agent.

We may conclude that Aristotle's distinction between accidental and intrinsic efficient causation, which the present chapter has shown to be presupposed by his account of voluntariness, allows him not only to provide a satisfactory explanation of why we are morally responsible for actions performed under compulsion, but also to accommodate the intuitions that appear to support the opposing verdict.

NOTES

1   All the MSS read *dei*. This makes the sentence hard to construe, since *dei* normally introduces an accusative-infinitive construction, but the main verb in the sentence is finite (*prattei*). Susemihl and Mingay and Walzer suggest emending *dei* to *aei*, which makes the sentence grammatically regular, but the point of *aei*, "always", in addition to the quantification expressed in *hosa*, is obscure. I prefer to keep *dei*, with the resulting anacolouthon, and interpret the two *hosa* . . . clauses in [B] to modify the originally intended subject of the accusative-infinitive clause dependent on *dei*. Had the original construction been carried through, Aristotle would have written *hekousia prattesthai* rather than *hekōn prattei* in 1225a11. Instead, the subject and mood of the main clause have been attracted into the subject and mood of the dependent clause, *hosa prattei ha mē bouletai* (1225a11).

2   One might wonder whether in this context "up to the agent" introduces a requirement additional to the requirement of internal causation. If so, then Aristotle is contradicting his general remarks about origins of action in *EE* ii 6, 1223a2–9; cf. *EN* 1110a17–18, 1113b20–1, 1114a18–19. I argue in detail against this interpretation in Appendix II.

3 This is not to deny, what Woods points out at 1225a8–19, that one's judgements about relative value may be causally relevant to one's development of an irresistible desire for a given alternative (Woods 1982, p. 144). I simply point out that such judgements are not necessary for the desire's actually being compulsive.

4 In this passage, Aristotle initially calls passions, rather than actions, involuntary or not up to one. But he proceeds to indicate that he thinks the actions performed as a result of such passions are not up to the agent (1225a23–5, 27–33). Presumably, the passion that is not up to one to bear and the action resulting from the passion are the alternatives faced by the agent. Since Aristotle thinks an action is up to me to do only if it is also up to me not to do, he would think that actions one performs in order to avoid unbearable passions are not up to one. If it is not up to me to leave a desire unsatisfied (because of its painfulness) then it is not up to me to satisfy the desire.

5 By contrast, the account of compulsion in *MM* i 15 cites examples and criteria only for rational compulsion ("doing something harmful in exchange for avoiding some greater ⟨evil⟩" – 1188b20). The previous chapter's definition of force (*bia*), however, includes as an example of forced movement a case in which a running horse is forced to change direction (1188b5–6), presumably by the rider pulling on the bit. This seems more like a case of psychological compulsion, although Aristotle here appears to include it under the rubric "force" rather than "compulsion."

6 It corresponds exactly to neither definition, but in its general form it is quite similar to that of *EE* ii 9. And the example of forced action offered immediately after the definition (A takes B's hand and uses it to strike C, 1135a27–8) is the same example offered in *EE* ii 8: 1224b13–15.

7 *Ph.* 196b24–9, 197a14; cf. *Met.* 1025a28–9, 1026b37–1027a5.

8 *Ph.* 194b16–20, 198a14–21; *Met.* 983a28–9.

9 *APst.* 73b10–16; *Met.* 1025a25–7; cf. *Ph.* 255b24–7. Accidental causes are not causes "properly speaking" (*oikeiōs legomena, Ph.* 195b3–4); they are not the "most exact" cause (*akrotaton aition*, 195b21–5) to cite.

10 Science, he regularly insists, does not concern itself with merely accidental connections (*APst.* 71b9–12, 87b19–27; *Met.* 1026b4–5).

11 *APst.* 73a34–b5. Here I am excluding from the class of accidents the *kath' hauta sumbebēkota* (intrinsic accidents) which Aristotle sometimes includes in the class of the accidental (cf. *Met.* 1025a30–4). These properties are *sumbebēkota* (accidents), on Aristotle's view, because they are not part of the essence (*to ti ēn einai*) of the entity in question, but they are *kath' hauto* (intrinsic) because they follow from the essence and hence can be demonstrated from the essence. Such properties are properly considered accidents in the ontological sense that they do not exist in their own right but only

as properties of things that exist in their own right. They differ from the wider class of accidents in that it is not an accident that they belong to the entities in question. Henceforth, unless indicated otherwise, I will not be referring to these intrinsic accidents (*kath' hauta sumbebēkota*) when referring to accidental properties.

12   *Ph.* 195b23–5; *Met.* 1027a4.

13   The causal power "naturally produces" its non-accidental effect: *Met.* 1026b10, 1027a1, 6; produces it "always or for the most part": *Met.* 1025a14–19, 1026b29–37; *Ph.* 196b34–197al. I discuss non-accidental production in more detail in Meyer 1992.

14   These two types of accidental efficient-causal relation are the ones involved in the production of the two different types of accidental occurrences identified by Richard Sorabji (Sorabji 1980, pp. 4–7). I have benefitted from Sorabji's illuminating discussion of the different types of Aristotelian accidents. Unlike him, I am not concerned here with the notion of an accidental occurrence, but with the accidental relation between efficient cause and effect. Focussing on the distinction between an accidental causal relation and an accidental occurrence solves a problem that Sorabji raises for Aristotle on p. 6, where he points out that an accidental property need not lack an intrinsic cause; while pallor may be accidental to a man, it need not be an accident that a particular man is pale. But in claiming that pallor is an accident of the man, all Aristotle claims is that pallor is accidental to the man – that the connection between pallor and man is only accidental. He does not thereby claim that the man's pallor is an accidental occurrence: that there is no intrinsic cause of this man's being pale.

15   This is why Plato insists (*Gorgias*, 464d) that the chef's culinary skill (*opsopoiikē*, sometimes rendered into English as "cookery") is a form of flattery: it produces pleasure but involves no knowledge of health.

16   Presumably the first scenario captures the way in which natural processes do not originate in the agent in the way voluntariness requires. At *EE* ii 6, 1223a10–13 Aristotle denies that we are responsible for what happens by nature, but in the *Physics* he defines a natural change as one that originates within the subject of change (192b8–193a1). Presumably this is because he identifies the voluntary agent in terms of the disposition (*hexis*) of his capacities for thought and desire, and this disposition is only accidentally related to the agent's nature.

17   For according to that account, a decision is a desire arrived at by figuring out how best to achieve a goal, and what the agent decides on is what he thinks will promote a given goal, rather than the goal itself. Here, by contrast, Aristotle claims that the agent decides on the goal, and not on the action that promotes it (*EN* 1113a9–14; *EE* 1226b4–9).

18 By *prohaireitai d' oudeis*, Aristotle cannot mean that no one does base actions (*phaula*) on decision (*prohairesis*), for he thinks that this is characteristic of the vicious person's activity (*EN* 1150b29–30). Nor can he mean that when one is compelled, one does not act on decision. The cases of compulsion are offered as examples of cases in which one must look to the decision rather than to the action in order to judge the agent's character. Therefore, the agent in such cases must be acting on decision.

19 Compare *EN* 1128a9–12, which claims that character is evident from its activities, and 1127a27–31, which denies that character is evident from actions that are performed for some ulterior motive.

20 Note that if they are considered with all the relevant qualifications, they are not contrary to the agent's desire. While it is contrary to the captain's desire to jettison the cargo, it is not contrary to his desire to do so when the lives of those on board ship are at stake.

5

Responsibility for Character: Its
Scope and Significance

◆

In the last chapter of the discussion of voluntariness in the *Nicomachean
Ethics* (*EN* iii 5), in a passage that has no parallel in either the *Eudemian
Ethics* or the *Magna Moralia*, Aristotle argues that we are responsible for
our states of character:

> People are themselves responsible for having come to be like this, by
> living without restraint, and for being unjust or intemperate – the
> ones by doing evil, the others by spending their time in drinking and
> the like. For the particular activities make them of this sort. This is
> clear from those who practice for any kind of contest or action, for they
> are continually exercising the activity. So to be ignorant that it is
> from exercising particular actions that one's states come to be is the mark
> of someone completely without perception. . . . If someone does know-
> ingly what will make him unjust, then he is unjust voluntarily. (*EN*
> 1114a4–13)

Modern accounts of moral responsibility often take responsibility for
character to provide the ultimate basis of moral responsibility.[1] According to these accounts, responsibility for character is a necessary condition both for responsibility for action and for the praiseworthiness and
blameworthiness of character itself. But nowhere else in Aristotle's
discussions of voluntariness have we found any reason to suppose that
Aristotle attaches this significance to responsibility for character. Indeed, *EN* iii 5 is the only place in those discussions where he argues for,
or even unambiguously asserts, the thesis that we are responsible for our

states of character.[2] So presumably this chapter should provide crucial evidence of the significance Aristotle attaches to the thesis of responsibility for character. In order to determine what significance Aristotle attaches to this thesis, we must first understand its scope. The best way to approach this issue is to consider a familiar objection that is often levelled at Aristotle's argument for the thesis.

1 On the Importance of Being Raised in Good Habits

Aristotle's argument that we are responsible for our states of character (*EN* 1114a4–13) appeals to his account of character formation, according to which states of character are formed by habituation. In the familiar phrase, "we become just by performing just actions, temperate by performing temperate actions, and brave by performing brave actions" (*EN* 1103a34–b2). He here supplements that account with the claim that when we engage in these character-forming activities we know that they will have this result (1114a12–13), and he concludes that the process of character formation satisfies the requirements for voluntariness that he has identified in *EN* iii 1: the process originates in the agent who knows what he is doing (1111a22–4).

Paradoxically enough, the account of character formation to which Aristotle appeals in this argument is often thought to undermine his conclusion that we are responsible for our states of character.[3] This is because Aristotle insists in that account on the importance of being properly habituated from an early age:

> And in a single account: the states result from similar activities, which is why one must display activities of a particular sort, for it is according to the differences between the activities that the states follow. So it makes no small difference whether one is habituated this way or that way right from youth (*euthus ek neōn*). Rather it makes a big difference, or rather all the difference. (*EN* 1103b21–5; cf. 1095b4–13, 1104b11–13, 1179b34ff.)

Clearly, we are not in control of the forces that influence our character development right from birth; our early moral educators are responsible for and in control of that. But then the patterns of habitual activity productive of our character dispositions would be already well entrenched in our dispositions by the time we emerge from the care of our early moral habituators, and so it would be unreasonable to claim that it is up to us to develop the states of character we do. Or so the objection goes.

This worry, in its strongest form, is somewhat exaggerated, for Aristotle clearly does not think that the habituation we receive from our earliest moral educators is sufficient to determine our states of character. In his remarks about moral education in *EN* x, he explicitly distinguishes two distinct stages of habituation, each of which is necessary for the development of our states of character and the second of which is up to the developing agents themselves:

> Nurture and ways of spending one's time (*epitēdeumata*) must be commanded by the laws, for things will not be painful once they have become ingrained in one's character (*sunēthē*). But it is presumably not sufficient for people to receive proper nurture and care when they are young. Rather even once they are mature (*andrōthentes*) they must spend their time on (*epitēdeuein*) them and become habituated to them. Concerning these things, and in general concerning the whole of life, we would need laws. (*EN* 1179b34–1180a4)

The first stage of habituation is the stage of "nurture and care". This stage is the earliest stage of moral education during which one's moral development is under the control of one's parents and other educators, but Aristotle here indicates that such early habituation is not sufficient for the development of a virtuous character. He explicitly distinguishes a second stage of moral habituation essential to the formation of character – the stage of adult life (*andrōthentes*, 1180a2) during which the ways we spend our time (*epitēdeumata*) continue to form our states of character.

It is clearly reasonable for Aristotle to distinguish these two stages of habituation, for the sorts of dispositions that the adult virtuous or vicious person will have concern a range of activities not within the scope of a child. The well-raised child will want to be virtuous, and will take pleasure in doing things she or he takes to be virtuous – but she will lack experience of a whole range of activity and emotion relevant to various virtues and vices. Consider, for example, the virtue of courage. The well-raised child will have listened to stories of courageous people and to music in the Dorian mode (cf. *Republic* 377a–383c, 386a–388d, 398d–399c), and will as a result desire to act bravely when he grows up. But he, as a child, has no experience of many of the fearful situations (*ta phobera*) in which the virtue of courage is exercised and acquired. Such situations as, for example, seeing the enemy advance, are naturally fear-provoking (cf. *EN* 1115b7–13) and hence painful and distressing to withstand. Even the well-raised child who desires to act bravely will feel fear and distress in these situations, and will find it difficult to stand his ground. The person newly emerging from a good *paideia* will therefore not find it easy to perform courageous actions in such situations, since he will be subject to strong counter-inclinations. He will require further habituation in order to develop the virtue of courage, and the activities involved in such habituation are ones he must undertake when he is adult (*andrōthentes*).

Upon reflection, it seems clear that when Aristotle claims, in his account of character formation, that we become virtuous by performing virtuous actions and vicious by performing vicious actions, the sorts of activities he has in mind belong to the second rather than the first stage of habituation:

> By their activities in exchanges with people some people become just, others unjust. By acting in dangerous situations and becoming accustomed to feel fear or confidence, some people become brave, others cowardly. And similarly with activities concerning appetites and anger: some people become temperate and gentle (*praoi*), others intemperate and irascible, by conducting themselves this way or that way in these situations. (*EN* 1103b14–21)

"Exchanges with people" (b14) and "dangerous situations" (b16) are clearly the domain of adult activities rather than those of a child. So too with the activities concerning the appetites and angers that make one temperate and gentle or intemperate and irascible (b18–21). While temperance is one of the first virtues early moral educators must begin to instill in a child, the full range of bodily pleasures and inclinations regarding which the temperate person must exert self-control are beyond the experience of a child (*EN* 1117b27–1118b8). Just as clearly, the sorts of activities Aristotle has in mind in *EN* iii 5 when he argues that we are responsible for our states of character belong to this stage of life: doing evil (*kakourgountes*), and spending one's time in drinking (1114a6). Since Aristotle claims that even the best early moral education fails to inculcate in the person educated a firm disposition to perform the right actions in one's adult life, it is perfectly reasonable of him to claim that it is up to the agent who has emerged from the care of his earliest moral educators to develop the states of character that he forms by his subsequent actions.

2 Full vs. Qualified Responsibility for Character

This is why the strongest form of the worry that Aristotle's views on character formation undermine his views on responsibility for character is exaggerated. But the worry can be reformulated. According to the scenario of moral development that Aristotle envisages, one's responsibility for one's states of character is of significantly limited scope. When the developing agent is about to embark upon the course of adult activities (*epitēdeumata*) that will complete or preclude the formation of a virtuous character, she already has a set of dispositions, albeit incomplete ones, that will identify certain goals and activities as worth pursuing and others as to be avoided. Only if the agent's earlier moral education has correctly identified the goals she should pursue in her activity will Aristotle be correct in claiming that the adult agent knows that the course of activity she is embarking upon will make her vicious (or virtuous). The course of activity such an agent pursues subsequent to this point will determine whether the character she develops will embody the goals she knows to be virtuous rather than the ones she knows to be vicious. This is why Aristotle claims such an agent is responsible for her goals (*EN* 1114b1–3, 22–4). But he has not shown that the agent is responsible for having the correct goals in the first place, at the crucial moment when she chooses between the alternative courses of action. Indeed, Aristotle's insistence that a correct early moral education is necessary for the development of a virtuous character (*EN* 1104b11–13) would seem to preclude such a possibility. While Aristotle's view of character formation is consistent with the thesis that we are responsible for our characters in a qualified way (on the assumption that our early moral education has already identified to us the correct goals to pursue), it appears to be inconsistent with the thesis that an agent is responsible for her character in the deepest sense (call it "full responsibility"), in which the moral quality of an agent's character is in no way due to factors beyond her control.

But do we have any reason to suppose that Aristotle intends his argument to establish that we have full, rather than simply qualified, responsibility for our characters? If he intends to argue for full responsibility, he must respond to the obvious objection that the person who has had a deprived childhood or a bad upbringing or environment will embark on the final stage of habituation with the wrong goals, but through no fault of his own. Aristotle, however, does not consider this objection to his argument, even though he does consider at some length other objections to his argument:

> Furthermore, it is ridiculous for the person doing injustice not to want (*boulesthai*) to be unjust, or the person acting intemperately not to want to be intemperate. If someone does knowingly what will make him unjust, then he is unjust voluntarily. This is of course not to say that whenever he wishes he will stop being unjust and will be just, for neither will the sick person become well in this way. If he got sick in this way, he is sick voluntarily, by living incontinently and disobeying the doctors. (*EN* 1114a11–16)

He addresses the objection that the person undertaking the course of activities that will make him unjust does not intend or want (*bouletai*) to become unjust (1114a11–13); and the objection that the person once unjust is unable not to be so (1114a13–21). He even anticipates, in the course of his positive argument, the objection that the agent does not know that like activities produce like states of character (1114a7–10). But he nowhere considers the objection that the agent, through no fault of his own, does not know that the actions he is performing are unjust and that therefore he is not responsible for becoming unjust.[4]

Furthermore, Aristotle appears to give us several explicit indications that he is arguing for qualified rather than full responsibility for character. In the last section of the chapter (1114a31–b25) he appeals more than once to the conclusion of his argument that we are responsible for our states of character, and in each case he states the conclusion with a qualifying demur. Each person is "responsible in a way" (*pōs aitios*) for his state of character (1114b2); "something also depends on him" (*ti kai par auton estin*, b17); and "we are co-causes in a way" (*sunaitioi pōs*) of our states (b23). These locutions appear to attribute to the agent only a qualified kind of responsibility for character, and to acknowledge the operation of other, perhaps even more important, causal factors.[5] Such qualifications would be problematic if Aristotle's thesis about responsibility for character attributed to us full responsibility for the moral quality of our characters. But they are perfectly consistent with the thesis of qualified responsibility for character – the thesis that, assuming that one's upbringing and social context provide one with the information about which sorts of activities are good and bad, it is up to us whether we develop a disposition to perform the good ones rather than the bad ones. These explicit qualifications therefore give us reason to suppose that Aristotle intends to defend the thesis of qualified rather than full responsibility for character.

Accepting this interpretation of Aristotle's conclusion has appeared problematic to many readers.[6] They assume that unless Aristotle succeeds in establishing the stronger thesis of full responsibility for character, his discussion of voluntariness fails to provide an adequate account of moral responsibility. Other readers, who accept that the qualified thesis is all Aristotle intends to establish, take this to indicate that Aristotle does not intend his account of voluntariness to be an account of anything we would recognize as moral responsibility.[7] Both sets of readers accept the common modern assumption that responsibility for character is the ultimate basis for moral responsibility, and they also assume, reasonably enough, that given such a view, only full responsibility for character, not qualified responsibility, would provide an ad-equate basis. But do we have any reason to suppose that Aristotle accepts this view about the basis of moral responsibility? I submit that we do not.

There are various passages in *EN* iii 5 that appear to various readers to either express or endorse aspects of this modern assumption about responsibility: 1113b17–19, 1114a3–5, and 1114b3–4 may appear to express the view that responsibility for action requires responsibility for character; 1114a21–31, the view that the praiseworthiness and blameworthiness of states of character requires that we be responsible for them. However, once we understand these passages in the context of the general argument of the chapter as a whole, the plausibility of this interpretation of them recedes. Indeed, we will see that the main point of the chapter is not even to establish that we are responsible for our states of character. While the thesis of responsibility for character is an important conclusion Aristotle argues for here, the main point of the chapter is to establish not this thesis but rather the thesis that virtuous and vicious actions are equally voluntary. The first stage of the chapter's argument introduces and argues for this thesis (1113b3–21); the second introduces independent evidence in support of this thesis (1113b21–1114a31); and the third addresses an argument against the thesis (1114a31–b25). Not until the second stage does Aristotle introduce and argue for the claim that our states of character are up to us (1114a3–21). In the third section Aristotle indicates that he takes this argument to show the falsity of a premise to an argument for the thesis that only virtuous actions are voluntary (1114b1–3, 22–4). But nowhere does he claim or imply that our responsibility for virtuous and vicious actions requires that the virtuous and vicious characters from which we act must be up to us[8] or that the praiseworthiness and blameworthiness of our states of character depends on this. To appreciate these points, let us examine the development of the chapter's argument.

3 The Asymmetry Thesis Introduced (*EN* 1113b3–21)

EN iii 5 begins by drawing together the topics addressed in the preceding discussion of voluntariness and related matters:

> Since the end is the object of wish, while the things that promote the end are objects of deliberation and decision, actions that concern these ⟨sc. the objects of deliberation and decision⟩ would be according to decision and voluntary. And the activities of the virtues concern these. So both virtue and, in the same way, vice are up to us. (*EN* 1113b3–7)

Aristotle tells us that the moral we are to draw from the preceding discussion of wish (chapter 4), deliberation (chapter 3), decision (chapter 2), and voluntariness (chapter 1) is that "both virtue and, in the same way, vice are up to us" (1113b6–7). After elaborating upon some of the reasons that support this conclusion (1113b7–17), Aristotle points out that we must accept this conclusion on pain of denying that we are responsible for our actions:

> Otherwise we must dispute what has just now been said and deny that a man is the origin and generator of his actions just as he is of his children. (*EN* 1113b17–19)

On the face of it, Aristotle appears to be introducing the thesis of responsibility for character because he thinks responsibility for character is necessary for responsibility for action. But this initial impression is mistaken, for the thesis that Aristotle introduces at 1113b6–7, as the moral we are to draw from the preceding chapters, is not the thesis of responsibility for character.

Certainly the conclusion Aristotle articulates at 1113b6–7 appears to be the thesis of responsibility for character. After all, virtue and vice, which the conclusion states are equally up to us, are in Aristotle's own view, states of character. Nonetheless, the argument Aristotle offers for that conclusion should make us hesitate to interpret it as asserting responsibility for character. For if we interpret the conclusion in this way, the argument, which proceeds as follows, is invalid:

(1) Actions concerning deliberation, decision, and wish are voluntary. (1113b3–5)
(2) The activities of the virtues ⟨and presumably also of the vices⟩ concern deliberation and decision. (1113b5–6)
(3) Therefore, "both virtue (*aretē*) and in the same way vice (*kakia*) are up to us." (1113b6–7)

This argument proceeds on the unstated assumption that what is voluntary is up to us. But even if we grant this presupposition, premises (1) and (2) entail simply that the activities of virtue and vice (that is, virtuous and vicious actions) are up to us. They do not entail that virtuous and vicious states of character are up to us. Therefore, in drawing his conclusion, (3), Aristotle is either making an invalid inference, or else he is using the terms 'virtue' (*aretē*) and 'vice' (*kakia*) to stand for virtuous and vicious activity, respectively.[9]

The latter alternative is confirmed by the argument that follows immediately (1113b7–14). Aristotle offers this argument as a further explanation (*gar*, b7) of his reasons for claiming that "both virtue (*aretē*) and in the same way vice (*kakia*) are up to us" at 1113b6–7. The first step of the argument is to establish that both virtuous and vicious actions are up to us if either is:

> For in those cases in which it is up to us to do something it is also up to us not to do it, and in cases in which no is up to us, so is yes. So if doing it, which is fine, is up to us, not doing it, which is bad, is also up to us. And if not doing it, which is fine, is up to us, doing it, which is shameful, is also up to us. (*EN* 1113b7–11)

In the second step, Aristotle explains that this conclusion, that virtuous and vicious actions are up to us, amounts to the claim that being virtuous and being vicious are up to us:

> And if it is up to us to do fine actions and shameful ones, and in the same way not to do them, and this is what it is to be good and bad, then it is up to us to be decent and base. (1113b11–14)

Aristotle's claim here that "being good" amounts to nothing other than performing fine actions, and that "being bad" amounts to nothing other than performing shameful actions, is quite puzzling in the light of his own explicit account of virtue and vice (*EN* ii 5–9; *EE* ii 1–5; *MM* i 5–9), which is his official account of what it is to "be good" and to "be bad" respectively (cf. *EN* 1105a10–13).[10] He explicitly defines the virtues and vices as states of the soul (*EN* 1106a10–12; *EE* 1220b7–20; *MM* 1186a10–19, 30–32), and explicitly distinguishes these states from the good and bad activities that they cause and are caused by (*EN* 1105a15–16, a17–26, b19–28; *EE* 1220a29–34). Performing a fine action is not sufficient for being virtuous.[11] To be virtuous one must have the state (*hexis*) that disposes one to perform such actions reliably and for the right reasons (*EN* 1105a28–33).

If Aristotle is to avoid contradicting his own explicit distinction between states and activities when he claims here that performing fine actions is what it is to be good and performing shameful actions is what it is to be bad (1113b11–14), then he must be using 'being good' and 'being bad' to refer to the performance of good and bad actions, rather than to the possession of virtuous and vicious states of character. So we have good reason to suppose that at the beginning of the chapter, when Aristotle introduces the thesis that "both virtue (*aretē*) and in the same way vice (*kakia*) are up to us" (1113b6–7), he is using 'virtue' and 'vice' in the same way he uses 'being good' and 'being bad' at 1113b13. That is, he is using them to refer to virtuous and vicious actions respectively rather than to virtuous and vicious states of character. He is not there making an invalid inference to the conclusion that our states of character are up to us. Rather, he claims that the moral to draw from his preceding discussion of voluntariness and related notions is that virtuous and vicious actions are equally up to us. So, contrary to our initial impression, Aristotle's remark at 1113b17–19 that we must accept this conclusion on pain of denying what has already been established in the preceding discussion – that we are the origins of our actions – in no way endorses the principle that responsibility for action requires responsibility for character. It simply reflects Aristotle's view that the preceding chapters, if they have succeeded in establishing that we are the origins of our actions, have established this for both good and bad actions alike.

Aristotle's use here of terms such as 'being good' and 'virtue' to refer to activities rather than states of character is perfectly natural Greek,[12] but it is potentially confusing, especially in the light of his own account of virtue and vice. Most likely he adopts this terminology because the opponents he has in mind use it to state their thesis. He articulates the opponents' thesis immediately after his own conclusion, at 1113b14, that "it is up to us to be decent and base":

> To say that no one is voluntarily wicked or involuntarily blessed seems
> in one respect true and in the other false. While no one is involuntarily
> blessed, vice is voluntary. (*EN* 1113b14–17)

These opponents accept the Socratic thesis that "no one does wrong
voluntarily."[13] I shall refer to this as the "Socratic asymmetry thesis"
since it entails that there is an asymmetry in voluntariness between our
good and our bad actions; that only our good actions, not our bad ones,
are voluntary. This thesis about actions is often stated by its proponents
using terminology that might equally well refer to states of character.[14]
This appears to be how the proponents of the thesis in Aristotle's time
articulated it (cf. *MM* 1187a5–19, b31, 20–1). Aristotle, in arguing
against that thesis here in *EN* iii 5, adopts his opponents' usage.

We can understand why Aristotle should be concerned to refute the
Socratic asymmetry thesis in the remarks that conclude his discussion
of voluntariness if we recall his motivation for introducing the discussion of voluntariness into the discussion of states of character in the first
place. As we saw in chapter 2, Aristotle is concerned to explain why
virtue is praiseworthy and vice blameworthy. These states of character
are praiseworthy and blameworthy respectively, he thinks, because they
are productive in the right way of good and bad actions. He develops
the account of voluntariness in order to capture these conditions of
production. It is therefore a constraint on his account that it count as
voluntary the actions produced by both virtue and vice. Hence he must
reject the Socratic asymmetry thesis, which claims that only the former
are voluntary. Aristotle intends to secure an account of voluntariness
that applies to vicious and virtuous actions alike, and in the final
chapter of his discussion (*EN* iii 5) he brings home the point that his
account of voluntariness succeeds in doing just this.

Our examination of the opening section of *EN* iii 5 (1113b3–21) does
not support the view that Aristotle attaches any particular significance
to the thesis of responsibility for character. Indeed, we have seen that
that section does not even introduce that thesis. Rather, it introduces
and argues against the Socratic thesis that there is an asymmetry in
voluntariness between virtuous and vicious actions. In the second
major section of the chapter (1113b21–1114a31) Aristotle does explicitly introduce and argue for the thesis that we are responsible for our
states of character. So let us turn to examine that section in order to see
what significance Aristotle attaches to the thesis of responsibility for
character.

4 Considerations Against the Asymmetry Thesis
(*EN* 1113b21–1114a31)

After concluding at 1113b21 that his discussion in the preceding chapters has established the voluntariness of both virtuous and vicious actions and hence the falsity of the Socratic asymmetry thesis, Aristotle goes on to adduce an additional set of considerations against the asymmetry thesis (1113b21–1114a31). He appeals to public practices of approbation and censure, and points out that these practices presuppose the falsity of the Socratic asymmetry thesis:

> And this ⟨sc. that we are the origins of our actions⟩[15] seems to be supported both by private individuals and by the lawmakers themselves. For they correct (*kolazousin*) and punish (*timōrountai*) those who perform wicked deeds, if they did so neither by force nor because of ignorance for which they are not themselves responsible, and they reward (*timōsin*) those who perform fine deeds, in order to encourage the latter and restrain the former. And indeed no one is encouraged to do things that are not up to us or voluntary, since there is no point to being persuaded not to be hot, pained, hungry or the like; for we will experience these things nonetheless. (*EN* 1113b21–30)

The point of these practices of reward and punishment is to have an effect on the future behavior of the agent rewarded or punished (b25–6), and they are meted out to both good and bad actions (b23–5). Aristotle therefore concludes that those who engage in these practices believe that the good actions they seek to encourage, as well as the bad actions they seek to discourage, are up to the agents who perform them. The participants in these practices implicitly agree with his contention that our good and our bad actions are equally up to us. These practices, Aristotle points out, presuppose the falsity of the Socratic asymmetry thesis.

In the context of this general line of argument Aristotle introduces and argues for the thesis that we are responsible for our states of character (1114a4–31). While his main argument for the thesis (1114a4–13) does not appeal to the presuppositions of these public practices, he indicates explicitly that the thesis is also supported by the presuppositions:

> Not only the vices of the soul are voluntary, in some cases those of the body are also – which we also reproach (*epitimōmen*). For no one reproaches

(*epitima(i)*) those who are ugly by nature, but rather those who are ugly because of lack of exercise and neglect. And similarly in the case of feebleness and deformity: no one would censure (*oneidiseie*) someone who is blind by nature or sickness or from a blow, but would rather pity him. But anyone would reproach (*epitimēsai*) someone who is blind from drinking too much or from any other excessive behavior. So in the case of bodily evils the ones that are up to us are reproached (*epitimōntai*), while those not up to us are not. And if this is so, then all the other evils that are reproached (*epitimōmenai*) would be up to us. (*EN* 1114a21–31)

In pointing out that certain practices of public censure and approbation of states of character presuppose that these states of character are up to us, and in endorsing that presupposition, does Aristotle in effect supplement his canonical account of the praiseworthiness of states of character[16] (which does not require that they be up to us), with the additional requirement that they be up to us? If so, then he is endorsing one aspect of the view that responsibility for character is the ultimate basis of all moral responsibility. But we should be wary of drawing this conclusion, for what is at stake in the present passage is the justification of certain public *practices*: reward or approbation (*timān*), censure (*oneidizein, epitimān*), and punishment (*kolazein, timōreisthai*). By contrast, what is at stake in his account of praiseworthiness is the justification of certain *attitudes*: praise (*epainos*) and blame (*psogos*). Aristotle gives us no reason to assume that what justifies the public practices must also justify the attitudes.[17] Indeed, the sort of justification he offers here for the practices is entirely different in kind from the justification of the attitudes he offers in his account of praiseworthiness. While Aristotle's account of the presuppositions of the practices indicates that their justification is prospective (their point is to encourage the development of virtuous character and discourage the development of vice), his account of praiseworthiness (*to epaineton*) indicates that praise and blame are justified retrospectively: based on the causal relation between the state of character that is the focus of the praise or blame and the good or bad activities it produces.[18]

So we may not yet conclude that Aristotle thinks the praiseworthiness and blameworthiness of states of character requires that we be responsible for them. But still, we may ask why Aristotle bothers to introduce the thesis of responsibility for character at this point in his argument against the Socratic asymmetry thesis. Perhaps his reasons for introducing the thesis will indicate after all that he does think responsibility for character is fundamental to our moral responsibility.

Immediately before he introduces the thesis that we are responsible for our states of character, and immediately after he has claimed that our public practices of approbation and censure presuppose contra Socrates that our good and bad actions are equally up to us, Aristotle points out that these practices also presuppose that certain cases of ignorance are up to us. He offers two examples:

> They also punish for the ignorance itself, if the person appears to be responsible (*aitios*) for the ignorance. For example, (1) there is a double penalty for those who are drunk, since the origin is in the agent. He is in control (*kurios*) of not getting drunk, and this is the cause (*aition*) of the ignorance. And (2) they also punish those who are ignorant of something in the laws which they ought to know and is not difficult, and similarly in other cases in which the agents appear to be ignorant due to carelessness, on the grounds that it is up to them to not be ignorant since they are in control (*kurioi*) of taking care. (*EN* 1113b30–1114a3)

Regarding the second example, Aristotle entertains the objection, "But presumably he is of the sort not to take care" (1114a3–4). It is in developing his response to this objection that he introduces the argument that we are responsible for our states of character:

> But still, people are themselves responsible for having come to be like this, by living without restraint, and for being unjust or intemperate – the ones by doing evil, the others by spending their time in drinking and the like – for the particular activities make them of this sort. (*EN* 1114a4–7)

In order to determine why Aristotle here introduces the thesis of responsibility for character, we must determine what force he sees in the objection "presumably he is of the sort not to take care" (1114a3).

In explaining why the agents in these two sorts of examples are responsible for being ignorant, Aristotle has appealed to the principle that the origin of an outcome is in the agent if the agent is in control (*kurios*) of its cause (*aition*). Of the agent whose ignorance is due to drunkenness, he says "the origin is in him, for he is in control (*kurios*) of not getting drunk, and this is the cause (*aition*) of his ignorance" (1113b32–3). Of the agents whose ignorance is due to carelessness (*ameleia*), he says: "it is up to them not to be ignorant, since they are in control (*kurioi*) of taking care" (1114a2–3). The objector, in claiming that an agent of the latter sort is "presumably of the sort not to take care" (a3–4), is taking this to be a reason to deny Aristotle's claim that the careless agent is in control of taking care.

But why does the objector think that:

(1)   the agent is careless;
       entails that
(2)   the agent is not in control of taking care?

Clearly, the objector does not appeal directly to the principle that an agent is not in control of an action (in this case, taking care) if he is not responsible for the disposition from which it proceeds. For she does not even affirm the antecedent of the principle. She claims simply that the agent is careless, not that he is not responsible for being careless.

But might she be appealing to the principle that if an activity (such as a particular failure to take care) is the expression of the agent's disposition, then the agent is not in control of that activity?[19] If this is how Aristotle understands the objection, then his reply, which does not challenge the principle, would be tacitly conceding its truth. In responding to the objection that the agent is still responsible for acquiring the disposition, Aristotle would in effect be claiming that even though the agent is not directly in control of the actions that proceed from his dispositions, he is still indirectly in control of those actions because he is responsible for acquiring those dispositions in the first place. To claim this would amount to allowing that responsibility for action does in fact depend on responsibility for character.

It would, however, be quite uncharitable to suppose that Aristotle endorses the principle that we are not in control of activity that is caused by our dispositions. For that principle contradicts some of the fundamental assumptions that motivate and guide Aristotle's inquiry into voluntariness. The goal of that inquiry, he tells us, is to identify the conditions in which the agent is the cause of his actions. In the *EE*, he explicitly states that these are the conditions in which the agent is in control (*kurios*) of his actions (*EE* 1222b20–2, 1223a6–9). And we have seen that, throughout the dialectical development of his account of voluntariness, Aristotle is consistently guided by the assumption that such actions are the ones produced by our character dispositions. Hence Aristotle's whole account of voluntariness presupposes that the actions we are in control of are precisely those that are produced by our character dispositions. To suppose that Aristotle endorses the contradictory principle here, in the final chapter of his discussion of voluntariness, would be quite unfair unless we had compelling independent reasons to interpret the passage in this way. But there is a much more plausible interpretation of the objector's presuppositions which does not require us to attribute the contradictory principle to Aristotle.

The objector clearly does think that the fact that the agent is dispositionally careless means he is not in control (*kurios*) of the carelessness that is the cause (*aition*) of his ignorance. But this thought does not depend on the general principle that we are not in control of activities caused by our dispositions. Rather it depends on the observation, particular to the case at hand, that the carelessness that is the cause of the ignorance is not an activity of the agent, but simply the careless disposition. To see this, it is useful to focus on a disanalogy between the case in which the agent's ignorance is due to drunkenness and the case in which it is due to carelessness. The drinker's ignorance is due to his having taken a certain number of drinks; this course of action is due to his decision to start drinking; and the decision in turn is an expression of the agent's dispositions. In this case we can identify separately the disposition and the activity it causes (the decision) and assign to each a discrete causal role in the explanation of the ignorance. But in the case of the careless person's ignorance, it is different. The careless person, unlike the drinker, does not make a conscious decision not to take care. He simply fails to take care without ever thinking about it. Nor is the failure to take care itself a distinct action produced by the agent's careless disposition. Clearly, the agent performed the actions which resulted in his ignorance because he was careless. But this carelessness was not a distinct activity precipitating those careless actions, in the way the drinker's decision is an activity distinct from his disposition to decide. Rather, the carelessness that Aristotle identifies as the cause (*aition*) of the ignorance at 1114a1–2 is the agent's careless disposition. Hence, when Aristotle claims of this agent that he is in control of the cause of his ignorance, the objector interprets this as claiming that the careless agent is in control of being careless. That is, the objector interprets "in control of taking care" in (2) as "in control of having a careless disposition." We may therefore explain her inference from (1) to (2) by attributing to her no stronger principle than:

(3)   Once an agent has acquired a disposition, he is no longer in control of having that disposition.

Aristotle's remarks in response to the objection (1114a4–21) indicate that he is prepared to concede (3) to the objector.[20] Once the agent is careless he may no longer be in control of *being* careless. But nonetheless, Aristotle insists, the agent was in the past in control of becoming careless, and for this reason he is now still responsible for being careless.

> If someone does knowingly what will make him unjust, then he is unjust voluntarily. This is of course not to say that whenever he wishes he will stop being unjust and will be just, for neither will the sick person become well in this way. If he got sick in this way, he is sick voluntarily, by living incontinently and disobeying the doctors. Back then, it was open to him (*exēn autō(i)*) not to be sick, but ⟨it is⟩ no longer open to him, now that he has let himself go, just as it is no longer possible for the one who has thrown the stone away to retrieve it. But all the same it was up to him to throw it, since the origin was in him. And so too for the unjust and the intemperate person, while it was open to them in the beginning not to become like this – which is why they are ⟨like this⟩ voluntarily – once they have become ⟨like this⟩ it is no longer ⟨open to them⟩ not to be ⟨like this⟩. (*EN* 1114a12–21)

Aristotle responds to the objector that even though the careless agent may no longer be in control of being careless, he is still relevantly similar to the drunk agent. The process whereby the careless agent became careless is relevantly similar to the process by which the drunk agent became drunk. Aristotle develops this point by comparing the process of character formation to the process of becoming ill rather than by comparing the development of a careless disposition to the process of getting drunk (1114a15–21), but the same point holds for the latter comparison.[21] Just as the careless person, once he has become careless, is no longer in control of not being careless, the drinker, once drunk, is no longer in control of not being drunk. However, at the beginning of the process whereby they came to be drunk, these agents were in control of initiating the course of activities that put them in these conditions. The transition is gradual and imperceptible from this original state of being fully in control to the later state of being no longer in control. But the fact that the agents had this control in the beginning is, nonetheless, sufficient to make them responsible for being in this condition:

> While we are in control (*kurioi*) of our states in the beginning, the progression in each case is not obvious, as in the case of infirmities. But

our states are voluntary for this reason: because it was up to us to conduct ourselves in this way or not. (*EN* 1114b32–1115a3)

Therefore, Aristotle responds to the objector, he is right, after all, to claim that the agent whose ignorance is due to carelessness was "in control (*kurios*) of the cause (*aition*) of the ignorance" (1113b32–1114a3).

Having examined the considerations that led Aristotle to introduce his claim that we are responsible for our states of character, we have seen no reason to suppose that Aristotle, or the opponent he is addressing, presupposes that responsibility for character is a necessary condition of responsibility for action. He introduces the thesis of responsibility for character in order to explain why our public practices of approbation and censure presuppose correctly that certain cases of ignorance are up to us. Insofar as Aristotle's defence of this presupposition invokes the principle that the agent is responsible for an outcome if he is in control of its cause (1113b32–1114a1), we may conclude at most that he is committed to the view that responsibility for character is sufficient for responsibility for the actions. We have as yet uncovered no reason to attribute to Aristotle the view that responsibility for character is the fundamental basis of all responsibility. But still, one might reasonably suspect that we have not yet identified the full significance Aristotle attaches to responsibility for character. To appreciate the full significance Aristotle attaches to the thesis, we need to understand why he thinks it is important to argue, in this context, that ignorance is something for which we can be responsible.

Since the asymmetry thesis that Aristotle is arguing against is a thesis about responsibility for actions, it is reasonable to wonder why Aristotle chooses this context to argue that we can be responsible for being ignorant, which is a state or condition rather than an action. Aristotle's introduction here of ignorance as an example of something that can be up to us is not an idle addition to the original list introduced at 1113b21–30. It is directly relevant to the asymmetry thesis, for the asymmetry thesis is motivated by the Socratic account of virtue and vice: the view that virtue is simply knowledge, and vice ignorance, of what one has reason to do. This account motivates the asymmetry thesis because it entails that all vicious action is due to ignorance; and from this Socrates concludes it is not up to the agent.

Aristotle's argument that we are responsible for our states of character directly challenges another implication of the Socratic account of virtue and vice. That account entails that simply knowing what is good is sufficient for acting virtuously (hence Socrates' denial of the possibility of incontinence) and that this is sufficient for having virtue. (The Socratic position allows for blurring the distinction between doing and being virtuous.) Aristotle, who insists contrary to Socrates that virtue involves non-cognitive aspects of the soul in addition to knowledge of the good (*MM* 1182a21–3), emphasizes the fact that the acquisition of virtue requires the training of these non-cognitive elements of the soul. It is not enough to know what is good; one must practice doing it if one is to have any chance of becoming good. He criticizes the implications of the Socratic intellectualist account of virtue at the end of his own account of character formation by habituation in *EN* ii:

> So it is well said that the just person comes to be from performing just actions, and the temperate person from performing temperate actions. Without performing these actions, no one will even be on the way to becoming good. Most people, however, do not perform these actions. Taking refuge in theory instead, they think that they are being philosophers and that in this way they will be good. They act like the sick who listen carefully to the doctors, but carry out none of the doctors' prescriptions. Just as the bodies of the latter will not be in good condition from this course of treatment, nor will the souls of the former be in good condition from philosophizing in this way. (*EN* 1105b9–18; cf. 1179b2–7)

I submit that the concerns expressed in this passage in *EN* ii 4 motivate Aristotle's argument, in *EN* iii 5, that our states of character are up to us.[22] If I am right, then in arguing that people are responsible for their states of character, Aristotle has in mind agents who have already had pointed out to them the sorts of activities that they must perform and avoid in order to develop a virtuous disposition. And he is claiming that such knowledge is insufficient to make them virtuous. Both virtue and vice are still open to those who possess such knowledge, and it is up to them whether they become virtuous by following the prescribed activities or vicious by following the proscribed activities.

On this reading of *EN* iii 5, Aristotle is not attempting to argue that, no matter what the circumstances in which we are raised and no matter what our range of experience and good or bad fortune, we are responsible for becoming good persons rather than bad persons. Rather, he has in mind a social context very much like the one in the Athens of his time where parents, educators, and other citizens participate in the moral education of the young.[23] In this context there is broad agreement about the types of actions that are, for example, unjust and intemperate, and one's family and society teach and remind the young person of these things. Up to a certain point in early moral education, parents and pedagogues habituate the young person in the performance of such activities. But at a certain point (the transition from *trophē* and *epimeleia* to adult activities described in *EN* x 9) it is up to the young person himself or herself to undertake the activities that will complete the process of habituation and in the end determine whether he or she becomes virtuous or vicious. This is the stage of moral education and development that Aristotle has in mind at 1114a4–21, when he claims that we voluntarily form our unjust and intemperate states of character by performing actions we know to be unjust and intemperate. He has in mind an agent who already knows that such actions are unjust and intemperate, because this knowledge is readily available from the education he has already received and from the publicly observable practices of censure and approbation. Such an agent is in a position analogous to that of the patient whose doctor has identified the action he must take to be healthy.[24] Just as it is up to the patient at this point to "disobey the doctors" and thereby become sick (1114a16; cf. 1105b14–16), it is up to the developing moral agent at this point to disregard the clear moral injunctions from his family and society, and thereby become vicious.

Once we understand that the asymmetry thesis, and the Socratic intellectualist account of virtue and vice that motivates it, are the targets of Aristotle's arguments in *EN* iii 5, and once we appreciate the role Aristotle's argument for responsibility for character plays in his argument against these Socratic theses, we have very good reason to suppose that he only intends his argument to establish qualified, rather than full, responsibility for character.

5 An Argument for the Asymmetry Thesis Considered (*EN* 1114a31–b25)

The final section of *EN* iii 5, 1114a31–b25, seems to many readers to provide the strongest evidence that Aristotle is arguing for full, rather than qualified, responsibility for character. If Aristotle is arguing for the stronger thesis then, given his insistence on the importance of early moral habituation, he has to be able to address the objection that at the end of that early habituation, the agent undertakes the subsequent character-forming activities in the light of goals that were inculcated in him by that early education and hence are not up to him. The final section of the chapter might appear to be addressing just such an objection, for it begins by articulating the objection that we are not in control of our goals:

> Someone might say that we all pursue the apparent good but are not in control of the appearance; that, rather, whatever sort of person someone is determines how the end appears to him. (*EN* 1114a31–b1)

It is, however, a mistake to suppose that the thesis of responsibility for character is at stake in this section of Aristotle's argument. Upon closer examination it turns out that the asymmetry thesis that is at stake in the rest of the chapter is also at issue in this section. To the extent that Aristotle invokes his thesis of responsibility for character in this section, he is arguing from it, not for it.

The objection Aristotle considers at 1114a31–b1 clearly does claim that we are not responsible for the way the good appears to us. But this claim is not in service of the thesis that we are not responsible for our states of character. First of all, the objection does not concern character-forming activities, but rather activities that express states of character: actions in pursuit of the good, which is determined by "what sort a person is" (1114a31). These are the sorts of actions that the Socratic asymmetry thesis concerns, and Aristotle's response to the objection indicates that he takes it to be offered in support of precisely that Socratic thesis.

Aristotle responds to the objection by posing a dilemma (1114b1–16), the first horn of which points out that the objector's premise conflicts with his argument that we are responsible for our states of character:[25]

> If, on the one hand, each person is himself responsible in a way for his state, then he is also in a way responsible for the appearance ⟨sc. of the good⟩. (*EN* 1114b1–3)

The second horn of the dilemma (b3–16) grants the objector's premise, but claims that his conclusion does not follow. It begins:

> If, on the other hand, no one (*mēdeis*)[26] is responsible for their wrong-doing but rather does these things due to ignorance of the good, think-

ing that through them he will achieve the best and the pursuit of the goal is not self-chosen but rather must grow naturally like eyesight . . . (*EN* 1114b3–7)

Aristotle here indicates how he takes the objector's argument to work. The objector infers from the premise, that our goals are not up to us but natural, to the conclusion that our wrongdoing is not up to us. After elaborating at some length upon what he takes to be the preposterous consequences of supposing our goals are determined in this way (1114b7–12), Aristotle makes the main point of his response:

If, then, these things are true, how is virtue any more voluntary than vice? For to both the good person and the bad person alike, the end appears and is set by nature or whatever means, and with reference to it they act in whatever way they do. (*EN* 1114b12–16)

His main point in this horn of the dilemma is that even if what the objector claims is true – that we are not responsible for our wrongdoing because we are not in control of the way the good appears to us (b3–5) – this does not establish that virtuous activity is any more voluntary than vicious activity. As in the opening section of the chapter, Aristotle here first states this as the claim that virtue (*aretē*) turns out to be no more voluntary than vice (*kakia*) (1114b12–13). But in his explanation of this claim in the following sentence, he clearly refers to the actions rather than the character of the virtuous and vicious person: "they *act* in whatever way they do" (b13–16). The objector Aristotle addresses in this third section objects not to Aristotle's immediately preceding argument that our states of character are up to us, but rather to his main contention in the chapter: that virtuous and vicious actions are equally up to us. Therefore, Aristotle's consideration of this objection cannot be taken as evidence that he is defending the stronger thesis of full responsibility for character.

Aristotle's concluding remarks in response to the objection confirm that the Socratic asymmetry thesis is what the objector is trying to establish:

Indeed, whether (a) it is not by nature that the end appears in the way it does to each person, but something also depends on him; or whether (b) the end is natural but virtue is voluntary because the good person does the other things voluntarily; vice would be no less voluntary. For the "because of himself" (*to di' auton*) would belong similarly to the bad person – in his actions even if not in his ends. (1114b16–21)

As in the case of the first dilemma he poses in response to the objection (b1–16), Aristotle here states the relevant claims using the terms 'virtue' and 'vice' rather than terms that refer unambiguously to virtuous and vicious actions. But he must be using 'virtue' and 'vice' here to refer to virtuous and vicious actions, for the last sentence (b20–1) indicates that the person whose vice is up to him is not responsible for his goals. But if he was responsible for his character, then he would be responsible for his goals. Therefore, the vice that is up to the agent of b20–1 must be vicious action, rather than vicious character.

Throughout *EN* iii 5 the main target of Aristotle's discussion has consistently been the Socratic asymmetry thesis about actions. His argument that we are responsible for our states of character is not the main project of the chapter. Rather, it is part of his many-pronged attack on the asymmetry thesis and the Socratic theory of virtue on which it rests. It does not follow from this, however, that Aristotle fails to attach independent significance to the thesis of responsibility for character. Indeed, Aristotle makes it very clear that he thinks the thesis is significant in its own right. After arguing in the second dilemma (1114b16–21) that the asymmetry thesis is false independently of whether he is right that we are responsible for our states of character, Aristotle proceeds to reaffirm emphatically that we are responsible for our states of character. He indicates that horn (a) of the dilemma is the one that states the truth:

> If in fact, as was stated, the virtues are voluntary (for we ourselves are in a way co-causes of our states, and by being of a particular sort we determine the character of our goals), then the vices would also be voluntary, and in the same way. (*EN* 1114b21–5)

Following these remarks, Aristotle concludes his general discussion of virtues and vices of character, and indicates that the thesis that these states of character are voluntary is one of the morals he wishes to draw from that general discussion:

> We have now spoken about the virtues in common: (i) giving their genus in outline, that they are means and states; (ii) that they are productive non-accidentally of the sorts of things that produce them; (iii) that they are up to us and voluntary; and (iv) ⟨that they do these things⟩ in the way right reason dictates. (*EN* 1114b26–30)

So we need not deny that Aristotle thinks responsibility for character has independent significance. The question we have been addressing, however, is what he thinks it is significant for. After examining the course of the chapter's argument in detail, we must conclude that Aristotle nowhere indicates that he thinks responsibility for character is significant because it is a necessary condition for responsibility for action,[27] or because it is necessary for the praiseworthiness or blameworthiness of states of character. His own account of praiseworthiness, as we have seen, indicates that (ii) rather than (iii) is what makes the virtues praiseworthy and the vices blameworthy, and nothing Aristotle says in this chapter indicates that he holds the contrary view. He is preoccupied in this chapter with resisting the Socratic asymmetry thesis, and the other implications of the Socratic account of virtue and vice on which it rests. His concerns in this context show that he thinks the qualified sort of responsibility for character he thinks we have is significant for our moral education, not for our moral responsibility.[28]

6 Moral Responsibility without Responsibility for Character?

Early on in our discussion of Aristotle's inquiries into voluntariness, in chapter 2, we concluded provisionally that the sort of praiseworthiness and blameworthiness for which Aristotle thinks voluntariness is necessary does not require that the agent be responsible for having the state of character in the light of which he is praised or blamed. Our examination in the present chapter of his explicit discussion of responsibility for character *EN* iii 5 has confirmed that conclusion. Some readers of Aristotle might accept this conclusion, but take it to establish that Aristotle's inquiries into voluntariness are not, after all, concerned with moral responsibility.[29] This is because they assume, as many modern theorists do, that when we hold someone morally responsible for an action, we are presupposing that its alternative is open to the agent in a very strong way that can be secured only if the agent is fully responsible for the morally relevant features of his character. We, on the other hand, have seen reasons in chapters 1 and 2 for supposing that Aristotle does intend his account of voluntariness to capture the conditions of moral responsibility. If, therefore, he has an adequate account of moral responsibility, he must be able to show what is wrong with this modern assumption about responsibility. He must be able to explain why the actions for which we are praiseworthy and blameworthy are up to us in a suitably strong way without invoking the thesis that we are responsible for our states of character. The next chapter considers Aristotle's resources for meeting this challenge.

NOTES

1 E.g., Williams 1985 and Roberts 1989.

2 The thesis may appear to be asserted at *MM* 1187a5–19, and at *EE* 1228a7–11, but as we saw in chapter 2, these passages do not adequately distinguish virtuous and vicious actions from virtuous and vicious states of character.

3 Engberg–Pedersen 1983, p. 246; Furley 1967, p. 194; Gauthier and Jolif 1970, ad 1114b1–3; Urmson 1988, pp. 59–61; Williams 1985, p. 38. The paradox is noted in Broadie 1991, p. 171.

4 Aristotle might appear to be addressing just such an objection at 1114a31 ff. But, as I argue below, he is not.

5 At *DA* 416a13–14, Aristotle indicates that a "co-cause" (*sunaition*) is not a cause "without qualification" (*haplōs*).

6 E.g. Urmson 1988, pp. 59–61; Furley 1967, p. 194.

7 Roberts explicitly argues for this conclusion (Roberts 1989), which seems also to be the view of Curren (Curren 1989). Williams, who agrees with Roberts that Aristotle is not interested in moral responsibility, finds it troubling that Aristotle should defend the thesis of responsibility for character (Williams 1985, p. 38).

8 On this point, I agree with Curren (1989), although for different reasons.

9 Engberg-Pedersen gives a slightly different diagnosis of the trouble with the chapter's opening argument (Engberg-Pedersen 1983, p. 241).

10 For this reason, Susemihl proposes to delete the phrase.

11 Indeed, it is not even necessary, for Aristotle allows that it is possible to have virtue and never exercise it, for instance, if one spent one's life asleep (*EN* 1098b33–1099a3).

12 As it is in English, where 'I was bad yesterday' refers to a bad action of mine, rather than to any of my states of character.

13 The corresponding passage in the *MM* explicitly identifies Socrates as the opponent (*MM* 1187a5–8). Cf. Plato, *Protagoras* 345d9–e2.

14 See chapter 2, n. 17.

15 The antecedent of *toutois* ("these things") in b21 is *tauta* ("these things") in b19, whose antecedent is *tois nun eirēmenois* ("what has just now been said") in b17, namely that a man is the origin of his actions no less than of his children (b18–19).

16 Explored in chapter 2.

17 Roberts does not distinguish between the practices and the attitudes (Roberts 1989, p. 25, n. 10). She denies that the latter are retrospective moral attitudes on the grounds that the former are not.

18 At *EN* 1179b11–13, Aristotle distinguishes those whose right actions are motivated by moral considerations from those who are motivated by the

prospect of rewards and sanctions. Presumably only the former agents satisfy his account of praiseworthiness, since only their motivation is non-accidentally productive of right actions.

19 So Furley 1967, pp. 189–90; Hardie 1980, p. 175; Joachim 1951, p. 106 (*ad* 114a3–31); and Thomson 1953 understand the force of the objection.

20 By contrast, at *Catg.* 13a23–31, he allows that it is possible for the vicious person to acquire a better state of character. For a discussion of the relation between this passage and *EN* iii 5, see Bondeson 1974 and Siegler 1968.

21 Even though carelessness is arguably not a state of character, it is, like states of character, a disposition.

22 Note that the medical analogy is dominant in both. In *EN* iii 5, when Aristotle considers the response that the person performing an unjust action does not necessarily want or intend (*bouletai*) to become unjust, he dismisses it by pointing to the weakness of the response in the medical case (*EN* 1114a11–16).

23 The situation is described a generation earlier, in the great speech in Plato's *Protagoras*, as one in which one learns the virtues in the same way one learns one's native language (325e–326a, 327e–328a).

24 Curren also emphasizes this claim, but does not see that it applies to a point in moral education before the agent has already achieved virtue (or vice) from societal habituation (Curren 1989). He thinks that Aristotle has in mind agents who have already formed virtuous characters as a result of nurture and upbringing, and that he believes it is up to these agents whether to maintain their virtuous character by acting virtuously. On my proposal, by contrast, Aristotle is thinking of agents who have not yet achieved virtue or vice of character, because they have not yet performed the adult activities he explicitly identifies as the second stage of habituation in *EN* x 9 (1179b34–1180a4).

25 This remark would be quite question-begging if the objector was arguing from this premise to the conclusion that we lack responsibility for our states of character. Although Aristotle does not here affirm explicitly the thesis that we are responsible for our states, presenting it instead as the antecedent of a conditional, his concluding remarks (1114b21–5) indicate that he does affirm the claim, and on the basis of the preceding argument.

26 At 1114b3–4, some MSS have *ei de mēdeis hautō(i) aitios tou kakopoiein* ("If no one is responsible for their wrongdoing"), while others have *ei de mē, oudeis* . . . ("if not, no one is responsible for their wrongdoing . . ."). With Irwin (1985a), Susemihl and Apelt (1903), and the ancient commentators, I follow the former reading. If the latter reading (followed by Bywater, Burnet, and most modern editors and commentators) is correct, then Aristotle is explicitly affirming the thesis that responsibility for action requires responsibility for character. But we have as yet no independent evidence that Aristotle subscribes to this thesis. And furthermore,

the reading itself gives Aristotle a very awkward argument in the context. It has Aristotle arguing: "if (a) we are not responsible for our states of character (*ei de mē*, 1114b3), then (b) we are not responsible for our wrongdoing (1114b3–5), and (c) having good goals would be natural (b5–12). And furthermore, this does not show that (d) virtue is more voluntary than vice (b12–16)." Theses (b) and (c) are supposed to be unacceptable consequences of the objector's argument, whose goal is to establish (d). But (b) will have no force against an objector who seeks to establish the asymmetry thesis (d), and (c) is hardly anything to worry the objector who has claimed that our goals are not in our control. On the reading I follow, the antecedent of the conditional extends from 1114b3–12 (as *ei de taut' estin alēthē* in b12 seems to indicate) and Aristotle argues: "if (b) and (c), then (d) still does not follow."

27 In fact, at 1114b17–20 (horn (b) of the second dilemma) Aristotle comes dangerously close to affirming outright that even if one is not responsible for the goals from which one acts, one's actions in pursuit of those goals can still be voluntary. To affirm this would be to deny that responsibility for character is necessary for responsibility for actions. Whether he in fact affirms this depends on whether in stating "but virtue is voluntary because the good person does the other things voluntarily" (b18–19) he states his own view or simply articulates what he takes to be the opponent's reason for claiming virtuous actions are voluntary.

28 Roberts, like Broadie 1991, pp. 166–74, agrees that the point of Aristotle's argument for responsibility for character is to establish that nature leaves room for habituation and educa-tion. But she takes this to indicate that Aristotle is not concerned with moral responsibility in the chapters in which he discusses voluntariness (Roberts 1989, pp. 30–1).

29 This is explicitly the position taken in Roberts 1989, pp. 30–1, and I take it to be in the spirit of Williams 1985.

6

Moral Agency and the Origination
of Action

◆

When we hold someone morally responsible for an action, we assume
that the sequence of causes that results in the action in some sense
begins with the agent. That is, we assume that the agent is not simply
a causal factor in the production of the action, but *the* causal factor to
which primary causal responsibility is attributable. The task of spe-
cifying exactly what this special causal status consists in is one of the
central, and most disputed, tasks of a theory of moral responsibility.
The task of the present chapter is to see how well Aristotle's conception
of voluntariness, and in particular the causal notions it presupposes,
accomplishes this task.

1   Origins, External Causes, and Self-Motion

Aristotle describes the causal role of the voluntary agent in terms that
appear to capture the special causal status that ascriptions of moral
responsibility presuppose. He insists that the voluntary action's origin
is in the agent, or alternatively, that the voluntary agent is its origin.[1]
He introduces the discussion of voluntariness in the *EE* by emphasizing
this causal role of the voluntary agent:

> Let us make a new beginning of our ongoing inquiry. All substances are
> naturally origins of a kind, which is why each is able to generate another
> of the same type – a man can generate men, an animal animals, and a

plant plants. But in addition to these things, man alone of the animals is also an origin of certain actions (*archē praxeōn*). (*EE* 1222b15–20)

As we saw in chapter 2, Aristotle's examples indicate that he takes the voluntary agent to be the efficient cause of his action: the cause whose canonical description is "that from which the primary origin of change or of rest is" (*Ph.* 194b29–30; 195a22–3), but that he also refers to as "that from which the change is" (*hothen hē kinēsis*, *Ph.* 195a8), or quite simply, "the origin of change" (*Ph.* 195a11), or "mover" (198a19).

In *EE* ii 6 he proceeds to explain that, in calling the agent the origin of his action, he means that the agent's causation of his action must not itself be caused by some further cause:

> If the fact that a triangle contains two right angles entails that a quadrilateral contains four, then the cause (*aition*) of this ⟨sc. that the quadrilateral contains four right angles⟩ is clearly the fact that the triangle contains two right angles . . . And if nothing else is the cause (*aition*) of the triangle's being like this, then this ⟨sc. the triangle's having two right angles⟩ is a kind of origin (*archē*) and cause (*aition*) of what comes after. (*EE* 1222b31–41)

Aristotle here states an instance of the general principle: if A is the cause (*aition*) of B, but C is the cause (*aition*) of A, then A is not the origin (*archē*) of B. His example invokes formal rather than efficient causes, and he does not indicate here exactly how the principle applies in the domain of efficient causation. His account of self-movement in the *Physics* supplies this explanation.

"The mover" (*kinoun*) is one of Aristotle's names for the efficient cause (*Ph.* 198a19, 24, 33). In *Ph.* viii 5, he distinguishes between two kinds of movers, one of which deserves the title "mover" more than the other does:

> There are two ways in which one thing can be moved by another. Either ⟨it is moved⟩ not because of the mover itself, but because of something else that[2] the mover moves; or ⟨it is moved⟩ because of ⟨the mover⟩ itself. And this ⟨sc. the mover⟩ either immediately precedes the result (*to eschaton*) or moves through several things.
>
> For example, the stick moves the stone and is moved by the hand which is moved by the man. But he does not do so by being moved by anything else (*tō(i) hup' allou kineisthai*).
>
> We say that both the first and the last mover moves, but the first is more (*mallon*) the mover. For it moves the last, and not the last the first,

and without the first the last will not move, while the first will move without the last. For example, the stick will not move if the man is not moving. (*Ph.* 256a3–13)

He here distinguishes between movers that move (that is, cause change – *kinein*) by being moved by something else (*tō(i) hup' allou kineisthai*), and movers that do not cause change in this way. He goes on to label this second sort of mover a "self-mover" (256a21, a33–b3). While Aristotle here acknowledges that both a self-mover and a non-self-mover can be said to move (*kinein*) the result, he insists that the self-mover deserves this label more than the other-moved (256a9–10). And later on in the chapter he indicates that the origin of movement must be a self-mover:

Indeed, if we had to investigate whether the cause of the movement – that is, the origin – is what moves itself or what is moved by something else, everyone would say the former is. (*Ph.* 257a27–30; cf. 241b34–7)

We may conclude that Aristotle, in calling the voluntary agent the origin of action, means that the agent is a self-mover. To understand how Aristotle explains the crucial causal status of the morally respons-ible agent as a genuine origin of action, we must therefore investigate what he thinks is involved in an agent's action being self-moved. If he had given any indication that he thinks an agent's responsibility for an action depends on the agent's prior responsibility for the disposition from which she performs that action, then we might have some reason to suppose that he thinks the agent is self-moved because she is in a sense self-created. But we have already established, in our discussion of Aristotle's views on responsibility for character, that we have no reason to attribute such a view to Aristotle. In any case, Aristotle's more detailed picture of the workings of self-movement makes it clear that the crucial causal fact about self-movement concerns the causation of the movement or action itself, not the prior causation of the dispositions involved in producing the movement or action.

Aristotle explains the special causal status he attributes to the self-mover by saying that its causation (*kinein*) of its movement is not itself a movement or change (*kinēsis*). This is what he means when he says that the aspect of the self-mover that causes the movement is "un-moved" (*akinēton*):

> So, of the whole, one aspect must be unmoved (*akinēton*) and the other
> will be moved. Only in this way can there be something that is self-
> moved. And since the whole moves itself, the one aspect will move
> (*kinēsei*) and the other will be moved (*kinēsetai*). (*Ph.* 258a1–4; cf.
> 243a14)

A moved mover causes movement (*kinein*) by exercising a causal power
whose exercise is itself also a movement (*kinēsis*); it fails to have primary
causal responsibility for the movement it causes because, according to
Aristotle, "anything that is in motion must be moved by something"
(*Ph.* 256a2–3). Hence a moved mover causes change "by being moved
by another". Since the moved mover's causal activity is itself a movement, we must ask, what mover moved it? In the case of the self-mover,
by contrast, Aristotle effectively blocks this troublesome question by
claiming that the self-mover is unmoved in causing its own motion.
This claim allows him to maintain that the chain of efficient causation
originates with, rather than simply involves, the self-mover. But exactly
what does Aristotle understand the self-mover's "unmoved moving" to
consist in?

Aristotle's account of self-motion is sometimes taken to be an expression of the view that moral agency involves the exercise of a type of
causality peculiar to the human self, a type of causality fundamentally
different from the sort of causality at work in the rest of nature. Rode-
rick Chisholm, for example, finds in Aristotle's account of self-motion,
a version of his own doctrine of agent-causation:[3]

> If we consider only inanimate natural objects, we may say that causation,
> if it occurs, is a relation between *events* or *states of affairs*. The dam's
> breaking was an event that was caused by a set of other events – the dam
> being weak, the flood being strong, and so on. But if a man is responsible
> for a particular deed, then, if what I have said is true, there is some event,
> or set of events, that is caused, *not* by other events or states of affairs, but
> by the agent, whatever he may be.

According to the theory of agent-causation, the agent's causation of his
action cannot be analyzed into any set of events, and hence it is not due
to any antecedent events. As a result, the agent's action is due to the
agent himself, and not to any antecedent event. The action's origin is
the agent precisely because the agent is a cause that is not an event.

Other interpretations of Aristotle allow that the agent's causation of
her action may be an event, but deny that this event is determined by

antecedent events.[4] Aristotle's account of self-motion might well appear to support such an indeterminist interpretation, for the account implies that nothing moves the agent to move himself, and it is natural to understand this to imply that the act of self-movement is causally undetermined. According to both sorts of interpretations, Aristotle's account of self-motion attributes to agents a type of causality that is importantly different from the type of causality at work in the rest of nature. Either it is an instance of a type of causality distinctive of moral agents, or it requires a radical discontinuity in the sequence of causes at work in the rest of the natural world. I would like to contest this presupposition of those interpretations. In Aristotle's view, the causal activity of self-movers is simply an instance of, rather than an exception to, the type of efficient causality at work in the rest of the physical world. But at the same time, Aristotle is able to justify his claims that human agents are the origins of their actions in the distinctive way his account of self-movement implies, and he is able to explain why only they, and not also other entities, are morally responsible for their causal activity.

2   The Unmoved Mover in the Moral Agent

What is the aspect of the self-moving moral agent that Aristotle considers to be the unmoved mover of the self-movement? We can find out by focussing on ways in which Aristotle's claims about self-movement reflect his claims about ordinary efficient causation. First of all, Aristotle claims both that: (a) the self-moving agent moves its own movement; and that (b) an unmoved mover, which is an aspect of the self-mover, moves it. He takes these two claims to amount to the same thing. He alternates between a similar pair of locutions when he discusses ordinary efficient causation. He typically calls substances – such as the sculptor or builder – efficient causes. But he sometimes calls a causal power of the substance the efficient cause – e.g. in *Ph*. ii 3, where he calls the sculptor's skill of sculpting the efficient cause (195a6–8). He takes these locutions to be equivalent. In virtue of this similarity, it would appear that the unmoved mover is the causal power in virtue of which the self-mover moves its own motion (see table 6.1).

But what is this causal power? Again, Aristotle's ordinary model of efficient causation points to the answer. Both the substance (the sculptor) and the causal power (the skill of sculpting) can be cited as the efficient cause of the statue because the skill is the causal power in terms of which Aristotle identifies the substance that is the efficient cause. It is qua possessing the skill of sculpting that the sculptor is the efficient cause of the statue. This is why Polycleitus, who happens to be the sculptor, is only the accidental cause of the statue (*Ph.* 195a32–5). These features of ordinary efficient causation indicate that the unmoved mover will be the causal power whose possession is essential to the self-mover, and that it will be the causal power in terms of which Aristotle identifies the self-mover.

So what is the causal power that makes the voluntary agent a self-mover, in the examples we are considering? Aristotle's introduction to the account of voluntariness indicates that he takes the voluntary acts of the self-movers he is interested in (those who are morally responsible for their voluntary activities) to be the products of their states of character (as we saw in chapter 2). This suggests that the agent's states of character, which together comprise her moral character, constitute the causal power Aristotle takes to be essential to the self-mover. So the agent's moral character would appear to be the unmoved mover of her voluntary activities. It is because of the causal role played by her moral

Table 6.1 Aspects of efficient causation

Efficient cause	Causal power	Activity	Effect
sculptor (*andriantopoios*)	sculpting skill (*andriantopoiikē*)	sculpting (*andriantopoiein*)	statue (*andrias*)
housebuilder (*oikodomos*)	housebuilding skill (*oikodomikē*)	housebuilding (*oikodomein*)	house (*oikia*)
self-mover	unmoved mover (*akinēton kinoun*)	moving (*kinein*)	movement (*kinēsis*)
agent	moral character (*hexis prohairetikē*)	acting (*prattein*)	action (*praxis*)
just person (*ho dikaios*)	justice (*dikaiosunē*)	doing-justice (*dikaiopragein*)	just thing (*dikaion ti*)
unjust person (*ho adikos*)	injustice (*adikia*)	doing-injustice (*adikein*)	unjust thing (*adikon ti*)
coward (*ho deilos*)	cowardice (*deilia*)	act the coward (*deilainein*)	(no name)
intemp. person (*ho akolastos*)	intemperance (*akolasia*)	act intemperately (*akolastainein*)	(no name)

character that the causal chain resulting in the agent's action goes back no further than the agent.

The suggestion that the agent's moral character is the unmoved mover of her voluntary actions derives support from Aristotle's emphatic distinction between states of character and the capacities for desire[5] of which they are dispositions (*EN* 1105b23–1106a12). He elsewhere tells us that the agent's faculty of desire is the moved mover by means of which the unmoved mover moves the action (*DA* 433b13–18; *MA* 701a1; cf. *Ph.* 256b14–20). By contrast, he insists that our states of character are not respects in which we are moved:

> In addition, according to the feelings, we are said to be moved, while according to the virtues and vices we are not said to be moved, but rather disposed in a certain way (*diakeisthai pōs*). (*EN* 1106a4–6)

Since the occurrent desire is the moved mover by means of which the unmoved mover moves, the unmoved mover must cause the occurrent desire by means of which the self-mover moves himself. And there is an intuitively obvious sense in which the agent's moral character, which is a set of dispositions of the agent's capacities for desire, causes occurrent desires.

If we reflect on the fact that the unmoved mover in these cases is a disposition of the agent's faculties of desire, we will be able to see how it is unmoved in causing these occurrent desires. That is, we will see that its causal influence is not exerted in a movement or change. A disposition of a set of capacities is a capacity of a higher order than the capacities of which it is a disposition. It determines in what circumstances these capacities will be exercised. Such a disposition is a standing condition that exercises its causal efficacy over these capacities whenever these capacities are in the conditions appropriate for their normal and unimpeded exercise. The disposition of an agent's capacities for feelings and desire is "at work" whenever the agent is awake. It does not move (*kinein*) the particular occurrent desires by means of which the agent moves himself by producing an occurrent activity of moving (*kinein*) whenever a particular desire is precipitated. Rather, its causal efficacy is continual, both when a particular capacity for desire is active and when it is not. The change that precipitates the exercise of a particular capacity for desire is not a change of the disposition, but rather a change in the external circumstances. The disposition, which "makes" the agent have a particular occurrent desire in these circumstances, is not moved or changed in exerting this causal influence. The movement that takes place when the disposition is exercised is that of the faculty of desire, not of the disposition. The disposition therefore satisfies the conditions for being the unmoved mover of the desire.

According to the interpretation I propose, those who interpret Aristotelian self-movement as an instance of agent-causation are in a way correct to deny that the causal activity of the unmoved mover is an event that causes the activity of the moved mover. However, my interpretation is completely contrary to the spirit of their interpretation. For the proponent of agent-causation supposes that actions originate with an agent because the sequence of events originated by the agent is not the result of any events prior to the agent's decision or desire; the activity of the agent-cause interrupts the flow of events. However, on the interpretation I propose, the unmoved mover is simply a disposition of the capacities that are exercised in a sequence of events. Its activity does not interrupt the flow of events, but is simply part of the mechanism that determines what will result from a given event.[6]

3 Worries about Determinism

One might worry, however, that the account I have just offered of the unmoved mover succeeds only at the price of undermining the plausibility of Aristotle's claim that we are self-movers. For the unmoved mover, on this picture, is a state of character, which on Aristotle's view is a disposition to act and react in certain ways in certain circumstances. For example, it determines at what objects one will become angry, how angry one will get, and what, if anything, one will do as a result of being angry.[7] So the presence of an object toward which one is disposed to be angry in a particular way is sufficient to precipitate that particular manifestation of anger. Indeed, it is natural, in English, to refer to these objects as the things that "make" us angry.[8] And Aristotle uses an equivalent locution in Greek: these objects of anger are the *empoiounta* (inducers) of our anger (*EN* 1125b30). But how could Aristotle reconcile this causal picture with his claim that we are self-moved? For if we are self-moved, then we must not be moved to act by anything other than ourselves. Aristotle's account of self-movement tells us that he thinks the state of character, rather than the external object, is what moves us to have the occurrent desire. But on what grounds can he deny that the external object that precipitates a given desire moves us to have it?[9]

The general worry expressed by these questions may be formulated as follows. If, given the agent's dispositions and the circumstances in which she acts, it is determined how the agent will act and react, then one cannot deny that external factors – such as the things that make us angry – move us to have the desires and make the decisions on which we act. Worries such as this motivate indeterminist interpretations of Aristotle's view. Alexander of Aphrodisias, for example, attributes to Aristotle the view that external circumstances, together with our dispositions, are not sufficient to determine how we will decide to act. I won't explain here why I think this indeterminist interpretation is mistaken.[10] Instead, I would like to examine the worry that motivates it: for even if indeterminism isn't Aristotle's explicit view, one might worry that Aristotle cannot defend his claims about self-movement without affirming indeterminism.

If the agent's moral character is a perfectly determinate disposition, how can Aristotle defend his presupposition that the external object that precipitates an agent's desire does not move (*kinein*) the agent to have it, while the disposition of which the precipitated desire is an expression does? The prospects for success appear bleak if we assume that Aristotle thinks anything whose causal activity precipitates a given result is thereby the efficient cause, or mover, of that result. But this assumption ignores the distinction Aristotle draws between accidental and non-accidental causes (*Ph.* 196b24–9), and the significance he attaches to that distinction:

> It is an accident that the builder should cure someone, since it is not the builder but the doctor who naturally produces (*poiein*) this. It is simply an accident that the builder is a doctor. And a cook (*opsopoios*), who aims at pleasure, might produce (*poiēseien an*) what is healthy for someone, but not in virtue of the skill of cookery. This is why we say it is an accident, and while there is a sense in which he produces ⟨something healthy⟩, he does not do so without qualification. (*Met.* 1026b37–1027a5)

As we saw in chapter 4, Aristotle denies that the accidental efficient cause of a result is properly said to be the producer, or efficient cause, of that result. He insists that the only causal claims worth taking seriously concern non-accidental causal relations, and explicitly includes his discussion of voluntariness within the scope of this claim (*EE* 1221b4–6).

These considerations suggest that Aristotle would be quite happy to allow that the external precipitator of the self-mover's desire is the accidental mover of that desire. For in such a case, the external object would no more deserve credit (or demerit) for the agent's desire than the chef would deserve credit for the patient's recovery. According to this suggestion, Aristotle would defend his claim that the origin of an action can be traced back only as far as the agent, and no farther, by claiming that external causal factors such as those that precipitate desires are at best the accidental causes of the agent's activity. While Aristotle does not explicitly articulate this argument himself, it follows a general strategy he adopts in other contexts.[11] Let us therefore see how it would apply to the present context.

4 Accidental vs. Non-accidental Antecedent Causes

In order to fill in the details of the argument, we need to know precisely what the self-moving agent is the non-accidental cause of. We saw in chapter 4 that Aristotle individuates the effects of efficient causes as finely as he individuates the causes themselves. When the doctor, who happens also to be a builder, cures someone, Aristotle claims that the doctor is the non-accidental cause while the builder is only the accidental cause of the cure (*Met.* 1026b37–1027a2). The builder is only the accidental cause of the cure because the builder is only accidental to the true efficient cause, the doctor. When the chef, who non-accidentally produces pleasant-tasting food, produces pleasant-tasting food that happens also to be healthy for someone, the chef is only the accidental cause of the healthy food (1027a3–5). This is because it is accidental to pleasant-tasting food to also be healthy. What, then, is the result that Aristotle thinks the moral agent is non-accidentally responsible for?

In Aristotle's usual examples of non-accidental efficient causation, the non-accidental result is the "natural" product of the characteristic activity of the efficient cause. For example, the characteristic activity of the housebuilder (*oikodomos*) is housebuilding (*oikodomein*), whose natural product is a house (*oikia*) (see table 6.2). The characteristic activity of the sculptor is sculpting (*andriantopoiein*), whose natural product is a statue (*andrias*) (*Ph.* 196b24–6; *Met.* 1026b6–10, 1027a1). Aristotle's general discussion of states of character (e.g. states of temperance, courage, cowardice) tells us that the characteristic activities of these states of character may be classified under the general headings of "doing justice" (*dikaiopragein*) and "doing injustice" (*adikein*) respectively. Furthermore, his discussion of justice and injustice tells us that to "do justice" is to bring about non-accidentally something just (*dikaion*), while to "do injustice" is to bring about non-accidentally something unjust (*adikon*):

> Just and unjust things being as we have said, someone does injustice and does justice whenever he does them voluntarily. Someone who does them involuntarily does not do injustice or do justice – except accidentally (*kata sumbebēkos*), for he does things to which being just or being unjust is accidental. (*EN* 1135a15–19)

These considerations indicate that just as the sculptor is the non-accidental cause of statues, and the builder of houses, the morally responsible agent, in Aristotle's view, is the non-accidental cause of just and unjust activities.

We are considering the proposal that when Aristotle claims that the moral agent is the origin of her activity not moved to act by anything else, he means that the agent is the non-accidental cause of that activity, and that any external object that precipitates that activity is only its accidental cause. In the problem that we are considering, the activity in question is the agent's desire. So we may dress out the hypothesis as follows: the agent is the non-accidental cause of an unjust desire, while the external object whose perception precipitates that unjust desire is only the accidental cause of an unjust desire.

In order to evaluate this hypothesis, we need to focus on Aristotle's account of the relation between an efficient cause and its "natural" product. We have seen in chapter 4 that Aristotle often explains what makes the non-accidental cause "naturally productive" of a result by claiming that the cause "always or for the most part" produces that result (*Met.* 1025a14–19, 1026b27–37). I take such claims to mean that in the normal conditions appropriate for its exercise, the non-accidental

Table 6.2 Examples of accidental production (a solid line indicates non-accidental connection, a dotted line accidental connection)

I	builder – – – – →	doctor	⎯⎯⎯→ health	
II		cook	⎯⎯⎯→ tasty food	← – – – – healthy
III		agent	⎯⎯⎯→ (un)just desire or action	
IV		external object	⎯⎯⎯→ desire or action	← – – – – (un)just

cause produces the result by exercising a causal power that will succeed in producing a result of this type unless it is impeded.[12] An accidental cause of a result, by contrast, exercises a causal power that, in its normal and unimpeded exercise, is no more likely to produce a result of this type than not.

Let us now consider why Aristotle would think that the external precipitator of the agent's unjust desire is only the accidental cause of that desire, while the agent's character is the non-accidental cause of that desire. Consider a simple example: a vicious person sees an untended pot of gold and decides to steal it. The pot of gold is the external object that precipitates in the agent the unjust desire to steal the gold.[13] But is the pot of gold the sort of thing that reliably precipitates in agents unjust desires? Considered in itself, does it have the power that, if unimpeded, will reliably produce unjust desires? Clearly not, for in itself it is no more productive of just desires than of unjust desires, for it is no more productive of desires to steal it than of desires not to steal it. Given the intrinsic features of the perceptual object, the pot of gold, it is accidental that its causal role in perception should result in an unjust desire (although perhaps it is not accidental that it should precipitate some desire concerning the gold). Whether the desire that results from perceiving the gold is just or unjust depends on more than the unimpeded exercise of the causal powers of the gold as perceptual object. Hence the gold is only the accidental cause of the unjust desire, and hence of the unjust action.[14] The gold is no more properly attributed responsibility for the injustice of the desire it precipitates than the cook should be held responsible for the healthiness of the food he produces (see table 6.2). If, by contrast, we consider the intrinsic features of the state of character from which the agent acts, and ask whether it is an accident that this state of character should produce an unjust desire and act, the answer is clearly "no". The unjust desire and action proceed from an unjust feature of the agent's character. While it is an accident that the pot of gold should produce an unjust desire, it is not at all an accident that the agent's character should produce an unjust desire.

One might object that although the pot of gold does not have the capacity reliably to produce in human agents the desire to steal, it still is reliably productive of such desires in agents of this type. That is, it has the power, if unimpeded, to induce, in agents with the disposition to steal if they can get away with it, in situations in which they can get away with it, the occurrent desire to steal. Just as the shoemaker has the power, if unimpeded, to turn nails and leather into a pair of shoes, the pot of gold has the power to turn such situations with such agents in them into situations in which the agent has the desire to steal.

Aristotle agrees that any request for an explanation – that is, any search for a cause – asks why one thing belongs to another (*Met.* 1041a10–b9). On the objection we are considering, the external object of perception is non-accidentally responsible for the fact that the agent, who is disposed to pursue such objects if she perceives them, has the additional property of actually desiring to pursue the object. But is this explanandum the same as the one assumed by Aristotle's claim that the agent is the origin of his action? In claiming that the vicious agent is the origin of the theft, surely Aristotle is thinking that the agent is responsible for the fact that, in a situation in which such an external object is present, the object is stolen rather than not. While we may be able, with sufficient ingenuity, to specify some situation involving the agent for which an external perceptual stimulus is the non-accidental cause, it is not within our power of stipulation to make the external object the non-accidental cause of the explanandum that is relevant to the claim that the agent is the origin of the action.

5 Distinctive Features of Moral Responsibility

We began this chapter with the question of how we are to understand the special causal status Aristotle attributes to the morally responsible agent, whose action is up to him both to do and not to do. We have seen that Aristotle articulates this special causal status in terms of his notion of a self-mover, and I have argued that his claims about the special causal status of self-movers can be justified by appeal to causal notions and distinctions that are ubiquitous in his natural philosophy. These are his notion of efficient causation and his distinction between accidental and non-accidental efficient causes. I have offered this interpretation of Aristotle's account of agency as an alternative to explanations that take the causal features of moral agency to be exceptions to or interruptions of the sort of causality at work in the rest of nature. In this respect, my interpretation of Aristotle attributes to him a view of agency that may be roughly described as "naturalist." It may be objected, however, that the very "naturalism" of the account I attribute to Aristotle renders it unfit to accomplish the theoretical task in which he employs it. For I claim that Aristotle takes claims about self-movement to justify ascriptions of moral responsibility, and that he takes claims about self-movement to be justified by non-accidental causal relations. But non-accidental causal relations are ubiquitous in nature, and are not restricted to morally responsible agents. Hence the account I attribute to Aristotle fails to account for the distinctive features of moral agency.

According to this objection, the account I attribute to Aristotle fails as an account of moral responsibility because it fails to identify a kind of causal relation that is distinctive of morally responsible agency. This objection derives its force from the intuition that only a very small class of entities that can enter into causal relations are morally responsible for the results they cause: while rocks, floods, viruses, non-human animals, children, and adult humans can be causally responsible for results, we suppose that only adult humans are morally responsible for the results they cause. But even if we grant the intuition, which I think we must, it does not follow that moral responsibility must be a distinctive type of causal relation, a specifically moral type of responsibility. Contrary to what the objector presupposes, moral responsibility might be an ordinary sort of causal responsibility for a distinctively moral type of outcome. According to this proposal, only certain types of agents can be causally responsible for the sorts of things for which one is attributed responsibility in ascriptions of moral responsibility. I think that this proposal captures Aristotle's position. While he clearly thinks that entities other than morally responsible agents can be non-accidental causes of outcomes, he thinks that only certain entities can be non-accidentally the cause of morally significant outcomes.

We are already in a position to see that just and unjust outcomes are the distinctive type of result of which morally responsible agents are non-accidentally productive. These are the outcomes an agent produces non-accidentally when acting from one of the just or unjust states of character (temperance, cowardice, etc.; see table 6.1). Aristotle's denial that the dispositions of animals, children (and presumably also inanimate objects) can be temperate, cowardly, etc. entails that these entities do not "do justice" or "do injustice" and hence that these entities can bring about just and unjust states of affairs only accidentally. Aristotle thinks that only certain agents can be non-accidental causes of the things for which one is morally responsible (just and unjust outcomes).

Aristotle nowhere gives a general definition of what makes a state of affairs just or unjust. Indeed, he insists that such an account cannot be given (*EN* 1104a1–10), and in the place of a general account offers us the doctrine of the mean (1104a10–11). But the doctrine of the mean says enough about the nature of the varieties of just and unjust states of affairs (the characteristic products of the various virtues and vices of character) for us to see that the sort of outcome he has in mind is indeed the sort of thing for which we think agents are morally responsible. For our present purpose, the salient features of the doctrine of the mean are these. Each type of justice or injustice concerns a certain type or types of activity. For example, cowardice and courage concern feelings such as fear and confidence and actions such as fight or flight. The state of character concerning a given range of activity disposes the agent to display or engage in that activity in a certain way in certain circumstances. The justice or injustice of a particular activity (e.g. flight or fear) depends essentially on these additional conditions: the "what, when, how, etc." in Aristotle's formula (1104b22–6; 1106a1, b21–3). Hence the thing for which one is blamed or praised is not, for example, getting angry, but rather getting angry in these circumstances, to this degree, etc:

> It is not the person who is afraid or the person who is angry who is praised, nor is it the person who is simply angry who is blamed, but rather the person who is so in a certain way (*pōs*). (*EN* 1105b32–1106a1; cf. 1104b24–6)

Aristotle's distinction between the salient activity involved in a given just or unjust state of affairs (e.g., being angry, striking back), and the complete set of conditions that make the state of affairs just or unjust (getting this angry at this sort of provocation and striking back at this person, in these circumstances . . .) corresponds, in effect, to a distinction between outcomes that are just or unjust only accidentally and outcomes that are just or unjust non-accidentally. A passage in *EN* v 9 illustrates the distinction:

> People say that doing injustice (*adikein*) is no less characteristic of the just person ⟨than the unjust⟩, on the grounds that the just person is no less able, indeed is more able, to do each of the things ⟨that the unjust person does⟩. For, ⟨they say⟩, he may very well have intercourse with a woman, or strike someone. And the brave person may well throw away his shield and turn and flee. But acting the coward (*deilainein*) and doing-injustice (*adikein*) is not the same as doing these things, except accidentally. Rather, it is to do these things in a certain condition (*to hōdi echonta tauta poiein*), just as doctoring and curing isn't simply cutting or not cutting, or giving medicine or not giving medicine, but rather doing it in this way (*hōdi*). (*EN* 1137a17–26)

Having sexual intercourse is only accidentally intemperate; striking someone is only accidentally insolent; and abandoning one's armour and fleeing is only accidentally cowardly. These sorts of activities are unjust (e.g. intemperate, insolent, cowardly) only in certain conditions (*hōdi echonta*), and the analogy between health and justice makes it clear that these conditions are the "when, where, how . . . etc." of the doctrine of the mean:

> In the case of health, it is easy to know honey and wine and hellebore and burning and cutting. But to know how one ought to apportion (*neimai*) them to produce health – that is, to whom and when – is so difficult as to make one a doctor. (*EN* 1137a14–17)

We can now see how Aristotle would articulate the claim that entities other than those that he thinks are the proper subjects of moral evaluation are only accidentally the cause of the sorts of things for which moral agents are non-accidentally responsible. He will agree that both classes of entity may bring about a state of affairs that is objectively just or unjust (e.g. a killing of someone who should not be killed, or in circumstances in which he should not be killed, . . . etc.). But he will insist that only morally responsible agents produce these just and unjust outcomes non-accidentally. All other entities produce justice and injustice in the way the cook of *Met.* vi 2 produces health. For example, as Aristotle himself claims earlier in *EN* v 9, these other entities may kill non-accidentally in circumstances that make the killing objectively unjust, but they still bring about the injustice only accidentally:

> Since doing (*poiein*) is said in many ways, it is possible even for inanimate things to kill – so too a hand, or a slave acting under orders – but they do not do-injustice (*adikei*), even though they do (*poiei*) unjust things (*ta adika*). (*EN* 1136b29–31)

But having seen how Aristotle would articulate the claim is not yet to see how he would defend it. Why should he think that only mature human agents are capable of producing just and unjust outcomes non-accidentally? Once Aristotle has drawn our attention to the multiplicity and complexity of the factors that make outcomes just and unjust, it is perhaps plausible to claim that inanimate entities cannot be sensitive to a wide enough range of considerations to be reliably productive of just or unjust outcomes. For example, a virus might be reliably productive of death, but it is completely insensitive to whether the death it produces satisfies the additional conditions that make it just or unjust. But why should Aristotle think that animals and children cannot be reliably productive of just and unjust activities? They are capable of the range of activities and resulting harms and benefits that are, in the appropriate circumstances, just and unjust. And Aristotle has no good reason to suppose that the motivations on which these beings act are necessarily so single-minded as always to be focussed on something as narrow as, for example, "striking back," rather than "striking back such and such a person, in such and such a circumstance, with such and such results." The actions of children, at any rate, can be sensitive to a fairly wide range of salient features of a situation. So why should Aristotle claim that there is no just or unjust outcome that children can produce non-accidentally?

What is it about the dispositions that Aristotle counts as states of moral character (temperance, courage, and so forth) that entails that only such a disposition can be non-accidentally productive of justice or injustice? As we saw in chapter 1, the distinctive feature of a state of character, on Aristotle's view, is that it is a *hexis prohairetikē* – a disposition that expresses the agent's conception of happiness. Aristotle must therefore think that only a disposition that expresses the agent's conception of happiness can be productive non-accidentally of just or unjust outcomes. But why should he think this?

To answer this question, we must return to the doctrine of the mean. Aristotle offers us the doctrine of the mean instead of a precise account of what makes a given activity just or unjust because he thinks justice and injustice – moral rightness and wrongness – cannot be given a reductive definition. One cannot specify in non-evaluative terms the features that make a given situation just or unjust. This is why he thinks the written law is necessarily inexact and requires interpretation by someone with the virtue of "equity" (*epieikeia*).[15] This conclusion is the legacy of Socrates' inquiries into the nature of virtue, which yield the inductive generalization that given any characterization, in non-evaluative terms, of courageous (or temperate, or just . . .) behavior it is relatively easy to imagine circumstances in which a token action of that type is not courageous (or temperate, or just . . .). Returning what you've borrowed is not intrinsically just (*Republic* 331c); standing firm in battle is not intrinsically courageous (*Laches* 190e–191e); self-restraint is not always temperate (*Charmides* 161a–b). Adding a further qualification to the initial specification will not succeed in identifying a type of activity that is intrinsically just, (or temperate, or courageous . . .) unless that further qualification introduces evaluative criteria into the specification.

The basic evaluative qualification that must be imported into the definition, in Socrates' view, and in virtually all of Greek Ethics, is the stipulation that the activity in question be good for the agent.[16] Aristotle follows this view.[17] So he must think that in order to be productive non-accidentally of a just outcome, one must, among other things, be productive of that outcome as something good. One must exercise a causal power that can produce good things non-accidentally. Now the causal power he thinks is distinctive of agents who produce just outcomes non-accidentally is a disposition for feeling and action that expresses the agent's conception of happiness. The agent's conception of happiness is a conception of what is good for the agent. So perhaps Aristotle's denial that children and non-human animals can produce just outcomes non-accidentally rests on the not so implausible view that one cannot produce good outcomes non-accidentally unless one acts from a conception of the good, and on the slightly more paradoxical yet still not impossible view that one cannot produce bad outcomes non-accidentally unless one acts from a conception of the good.

Aristotle, of course, never articulates such a thesis. However, he does claim explicitly that reason, the faculty crucially involved in activity for the sake of happiness, is necessary for perceiving alternatives as just and unjust:

> Reason is for indicating the beneficial and the harmful, and so too the just and the unjust. For this distinguishes a human being from the other animals — that he alone has perception of good and bad and just and unjust and the rest. (*Pol.* 1253a14–18)

And one might reasonably suppose that Aristotle thinks one must be able to perceive alternatives as good and bad, or as just and unjust, if one is to be reliably productive of outcomes that are good and bad or just and unjust.

The ultimate plausibility of Aristotle's account of moral responsibility will depend on the defensibility of this suggestion, which I do not know how to work out in detail. But the main goal of my project is now complete. We have seen that Aristotle is concerned with the topic of moral responsibility, and that his inquiries into the subject of voluntariness are theoretical attempts to identify the conditions in which agents are morally responsible for their actions. His conception of moral responsibility is unlike many modern ones in that it does not require responsibility for character, but this feature of his view does not entail that he cannot assign to agents the special causal status essential for truly moral responsibility. This special causal status can moreover be articulated and defended without invoking types of causality additional to or inconsistent with the ordinary variety at work in the natural world. Aristotle's view, if successful, shows us that we need not give up the characteristic presuppositions of morality in order to reconcile ourselves to our status as natural creatures.

NOTES

1 On the equivalence of these two locutions, see chapter 2, n. 6.

2 *ho* in *ho kinei to kinoun* might be either nominative or accusative, and if nominative, then *to kinoun* is the (accusative) object of the verb *kinei* rather than its (nominative) subject. My translation takes *ho* to be the accusative object of the verb, and *to kinoun* to be its subject. This makes the contrast at 256a4–5 between (a) being moved by something moved by the mover itself and (b) being moved by the mover itself. On the alternative translation, instead of (a) we would have (a') being moved by something that moves the mover itself. But this is awkward, since the example Aristotle provides at 256a6–8 indicates that the mover itself (the antecedent of *touto* in 256a5) is not moved by anything else.

3 Chisholm 1964, p. 28.

4 Interpreters who claim that there is no set of antecedent conditions sufficient to determine the agent's decision to act include Alexander of Aphrodisias, *De Fato* xi–xv.

5 He explicitly says here that they are dispositions of our faculties for feelings (*pathē*), but he offers the list of these faculties in enumeration of the capacities of the soul that he initially introduces collectively in *EN* i 13 as the faculty of desire (1102b30).

6 I give a fuller discussion and criticism of the view that Aristotelian self-motion is an instance of agent-causation in Meyer (1994).

7 *EN* 1105b25–8, 1125b31–1126a3. The latter passage, which includes the activity *chalepainein* (being difficult) in the domain of the exercise of anger, indicates that the disposition concerning anger determines what actions one does while angry, not simply how angry one feels. In chapter 1, we saw that Aristotle generally includes both feelings and actions in the domain of the exercise of the capacities for feeling.

8 Or make us sad, or move us to pity.

9   There are a number of passages in which Aristotle may appear to admit
    that external objects move the self-movers to have the occurrent desires
    by means of which they move themselves (*MA* 700b24–9; *DA* 433a17–21;
    Ph. 253a9–20, 259b6–14). I argue against such an interpretation of these
    passages in Meyer 1994.

10 I defend this interpretation of Alexander and criticize his interpretation
    of Aristotle in Meyer (forthcoming).

11 In *Ph.* viii 4, 254b34–255b31, Aristotle solves the problem of reconciling
    his claim that elemental motions are natural (and hence internally caused)
    with his claim that they are moved by something other than themselves
    (255a2–4) by proposing that the external causes of these motions move
    the elements only accidentally (255b24–7).

    In *Met.* vi 3, in arguing for the thesis that not every occurrence is
    the result of a non-accidental cause (1027a29–32), he indicates that if the
    thesis is false, the causal chain of anything that happens can always be
    traced indefinitely far back into the past (1027a32–b7); but that if it is
    true, then some causal chains go back only so far – to an origin that cannot
    be traced back to anything else (1027b11–12). Such an origin is one whose
    coming into being has no cause (1027b13–14). But the accidental is what
    lacks an origin of coming into being (1026b22–4, 1025a28–9). As in
    Ph. viii 4, Aristotle here defends the claim that X is the origin of some-
    thing by claiming that X's causal antecedents are only its accidental cause.

    Similarly, in *De Int.* 9, Aristotle rejects a thesis of necessity quite similar
    to that of *Met.* vi 3, on the grounds that it entails, among other things,
    that (a) nothing happens accidentally, and (b) human deliberation is
    not the origin of action. Theses (a) and (b) are related, I propose, in the way
    the analogous claims are related in *Met.* vi 3. Aristotle is not claiming that
    the outcome of deliberation is by chance, but rather that its external
    antecedents are only its accidental causes.

12 I defend this interpretation in Meyer 1992.

13 It does not matter whether this desire results from deliberation or from
    simple perception. If it results from deliberation it is still a result of the
    agent's deliberative disposition and hence is "triggered" by the external
    object in a way relevantly similar to the triggering of a desire unmediated
    by deliberation.

14 By contrast, an external object of perception that is the non-accidental
    cause of a desire it precipitates would be an object that any human being
    would react to in the same way. The naturally fearful things, which
    Aristotle says any sensible person would fear (*EN* 1115b8–10) would be
    examples of external causes that do move the agent to have the desire or
    feeling they "make" (*empoiein*) him have.

15 *Rhet.* 1374a25–b1.

16 For example, it underlies Plato's insistence, in *Laws* ix, that no one volun-
    tarily brings about an injustice.

17 The usual evaluative qualification he adds to the non-moral specification of the virtuous action is *kalon* (noble) rather than *agathon* (good) – as for example in his claim that courage is a disposition concerning a "noble death" (*EN* 1115a32–4). But he maintains that only activity in pursuit of the noble secures goods that are truly good for the agent who secures them (*EE* 1248b26–37). He too thinks that just activity is necessarily good for the agent.

Appendix I
Varieties of Knowledge and Ignorance

Aristotle says various conflicting things, in the different ethical works, about the kind of knowledge that voluntariness requires. These different positions become intelligible on the interpretation for which I have been arguing. That is, if we suppose that Aristotle evaluates proposed criteria for voluntariness by considering whether they entail the voluntariness of actions for which the agent is praiseworthy and blameworthy, and if we suppose that his goal is to count as voluntary all activity of which the agent's moral character is the cause, then we can understand why he says what he does about the voluntary agent's knowledge.

It is reasonable to suppose that Aristotle's articulation of the cognitive criteria for voluntariness and involuntariness should provide evidence of the theoretical goals of his inquiry into voluntariness. As we saw in chapter 2 Aristotle insists, in all three of the ethical works, that voluntary actions are those that originate in the agent, are up to the agent, and of which the agent is causally responsible (*aitios*). He uses these locutions interchangeably. That is, he indicates that voluntariness is a causal relation between an agent and an action, and that the nature of voluntariness can be captured by this single causal condition, alternatively described by these different locutions. But when Aristotle comes to define voluntariness he requires not only that the origin of the voluntary action be in the agent, or that it be up to the agent, but also that the agent know what he is doing.[1] He does not indicate that in adding the requirement of knowledge he admits the simple causal criterion to be inadequate. So, it is reasonable to suppose that the requirement of knowledge expresses Aristotle's assessment of what it takes for the action to originate in the agent; that it expresses a necessary condition for satisfaction of the causál condition he initially mentions as being constitutive of voluntariness.[2] If, as chapters 2 and 3 have established, Aristotle intends his account of voluntariness to capture the conditions in which agents are praiseworthy and blameworthy for their actions and thinks they are praiseworthy and blameworthy for the actions produced by their moral character, then we should expect that in articulating the cognitive requirements for voluntariness, he will be sensitive to these considerations. That is, we should expect that he will reject versions of the cognitive requirement that fail to count as voluntary praiseworthy and blameworthy activity, and that the activity he will judge praiseworthy and blameworthy will be activity that is produced by the agent's moral character. If we examine the various cognitive requirements for voluntariness that Aristotle articulates in his different discussions of voluntariness, we will see that his articulation of the requirement is sensitive to precisely these considerations.

In his various discussions of voluntariness and involuntariness, Aristotle claims that the voluntary agent must know the "particulars" but need not know the "universals" concerning his action. He claims that the agent whose involuntariness is due to ignorance must not only act "in ignorance" (*agnoōn*) of what he does but also "because of ignorance" (*di' agnoian*). And he appears to be of two minds on the question whether the agent who acts in culpable ignorance of particular facts satisfies the cognitive condition for involuntariness. We will see that Aristotle requires knowledge only of particulars for voluntariness because no other kind of ignorance can keep the agent's character from being productive of the action in question. His discrimination between action performed in ignorance and because of ignorance shows that he is willing to call "because of ignorance" only those actions of which the agent's character is not productive. Finally, his remarks about culpable ignorance and its relevance for voluntariness and involuntariness are motivated by his desire to capture, with his account of voluntariness, those actions produced by the agent's character.

1 Universal and Particular Knowledge

In *MM* i 16, when Aristotle concludes that voluntary action is what is done "from thought" (*ek dianoias*), he does not elaborate upon the sort of thought he has in mind. His examples in fact indicate some confusion over whether the thought in question is something like premeditation, or rather something like knowledge of the consequences of one's actions (1188b28–37).[3] In the corresponding passage in *EE* ii 9, Aristotle interprets the requirement of 'thought' as a requirement of knowledge, and illustrates the sort of knowledge he has in mind as follows:

> Knowing either whom or how or with what result (*ē hon ē hō(i) ē hou heneka*) – i.e., sometimes one knows this is one's father, but one does not act in order to kill him but rather to preserve him, as the daughters of Pelias did; or one might know this is a drink but think that it is a love potion and wine when in fact it is hellebore. (*EE* 1225b2–5)

In *EN* v 8, a book common to the *EE* and *EN* that repeats an account of voluntariness similar in many respects to that of *EE* ii 9 and appears to be referring back to it, Aristotle gives a similar illustration of the sort of knowledge voluntariness requires:

> knowing and not being ignorant either of whom or how or with what result (*mēte hon mēte hō(i) mēte hou ⟨heneka⟩*) – for example: whom one hits (*tina*) and with what (*tini*) and for the sake of what (*tinos heneka*) . . . It is possible for the person hit to be your father but that you know only that he is a man or one of the company and not that he is your father. (*EN* 1135a24–30)

In *EN* iii 1, as in *EE* ii 9, Aristotle requires knowledge for voluntariness. His list of the relevant types of knowledge, and his examples, coincide with his illustration and examples of the relevant type of knowledge in *EE* ii 9 and *EN* v 8:

> The person who is ignorant of one of these things acts involuntarily. It is presumably not a bad idea to enumerate them, what and how many they are: certainly who acts, what is done, and concerning what, or in what; sometimes also with what (for example, with what instrument), and for the sake of what (for example, preservation), and how (for example, lightly or strongly). (*EN* 1111a2–6)

The examples he gives include:

> One might intend to show off the catapult, but set it off. And one might take one's son for the enemy, as Merope did; or think that the spear is

blunted, when it is really pointed; or that a rock is pumice stone; and one might make someone drink in order to save him, but kill him instead. And while intending just to touch someone, as wrestlers do, one might strike him instead. (*EN* 1111a10–15)

Unlike *EE* ii 9 and *EN* v 8, Aristotle here in *EN* iii 1 explicitly distinguishes the kind of knowledge necessary for voluntariness from a different kind of knowledge:

Certainly every wicked person is ignorant of what one must (*dei*) do and what one must refrain from (*aphekteon*), and because of such error people become unjust and generally bad. But "involuntary" is not intended to apply to the case of someone who is ignorant of what is beneficial (*ta sumpheronta*), for ignorance in one's decision (*prohairesei*) does not cause involuntariness but rather wickedness. Nor yet does ignorance of the universal (for one is blamed on account of that), but rather ignorance of the particulars (*hē kath' hekasta*) concerning and constituting the action. In these cases there is both pity and excuse, for someone who is ignorant of one of these things acts involuntarily. (*EN* 1110b28–1111a2)

Aristotle here identifies the sort of knowledge required for voluntariness by describing the sort of ignorance that can render an action involuntary.[4] He describes the kind of ignorance that can make an action involuntary as ignorance of "the particulars" (*ta kath' hekasta*). He contrasts this kind of ignorance with ignorance that he variously describes as: ignorance of what one ought (*dei*) to do (1110b28); ignorance of what is beneficial (*ta sumpheronta*) (1110b30–1); and ignorance in one's decision (*prohairesei*) (1110b31).

Aristotle here invokes a distinction between two types of thought involved in the causation[5] of action, a distinction he makes frequently both inside and outside the ethical works. He regularly distinguishes between two kinds of "premises" (*protaseis*) involved in the inference that explains the occurrence of an action. He regularly labels one kind of premise "universal" (*hē katholou*), the other premise "particular" (*hē kath' hekasta*).[6] The "universal" premise is a thought about what sorts of things are good or bad for one, and generally takes the form of a claim that one ought (*dei*) to do something, alternatively expressed in the gerundive.[7] The "particular" premise is a thought that a particular object or alternative satisfies the conditions that the universal premise puts forth as desirable or to be done. The particulars are the sorts of things one can perceive.[8] For example, the universal premise might be that stagnant water is bad, and the particular premise that this water is stagnant (*EN* 1142a20–3). Both sorts of premise are involved in the causation of the action:

> One can also consider scientifically (*phusikōs*) the cause ⟨of action⟩ in the following way. For one belief (*doxa*) is of the universal (*katholou*), while the other is of the particulars, which perception controls. When one thing results from them, it is necessary that the soul affirm the conclusion or – in the case of thoughts about production – it is necessary that action immediately follow. For example, if one ought to (*dei*) taste anything sweet, and this particular thing is sweet, it is necessary that the agent who is able and unimpeded do this ⟨sc. taste this⟩. (EN 1147a24–31)

Here Aristotle indicates that the combination of these two premises results in action of necessity, unless something impedes it.[9] He makes the same point at *MA* 701a15–16.

Both kinds of premise, the universal and the particular, can be true or false. One can be mistaken in one's objects of pursuit (i.e., think one ought to do a certain kind of thing when one really ought not to). Or one can be mistaken in one's beliefs about the particular situation in which one applies one's beliefs about what one ought to do. The difference between such mistakes is the difference between believing mistakenly that it is permissible to pull the trigger of a loaded gun, and mistakenly believing that the gun whose trigger one pulls is not loaded.

Aristotle in *EN* iii 1 indicates that voluntary action requires knowledge of the particular premise, but is compatible with ignorance of the universal premise. While he does not here use 'universal' (*katholou*) as the general label for this type of ignorance, his examples indicate that this is the sort of ignorance he has in mind. For example, he first describes this ignorance as ignorance of what one ought (*dei*) to do (1110b28) – which at *EN* 1147a25–31 he gives as an example of a universal premise (cf. *DA* 434a16–19).[10] He next describes it as ignorance of what is beneficial (*ta sumpheronta*), explaining this (*ou gar*, 1110b31) as "ignorance in one's decision (*prohairesei*)" (b31). The thought that something is healthy or bad for one are examples he has given elsewhere of the universal premise (1141b14–22, 1142a20–3). Being healthy and being bad for one are specific ways in which something can be (or fail to be) beneficial (*sumpheron*). Ignorance about such matters counts as "ignorance in the *prohairesis*" because such benefits are the goals (*telē*) in the light of which one deliberates, the result of such deliberation being a *prohairesis*; for example, health is the goal in the light of which the doctor deliberates (*EN* 1112b12–20).[11] It is somewhat surprising that Aristotle here uses the label 'universal' for another kind of knowledge added to the list, instead of a general category into which the preceding types of knowledge fall.[12] However, this should not keep us from concluding that Aristotle here, in *EN* iii 1, unambiguously claims that knowledge of the sort to which he elsewhere applies the general label 'universal' is not necessary for voluntariness.

Aristotle appeals to considerations of blameworthiness and character when he explains why knowledge of the universal premise is not necessary for voluntariness. He begins his description of the types of ignorance that do not make actions involuntary by saying that it is the sort of ignorance the bad person (*ho mochthēros*) has (1110b28). Such ignorance, he goes on to say, is a cause not of involuntariness but of wickedness (1110b31–2). Ignorance of the universal is not a feature of an action that makes it involuntary but is rather a feature of an agent that makes the agent bad (*mochthēros*). Finally, he claims, ignorance of the universal is a reason for blame (1110b32–3). These considerations show that Aristotle intends his account of voluntariness to capture the conditions in which agents are praiseworthy and blameworthy for what they do. And they confirm the suggestion that an evaluation of the agent's moral character is central to the judgements of praiseworthiness and blameworthiness.

Furthermore, if we reflect upon the different causal roles played in the causation of action by universal and particular thoughts, Aristotle's restriction of the requirement of knowledge for voluntariness to knowledge of particulars supports the interpretation that Aristotle thinks actions produced by the agent's moral character are voluntary. In claiming that ignorance of the universal is a cause of wickedness (1110b31–2), Aristotle tells us, reasonably enough, that an agent's universal beliefs, his beliefs about the sorts of things it is worthwhile to do, are constitutive of his character. This is because "universal" beliefs are constituted by the agent's standing desires – his dispositions to have certain occurrent desires in particular circumstances. Such dispositions are part of the agent's character. The particular beliefs, by contrast, are not states of one's persisting character. They are simply occurrent states that represent the circumstances in which the agent finds himself. Such beliefs supply the information that engages a particular standing desire, and produces an occurrent desire for the action. In order for the character, the set of standing desires, to be productive of an action in the appropriate way, the particular beliefs must be true, but the "universal" beliefs need not be.

It is easy to see how actions involving and even depending on ignorance of what one should do do not thereby fail to be produced by and expressive of the agent's character. Such ignorance is constitutive of the agent's character. It is also easy to see how ignorance of particular facts can keep the action actually performed from depending on one's character. For example, if Oedipus knew that the old man he met at the crossroads was his father, then the action he performed would have depended on his "universal" beliefs about how one should (*dei*) treat one's father. In such circumstances his action would have shown him to be vicious regarding his parental obligations. However, in the circumstances in which he acted, he did not know that the old man was his father, and hence we cannot conclude from the fact that he killed his father that he has the corresponding vice. Given his ignorance of this crucial fact, we have no reason to suppose that his attitudes toward his father were engaged at all in the action. Since one's beliefs about the particular facts about one's action play an important role in the process whereby one's character is productive of one's actions, it seems reasonable for Aristotle, in his account of voluntariness, to require that these beliefs not be mistaken.

The best explanation of Aristotle's account of the sort of thought or knowledge necessary for voluntariness is that he modulates the requirement in order to preserve the result that actions produced by the agent's moral character, and indicative of that character, are voluntary.

2 "In Ignorance" vs. "Because of Ignorance"

The preceding explanation of Aristotle's motive for restricting the sort of knowledge necessary for voluntariness to knowledge of particulars allows us to understand a further distinction Aristotle makes between types of ignorance: the distinction between acting "because of ignorance" (*di' agnoian*) and merely acting "in ignorance" (*agnoōn*). He makes this distinction in two places – once in *EN* iii 1 (1110b24–7) and once in *EN* v 8 (1136a5–9). Let us first examine the distinction as Aristotle introduces it in *EN* iii 1, immediately before his distinction between universal and particular ignorance:

> Acting because of ignorance is different from acting in ignorance. For the person who is drunk or angry does not act because of ignorance, but rather because of one of the things mentioned ⟨sc. being drunk or being angry⟩ – although not in knowledge but in ignorance. (*EN* 1110b24–7)

Immediately after he makes this distinction, Aristotle proceeds to distinguish between universal and particular ignorance, claiming that only the latter makes an action involuntary (1110b28–33). He does not indicate that the second distinction, concerning the content of the ignorance, introduces a requirement additional to the requirement introduced by the first distinction: that the involuntary agent act because of ignorance. On the contrary, the second distinction begins in a way (*agnoei men oun*, 1110b28) that suggests it provides further support for the requirement expressed in the first distinction. It is therefore natural to interpret the distinction between acting in ignorance and acting because of ignorance as corresponding to the distinction between acting with ignorance of the universal and acting with ignorance of the particulars. On this interpretation, the angry person and the drunk are ignorant of what they should do. The angry person, for example, desires to harm the object of his anger, his anger mistakenly presenting this goal as permissible or required. The person who is drunk has his inhibitions lessened, and will undertake to do things he would think inappropriate if he were sober.[13]

Aristotle also distinguishes between acting in ignorance and because of ignorance at the end of *EN* v 8:

> Some involuntary actions are excusable (*sungnōmonika*), while others are not. For those errors that people commit (*hosa . . . hamartanousi*) not only in ignorance (*agnoountes*) but also because of ignorance (*di' agnoian*) are excusable. But those they commit not because of ignorance but rather in ignorance due to a feeling (*pathos*) that is neither natural nor human are not excusable. (*EN* 1136a5–9)

It is, however, hard to see how the distinction invoked here can be interpreted in the same way as I have suggested it is natural to interpret it in *EN* iii 1. The ignorance that here counts as ignorance "in which" but not "because of which" the agent acts cannot be ignorance of the universal, for Aristotle indicates here that the action performed in such ignorance counts as involuntary. The ignorance in question therefore seems to be ignorance of particulars. And it is easy to see why Aristotle should here want to draw the distinction between acting in ignorance of particulars and acting because of such ignorance. In the account of voluntariness and involuntariness presented earlier in the chapter, Aristotle describes the types of involuntary actions involving ignorance as actions which are unknown (*agnooumenon*, 1135a31–3), and his examples make it clear that the ignorance in question is ignorance of the particulars (1135a28–30). Unlike *EE* ii 9 and *EN* iii 1, he does not explicitly require that such actions be "because of ignorance." Hence it is reasonable to suppose that these remarks at the end of *EN* v 8 serve to distinguish between actions that are performed in ignorance of the particulars from those that are performed both in such ignorance and because of it.

So the distinction between acting "in ignorance" and acting "because of ignorance", if Aristotle intends the same distinction in *EN* v 8 and *EN* iii 1, does not simply correspond to the distinction between acting with universal and acting with particular ignorance. Rather, Aristotle must intend the distinction to capture the contrast between some other pair of properties. The property he intends to capture with the label "in ignorance but not because of ignorance" must be a property common both to actions performed due to ignorance of the universal (as in *EN* iii 1) and to actions performed in ignorance of particulars due to "a feeling neither natural nor human" (as in *EN* v 8, 1136a8–9). In order to identify the common feature of these two cases, we need first to identify the feelings that count as "neither natural nor human" (1136a8–9).

A reasonable guide to the interpretation of "a feeling neither natural nor human" at 1136a8–9 is Aristotle's remark that:

> What an agent does in knowledge but without prior deliberation is an injustice (*adikēma*) – for example, actions due to spirit (*thumos*) and other feelings that are necessary or occur naturally to human beings. (1135b19–22)

Such cases are cases of voluntary, rather than involuntary activity, but the natural and necessary feelings referred to here are probably the same as the "natural and human" feelings referred to at 1136a8–9. Aristotle proceeds to say that such actions as these are not due to vice (*dia mochthērian*, 1135b24). He cannot mean by this remark that no action is due to vice if it results from any of the kinds of feelings for which we naturally have the capacity in our souls,[14] for this would conflict with his account of virtue and vice as dispositions to have and act in the light of these feelings.[15] Rather, he must have in mind a particular class of feelings which do not express the agent's moral character. If he has in mind particular token feelings that anyone in the same situation would feel, feelings that are for this reason "natural and necessary", then he would have grounds for claiming that such actions are not due to vice. Rather, they would be due to human nature, and hence not proper to one's character. Let us suppose, therefore, that these are the feelings to which Aristotle refers at 1136a8–9.

On this interpretation, ignorance that is of particulars but due to feelings that are natural or human (1136a8–9) would be ignorance that is not due to the agent's character, since such feelings are natural and hence not within the scope of character. Ignorance of particulars that is due to feelings not of this type, however, is due to the agent's character, since such feelings are not natural and hence are within the scope of character. On this interpretation, the actions that, according to *EN* v 8, are performed both in ignorance of particulars and because of such ignorance are cases of actions in which the agent's character is not responsible for the ignorance. And actions that are performed merely in such ignorance but not because of it are actions in which the agent's character is responsible for the ignorance and derivatively for the action. In this respect, the distinction between acting merely in ignorance and acting because of ignorance in *EN* v 8 corresponds to the distinction in *EN* iii 1. For in *EN* iii 1, the ignorance that fails to count as ignorance "because of which" the agent acts is, as in *EN* v 8, ignorance that is a product of the agent's character.

In both *EN* v 8 and *EN* iii 1 the ignorance that fails to count as ignorance "because of which" the action occurs is ignorance that is either constitutive of or produced by the agent's moral character. But why should the fact that the ignorance in question stands in this relation to the agent's moral character give Aristotle reason to deny that the action is "because of ignorance". After all, the ignorance in question plays a causal role in the action. Aristotle's reason for denying that such ignorance is ignorance "because of which" the action occurs is intelligible if he intends "because of ignorance" to capture "because of ignorance and not because of the agent". This, I propose, is what the distinction between acting in ignorance and because of ignorance means for Aristotle. Aristotle's judgements about whether an action is because of the agent (rather than because of his ignorance) depend on his assessment of whether the ignorance in question is a product or feature of the agent's character. Aristotle's judgements about whether actions are due to ignorance are explicable on the hypothesis that he thinks voluntary actions are not due to ignorance and that actions produced by one's character are voluntary.

3 Culpable Ignorance

The discussion of *EN* iii 1 seems to allow that any action involving ignorance of particulars is thereby due to ignorance of particulars (1111a15–18). But *EN* v 8, on the interpretation offered above, gives reason to suppose that not all such ignorance renders the action "because of ignorance". If the agent's character is responsible for that ignorance of particulars, then *EN* v 8 does not count that action as "due to ignorance". (I shall refer to such ignorance as "culpable ignorance".) *EN* v 8 does not claim that culpable ignorance of particulars keeps an action from being involuntary. It simply claims that the culpability of the ignorance affects the propriety of giving "forgiveness" (*sungnōmē*) for the involuntary action. An action performed in ignorance of particulars is, according to *EN* v 8, involuntary, but such an involuntary action does not merit *sungnōmē*. But even though *EN* v 8 does not claim that culpable ignorance renders an action voluntary, one might wonder whether it does not provide a reason for such a claim. After all, if Aristotle thinks the activity produced by the agent's character is voluntary, then action performed in culpable ignorance of particulars would seem to be voluntary. Aristotle explicitly discusses culpable ignorance in two places in his discussions of voluntariness: in *EN* iii 5, 1113b23–1114a3 and in *EE* ii 9, 1225b11–16.

In *EN* iii 5, Aristotle claims that an agent who does something bad is responsible for it unless the action is due to force or due to ignorance for which the agent is not responsible (*di' agnoian hēs mē autoi aitioi*) (*EN* 1113b23–5). It is not clear that the ignorance in question is ignorance of the particular facts rather than ignorance of what one should and should not do (ignorance of the universal). Since the chapter is one in which Aristotle argues that agents are responsible for their states of character, it is possible that the ignorance for which one is responsible is ignorance of what one ought to do. However, if the ignorance in question is supposed to be ignorance of the particulars, and if Aristotle continues to maintain the view that one is blameworthy only for voluntary actions, then these remarks indicate that Aristotle's definition of voluntariness in *EN* iii 1, requiring knowlege of the particulars, needs to be revised.

Aristotle does not address this question explicitly in *EN* iii 5. This silence might be further evidence that particular ignorance is not the sort of ignorance he has in mind when he refers to "ignorance for which the agent is responsible" at 1113b24–5. However, even if this ignorance is simply ignorance of the "universal", there still remains an unclarity and tension in Aristotle's account, for in his argument that our states of character (and hence our ignorance of the universal) are volun-tary (1114a4–13) he does not establish that we knowingly do what will produce these states of character in us; rather, he establishes simply that we have no excuse for not knowing this (1114a9–10). This claim would serve the conclusion that character development is voluntary only if culpable ignorance did not count as the sort of ignorance that makes an action involuntary.

A similar problem arises, in more explicit terms, in *EE* ii 9. In his preliminary discussion of voluntariness and involuntariness, Aristotle requires that the action whose involuntariness is due to ignorance must be "because of ignorance non-accidentally" (1225b5–6). Presumably the addition of "non-accidentally" to "because of ignorance" is intended to rule out cases in which the ignorance of particulars doesn't play the relevant causal role in the production of the action. Aristotle does not indicate what sorts of particular ignorance he would take to be only accidentally involved in the production of the action. He might, for example, have in mind something like this. Oedipus strikes the old man at the cross-roads not knowing that the old man is a Theban. But his ignorance that the old man is from Thebes has no effect on whether he strikes him, since he would do the same even if he knew this. Even though Oedipus does not voluntarily strike the Theban, his ignorance that the old man is a Theban does not undermine the claim that he voluntarily strikes the old man at the crossroads.[16]

Aristotle, however, also might intend the remark, about being due to ignorance non-accidentally, to be interpreted in the light of certain remarks about culpable ignorance which he appends to the definition of voluntariness and involuntariness:

> Knowledge and knowing are twofold – one being to have the knowledge, the other to use it. The person who has but does not use the knowledge might rightly be said not to know. But he might also not rightly be said not to know, for example if he failed to use it due to carelessness. Similarly too, the person not having the knowledge might be blamed, if he fails, due to carelessness or pleasure or pain, to have some knowledge that is easy or necessary to have. So let these things be added to the definition. (*EE* 1225b11–16)

Aristotle's remarks here are clearly motivated by the thought that agents who act in culpable ignorance are blameworthy, as he remarks explicitly in discussing the second type of culpable ignorance. He does not, however, appear to have clearly thought through the implications that these remarks are to be "added to the definition". It is not clear what the second case is supposed to add, since it only claims that such agents are blameworthy, not that they are voluntary. Does he intend that such agents act voluntarily? If so, then he cannot require knowledge for voluntariness, as he has just done in the definition above. This would not be a simple addition to but an amendment of the definition.

Aristotle does not resolve these issues, or even address them explicitly. For our present purposes, it is sufficient to note that Aristotle's assessment of whether a given type of ignorance keeps an action from being voluntary is sensitive to his judgement about whether the agent is blameworthy for the action in question. Aristotle's unresolved difficulty here about whether knowledge is necessary for voluntariness, or whether culpable ignorance would suffice, is explicable in the light of the assumption that, in his account of voluntariness, he is seeking to capture the conditions in which an agent is praiseworthy or blameworthy. And, as we have had occasion to observe at various points in chapter 3, the judgements about praiseworthiness and blameworthiness against which Aristotle checks proposed criteria for voluntariness are closely connected to assessments of the agent's moral character. That is, the praise and blame for which he thinks voluntariness is a necessary condition are the retrospective moral evaluations of concern to moral responsibility.

NOTES

1 *EN* 1111a22–4; *EE* 1225b8–10; cf. *EN* 1135a23–8. Only the definition in the *MM* states a single criterion: that the action be "from thought" (1188b26; cf. b38).

2 For example, the requirement of knowledge in *EE* ii 9's definition of voluntariness is stated: "not in ignorance and because of oneself" (*mē agnoōn kai di' hauton*, 1225b8–9). And the recapitulation of the definition at *EE* ii 10, 1226b30–2 shows that the "and" (*kai*) in this articulation of the condition is epexegetic, for the equivalent condition is there stated as: "because of oneself and not because of ignorance" (*di' hauton kai mē di' agnoian*, 1226b31–2).

3 In this respect, the *MM*'s definition reflects contemporary legal criteria, according to which *pronoia* (forethought) is considered necessary for voluntariness, but what counts as *pronoia* ranges widely (cf. *MM* 1188b35). The *MM* cites a trial in the Areopagus as evidence in favour of its definition

(1188b31–7). Plato, in *Laws* ix counts as involuntary (*akōn*) agents who act unintentionally (865a–c), but counts as voluntary (*hekōn*) only agents who act from the deliberate forethought and plotting characteristic of consummate and incurable vice (869e–873c). He refuses to count as either voluntary or involuntary actions performed in knowledge, but prompted by anger (866d–868a), indicating that there is considerable controversy about the voluntariness of such cases (867b). These controversial cases would seem voluntary if mere awareness satisfied the cognitive condition for voluntariness, but involuntary if prior deliberate intent is required.

4 That is, if supplemented by pain or regret (*EN* 1111a20–1).

5 *EN* 1147a24–6 makes it clear that to state the two types of thought is to state the cause (*aitia*) of the action in the manner of the natural scientist (*phusikōs*, 1147a24).

6 The distinction invoking the terms 'universal' and 'particular' is made at *EN* 1112b33–1113a2; common book *EN* 1141b14–22, 1142a20–23, 1147a25–31. The same distinction is made, but without the labels 'universal' and 'particular' at *DA* 434a16–19 and *MA* 701a10–11.

7 Universal premise about what is good or bad: *EN* 1141b14, 1142a20; of the form *dei* (ought): *EN* 1147a29, *DA* 434a18; expressed in the gerundive (e.g., *badisteon, poiēteon*): *MA* 701a13, 14, 16.

8 *EN* 1142a27–30, 1143b5, 1147a26, 1113a1–2; cf. 1109b18–26, 1126b2–4.

9 On the absence of impediment, see *Met.* 1048a16–21.

10 In the same phrase he also uses the gerundive (*aphekteon*) (1110b29), the form he uses in *MA* 7 to give the universal premise, although he does not there use the terminological distinction between universal and particular.

11 On error about the universal as error involved in deliberation: *EN* 1142a20. On the relation between the goals and the results of deliberation as the relation between universal and particular: *EN* 1112b33–1113a1.

12 I would explain this more restricted use of 'universal' as follows: *to d' akousion bouletai . . . en hois kai peri ha hē praxis* (1110b28–1111a1) is a *de*-clause in contrast with the *men*-clause: *agnoei men oun pas ho mochthēros . . . kakoi gignontai* (b28–30). The types of ignorance listed in the *de*-clause (of the beneficial, in the *prohairesis*, of the universal) therefore are all supposed to be of the same type as the types of ignorance in the *men*-clause (of what one should (*dei, -teon*) do). The *oud'* in *oud' hē katholou* (b32) effects a contrast between ignorance of the *sumpheronta* (which is ignorance in the *prohairesis*, as indicated by the *gar* in b31) and ignorance of the universal. The intended contrast is probably between ignorance of the highest goals in the light of which one deliberates, and the subordinate goals that contribute (*sumpherei*) either instrumentally or intrinsically to those goals. The intended contrast is between ignorance of whether one should act justly and ignorance of whether returning this deposit is just. Good

intentions do not excuse, Aristotle indicates, if one is ignorant about how to execute them.

13   Further support for the interpretation that, in *EN* iii 1, actions performed in ignorance of particulars are thereby because of ignorance comes from 1111a15–18, where Aristotle indicates that he takes simply being ignorant of one of the particular facts to satisfy the condition of acting because of ignorance of such facts.

14   *EN* 1106a9; cf. *EE* 1220b7–8.

15   In *Rhet.* i 13 he claims explicitly that actions due to feelings can be due to wickedness (*apo ponērias*) (*Rhet.* 1374b9–10; omitted by one MS and William of Moerbeke).

16   This explanation was suggested to me by Terence Irwin.

Appendix II
"Up to Us" and the Internal Origin

———————————— ◆ ————————————

In several places in both the *EE* and *EN*, Aristotle indicates quite explicitly that if an action's origin is in me, then it is up to me to do and not to do.[1] For this reason, I interpret Aristotle's claim in *EE* ii 8, that compelled actions are not up to the agent, as expressing the same point as the *MM* makes in claiming that compelled actions are due to externals (*MM* 1188b19). That is, both the *EE* and *MM* take compelled actions to be not up to the agent because they are not internally caused. By contrast, the *EN* takes such actions to be up to the agent because they are internally caused (1110a15–18). This is why I diagnose Aristotle's conflicting views about the voluntariness of compelled actions as based on conflicting views about whether the compelled action's origin is in the agent.

However, Aristotle's discussion of compulsion in *EE* ii 8, in particular his admission that some actions due to unbearable desires are not up to the agent (*EE* 1225a19–27), naturally raises the suggestion that he thinks the requirement, that the voluntary action be up to the agent, expresses a requirement in addition to (and hence not entailed by) the requirement that the action's origin be in the agent. For actions due to unbearable desires seem to originate within the agent, but Aristotle claims they are not up to the agent. We have already seen, in examining the Eudemian account of compulsion, that Aristotle denies that such actions originate in the agent in the way voluntariness requires (that is, non-accidentally). Nonetheless, the suggestion (that the requirement that the voluntary action be up to the agent is not entailed by the requirement that the action's origin be in the agent) also derives some support from the definition of voluntariness Aristotle articulates in *EE* ii 9. He there claims that a voluntary action must be: (a) up to the agent not to do; and (b) performed knowingly and because of the agent (1225b8–10). Condition (b) presumably expresses the requirement that the action originate in the agent. But if an action's origin's being in the agent entails that it is up to the agent to do and not to do, why does Aristotle make (a) an explicit requirement?

We can see why Aristotle explicitly states both (a) and (b) in his Eudemian definition of voluntariness, even if he thinks that it follows from the fact that an action's origin is in the agent that it is up to the agent to do and not to do, if we note that Aristotle's account of the conditions in which something is up to us admits of both a wide and a narrow interpretation. He identifies the sort of action that is "up to us" in the course of identifying the proper objects of deliberation:

> One does not deliberate about eternal things, such as the cosmos and the diagonal's being incommensurate with the side. Nor does one deliberate about changing things that always happen in the same way – whether of necessity or by nature or because of some other cause (*di' allēn tina aitian*) – such as the orbits and the risings ⟨sc. of the celestial bodies⟩. Nor about what happens by chance, e.g. finding treasure. Nor about men in general – for example, no Spartan deliberates about how the affairs of the Scythians would be best conducted. For none of these things can come about through us, and we deliberate about what is up to us and what we can do (*tōn eph' hēmin kai praktōn*). (*EN* 1112a21–31; cf. *EE* 1226a21–33)

The general feature of things that are up to us, Aristotle tells us here, is that they "might happen through us" (*ha di' hēmōn genoit' an* – 1112a30). And he goes on to say that anything with its origin in us is thereby something that "might happen through us" (*EN* 1112b27–8). The only positive characterization of the things that "might happen through us" offered here is that they are things we can do (*prakta*). Presumably, these are the sorts of things that we can bring about by our faculties of thought and desire (cf. *MA* 703b8–11).

Aristotle, in this context, clearly has in mind what I will call the wide notion of what is up to us. According to this notion, an action is up to us in the wide sense if it is the sort of thing that can occur as the result of our thought and desire; it is of the sort that, if we choose to perform it, we will generally succeed in bringing it about. But we can also identify a narrower notion of what is up to us. An action is up to us in the narrow sense if it actually occurred as the result of our thought and desire. Not every action or outcome that is up to me in the wide sense will be up to me in the narrow sense. The fact that a given outcome is the sort of thing I can bring about if I choose to does not entail that it actually occurred as a result of my choice. For example, hitting my neighbour may be something that is up to me in the sense that it is within the scope of my thought and desire. I can bring it about by simply choosing to do it. But a particular instance of hitting my neighbour may occur not as the result of my thought and desire, and indeed in opposition to them – as in the example of forced action at *EE* 1224b13–14 and *EN* 1135a27–8 where someone takes my hand and uses it to strike my neighbour. We might say that the action of hitting my neighbour that occurs in this example is of a sort to be up to me (since it is the sort of thing I can do by exercising my powers of thought and desire) but that its occurrence was not up to me (because these capacities did not in fact bring it about).

Aristotle uses 'up to us' in these two different senses in his definition of voluntariness in *EN* v 8. We will see this if we understand why he denies there that natural processes are voluntary:

> We also undergo knowingly many of the things that obtain by nature, none of which is either voluntary or involuntary – for example, growing old and dying. (*EN* 1135a33–b2)

He has in the immediate context provided a definition of voluntariness that makes it clear why such processes fail to be voluntary:

> By voluntary I mean, as was said earlier, whatever of the things that (i) are up to him, that (ii) someone does knowingly and not in ignorance (either of whom, or how . . .), and each of these (iii) neither accidentally nor by force (as in a case where someone takes one's hand and uses it to strike another, for this is not up to him). (1135a23–8)

Aristotle denies that natural processes are up to us (*EN* 1112a25; *EE* 1223a11–12). So he must think they fail to satisfy the first condition for voluntariness given in this definition. Aristotle's claim that natural processes are not involuntary either (1135b1–2; also made at *MA* 703b3–11) is initially puzzling, for immediately before making this remark about natural processes, he has also defined conditions for involuntariness:

So what is [i] unknown; or [ii] not unknown but not up to him; or [iii] forced, is involuntary. (*EN* 1135a31–3)

Given that natural processes are not up to us, and given that we know they are occurring (1135b1), they would seem to satisfy the second condition for involuntariness, contrary to Aristotle's explicit claim two lines later.[2]

This difficulty disappears once we remark that "up to us" plays two roles in the definitions of voluntariness and involuntariness. This is clearly the case in the definition of voluntariness, where the requirement that the action be up to the agent occurs twice: once in the initial requirement that the action be up to the agent, and once again in the requirement that the action not be forced – a requirement which the parenthesis at 1135a27–8 identifies as requiring that the action be up to the agent. The first statement of the requirement that the action be up to the agent (= (i) in the definition of voluntariness) is reasonably interpreted as requiring that the voluntary action satisfy the condition for being up to the agent given in *EE* 1226a21–33 and *EN* 1112a21–31: that it be the sort of thing the agent can bring about by thought and desire. But an action can satisfy this condition, yet still occur as a result of causes other than the agent's thought and desire – as in the case of force, where someone else's thought and desire bring it about. So the second statement of the requirement that the action be up to the agent (in (iii) in the definition of voluntariness) requires that the action, which satisfies the wide conditions for being up to the agent expressed in (i), also satisfy the narrow conditions for being up to the agent expressed in (ii): that it have actually been due to the agent's thought and desire. Finally, we need only note that a requirement like (i) in the definition of voluntariness, must be presupposed in the definition of involuntariness at 1135a31–3.[3] Given this presupposition, natural processes fail to be involuntary for the same reason that they fail to be voluntary: they are not the sort of thing that our thoughts and desire control.

To summarize, the account of voluntariness in *EN* v 8 twice states the requirement that the action be up to the agent. The first time it requires that the action be the sort of thing that can be brought about by the agent's thought and desire; the second time it requires that the action have been actually brought about by the agent's thought and desire. This definition is very similar to the definition of voluntariness in *EE* ii 9. One salient respect of similarity is that it begins with the requirement that (a) the action be up to the agent, and then adds the requirement that (b) the action be due to the agent. The preceding analysis of the definition in *EN* v 8 provides a natural explanation of these two conditions. Condition (a) requires that the voluntary action be the sort of thing that can be brought about by the agent's thought and desire; and condition (b) requires that the voluntary action have been actually brought about by the agent's thought and desire. On this interpretation, we have no reason to suppose that Aristotle here indicates that an action can originate in the agent in the way voluntariness requires, yet not be up to the agent to do and not to do.

NOTES

1 *EE* 1223a2–9; *EN* 1110a17–18, 1113b20–1, 1114a18–19.

2 Kenny concludes on the basis of this that such processes are up to us (Kenny 1979, p. 8), but he fails to note that his interpretation entails that natural processes turn out to be voluntary, since they would satisfy the definition of voluntariness at 1225a23–8. Irwin proposes to avoid the difficulty by deleting "nor involuntary" (*out' akousion*) at 1135b1–2 (Irwin 1985a, ad loc.). But there is no textual warrant for such a deletion, and *MA* 703b3–11 provides independent evidence that Aristotle really does think such processes are neither voluntary nor involuntary. The solution I will propose allows us to make sense of Aristotle's text.

3 Some such condition must be presupposed or else anything of whose occurrence an agent were unaware would count as an involuntary action of hers – according to the first clause of that definition; so would occurrences of which he or she were aware but which were done by other agents in other places – according to clause [ii]. The government of the Scythians would be an involuntary action of the Spartan referred to at *EN* 1112a29! And, according to [iii], anything that occurs by force anywhere would be an involuntary action of mine.

Bibliography

Ackrill, J. L. 1978: Aristotle on action. *Mind*, 97, 595–601.

——1980: Aristotle on eudaimonia. In A. O. Rorty (ed.), *Articles on Aristotle's Ethics*, Berkeley: University of California Press.

Adkins, A. W. H. 1960: *Merit and Responsibility*. Oxford: Clarendon Press.

Annas, J. 1982: Aristotle on inefficient causes. *Philosophical Quarterly*, 32, 311–26.

——1992: Ancient ethics and modern morality. *Philosophical Perspectives*, 6, *Ethics*, 119–36.

Anscombe, G. E. M. 1963: Two kinds of error in action. *Journal of Philosophy*, 60, 393–401.

——1965: Thought and action in Aristotle. In R. Bambrough (ed.), *New Essays in Plato and Aristotle*, London and New York. Reprinted in J. Barnes, M. Schofield, R. Sorabji (eds), *Articles on Aristotle*, vol. 2. New York: St Martin's Press, 1977.

Aquinas: *In decem libros Ethicorum Aristotelis ad Nicomachum Expositio*. A. M. Pirotta, P. Martini, and S. Gillet (eds), Taurini, Italy: M. E. Marietti, 1934.

Aspasius, *In Ethica Nicomachea Commentaria. Commentaria in Aristotelem Graeca*, vol. 19. G. Heylbut (ed.), Berlin: G. Reimer, 1889.

Audi, R. 1974: Moral responsibility, freedom and compulsion. *American Philosophical Quarterly*, 11, 1–14.

Austin, J. L. 1956–7: A plea for excuses. *Proceedings of the Aristotelian Society*, 57, 1–30. Reprinted in his *Philosophical Papers*, Oxford: Clarendon Press, 1961.

——1967: *Agathon* and *eudaimonia* in the *Ethics* of Aristotle. In J. M. E. Moravcsik (ed.), *Aristotle*, New York: Macmillan.

Barnes, J. 1980: Aristotle and the methods of ethics. *Revue Internationale de Philosophie*, 34, 490–511.

Bigelow, J., Dodds, S. and Pargetter, R. 1988: Against the will. *Pacific Philosophical Quarterly*, 69, 307–24.

Bondeson, W. 1974: Aristotle on responsibility for one's character and the possibility of character change. *Phronesis*, 19, 59–65.

Brickhouse, T. C. 1991: Roberts on responsibility for character in the *Nicomachean Ethics*. *Ancient Philosophy*, 11, 137–48.

Broadie, S. 1991: *Ethics with Aristotle*. New York: Oxford University Press.

Burnet, J. 1900: *The Ethics of Aristotle*. London: Methuen.

Burnyeat, M. F. 1980: Aristotle on learning to be good. In A. O. Rorty (ed.), *Essays on Aristotle's Ethics*, Berkeley: University of California Press.

Charles, D. 1984: *Aristotle's Philosophy of Action*. Ithaca: Cornell University Press.

Chisholm, R. 1964: Human freedom and the self. The Lindley Lecture, Department of Philosophy, University of Kansas. Reprinted in G. Watson (ed.), *Free Will*, New York: Oxford University Press, 1982.

Cooper, J. M. 1973: The *Magna Moralia* and Aristotle's moral philosophy. *American Journal of Philology*, 94, 327–49.

——1975: *Reason and Human Good in Aristotle*. Cambridge: Harvard University Press.

——1981: Review of A. Kenny, *The Aristotelian Ethics*. *Nous*, 15, 381–92.

Curren, R. 1989: The contribution of *Nicomachean Ethics* iii 5 to Aristotle's theory of responsibility. *History of Philosophy Quarterly*, 6, 261–77.

Davidson, D. 1967: Causal relations. *Journal of Philosophy*, 64, 691–703. Reprinted in Davidson 1980.

——1973: Freedom to act. In Ted Honderich (ed.), *Essays on Freedom of Action*, London: Routledge & Kegan Paul, 1973. Reprinted in Davidson 1980.

——1980: *Essays on Actions and Events*. Oxford: Oxford University Press.

Dirlmeier, F. A. 1958: *Aristoteles, Magna Moralia*, Berlin: Akademie–Verlag.

——1962: *Aristoteles, Eudemische Ethik*, Berlin: Akademie–Verlag.

Dodds, E. R. 1951: *The Greeks and the Irrational*. Berkeley: University of California Press.

Dyer, R. R. 1965: Aristotle's categories of voluntary torts (*EN* 1135b8–25). *Classical Review*, 25, 250–2.

Engberg–Pedersen, T. 1983: *Aristotle's Theory of Moral Insight*. Oxford: Clarendon Press.

Everson, S. 1990: Aristotle's compatibilism in the *Nicomachean Ethics*. *Ancient Philosophy*, 10, 81–99.

Fine, G. 1987: Forms as causes: Plato and Aristotle. In A. Graeser (ed.), *Mathematics and Metaphysics in Aristotle*, Bern: P. Haupt.

Frankfurt, H. 1971: Freedom of the will and the concept of a person. *Journal of Philosophy*, 68, 5–20. Reprinted in G. Watson (ed.), *Free Will*, Oxford: Oxford University Press, 1980.

——1973: Coercion and moral responsibility. In T. Honderich (ed.), *Essays on Freedom of Action*, London: Routledge & Kegan Paul.

——1987: Identification and wholeheartedness. In F. Schoeman (ed.), *Responsibility, Character and the Emotions*, Cambridge: Cambridge University Press.

Frede, M. 1980: The original notion of cause. In M. Schofield, M. Burnyeat, and J. Barnes (eds), *Doubt and Dogmatism: studies in Hellenistic epistemology*, Oxford: Clarendon Press.

Freeland, C. 1982: Moral virtues and human powers. *Review of Metaphysics*, 36, 3–22.

Fritzsche, A. T. H. 1851: *Aristotelis Ethica Eudemia*. Regensburg: G. I. Manz.

Furley, D. J. 1967: Aristotle and Epicurus on voluntary action. In *Two Studies in the Greek Atomists*, Princeton: Princeton University Press. With revisions, in J. Barnes, M. Schofield, and R. Sorabji (eds), *Articles on Aristotle*, Vol. 2, New York: St Martin's Press, 1977.

——1978: Self-Movers. In G. E. R. Lloyd and G. E. L. Owen (eds), *Aristotle on Mind and the Senses: Proceedings of the Seventh Symposium Aristotelicum*, Cambridge: Cambridge University Press. Reprinted in A. O. Rorty (ed.), *Essays on Aristotle's Ethics*, Berkeley: University of California Press, 1980.

Gauthier, R.-A., and Jolif, J. Y. 1970: *Aristote: l'Ethique à Nicomaque*. 2nd edn, 2 vols. Louvain: Publications Universitaires.

Gert, B. and Duggan, T. G. 1979: Free will as the ability to will. *Nous*, 13, 197–217.

Gill, C. 1986: The question of character and personality in Greek tragedy. *Poetics Today*, 7, 251–73.

——1990: The character-personality distinction. In C. Pelling (ed.), *Characterization and Individuality in Greek Literature*, Oxford: Clarendon Press.

Grant, A. 1885: *The Ethics of Aristotle*, 4th edn. London: Longmans, Green, and Co.

Haksar, V. 1964: Aristotle and the punishment of psychopaths. *Philosophy*, 39, 323–40.

Halliwell, S. 1986: *Aristotle's Poetics*. London: Duckworth.

Hamburger, M. 1951: *Morals and Law: the growth of Aristotle's legal theory*. New Haven: Yale University Press.

Hardie, W. F. R. 1968: Aristotle and the free will problem. [Reply to Huby 1967.] *Philosophy*, 43, 274–8.

——1980: *Aristotle's Ethical Theory*, 2nd edn. Oxford: Clarendon Press.

Heinaman, R. 1988: Compulsion and voluntary action in the *Eudemian Ethics*. *Nous*, 22, 253–81.

Huby, P. 1967: The first discovery of the freewill problem. *Philosophy*, 42, 353–62.

Hursthouse, R. 1984: Acting and feeling in character: *Nicomachean Ethics* 3.i. *Phronesis*, 29, 252–66.

Hutchinson, D. S. 1986: *The Virtues of Aristotle*. Boston: Routledge & Kegan Paul.

Irwin, T. H. 1978: First principles in Aristotle's ethics. In P. A. French, T. E. Uehling Jr and H. K. Wettstein (eds), *Studies in Ethical Theory*, Midwest Studies in Philosophy, Vol. 3, Morris: University of Minnesota.

——1980a: The Aristotelian Ethics and Aristotle's theory of the will. Review of A. Kenny, *Aristotle's Theory of the Will. Journal of Philosophy*, 77, 338–55.

——1980b: Reason and responsibility in Aristotle. In A. O. Rorty (ed.), *Essays on Aristotle's Ethics*, Berkeley: University of California Press.

——1981: Aristotle's method of ethics. In D. J. O'Meara (ed.), *Studies in Aristotle*, Washington: Catholic University Press.

——1985a: *Aristotle, Nicomachean Ethics*. Indianapolis: Hackett Publishing Co.

——1985b: Aristotle's conception of morality. *Proceedings of the Boston Area Colloquium in Ancient Philosophy*, 1, 115–43.

——1988: *Aristotle's First Principles*. Oxford: Clarendon Press.

Joachim, H. H. 1951: *Aristotle, The Nicomachean Ethics*. D. A. Rees (ed.). Oxford: Clarendon Press.

Jones, J. 1962: *On Aristotle and Greek Tragedy*. London: Chatto & Windus.

Kenny, A. 1979: *Aristotle's Theory of the Will*. New Haven: Yale University Press.

Kosman, L. A. 1980: Being properly affected: virtues and feelings in Aristotle's Ethics. In A. O. Rorty (ed.), *Essays on Aristotle's Ethics*, Berkeley: University of California Press.

Kraut, R. 1989: *Aristotle on the Human Good*. Princeton, New Jersey: Princeton University Press.

Lear, J. 1988: *Aristotle and the Desire to Understand*. Cambridge: Cambridge University Press.

Lee, H. D. P. 1937: The legal background of two passages in the NE. *Classical Quarterly*, 31, 129–40.

Lloyd, G. E. R. 1968: The role of medical and biological analogies in Aristotle's ethics. *Phronesis*, 13, 68–83.

Loening, R. 1903: *Die Zurechnungslehre des Aristoteles*, Jena: Gustav Fisher.

Loomis, W. T. 1972: The nature of premeditation in Athenian homicide law. *Journal of Hellenic Studies*, 92, 86–95.

Maschke, R. 1926: *Die Willenslehre im griechischen Recht*. Berlin: Georg Stilke. Reprinted, New York: Arno Press, 1979.

MacDowell, D. M. 1963: *Athenian homicide law in the age of the orators*. Manchester: University Press.

McDowell, J. 1978: Are moral requirements hypothetical imperatives? *The Aristotelian Society Supplement*, 52, 13–29.

——1979: Virtue and reason. *Monist*, 62, 331–50.

——1980: The role of eudaimonia in Aristotle's Ethics. In A. O. Rorty (ed.), *Essays in Aristotle's Ethics*, Berkeley: University of California Press.

——1988: Comments on 'Some rational aspects of incontinence' by T. H. Irwin. Spindel Conference, 1988. *Southern Journal of Philosophy*, 27 (Supplement), 89–102.

Mele, A. R. 1981: Choice and virtue in the *Nicomachean Ethics*. *Journal of the History of Philosophy*, 19, 405–23.

Mele, A. R. 1984: Aristotle's wish. *Journal of the History of Philosophy*, 22, 139–56.

Meyer, S. S. 1992: Aristotle, teleology and reduction. *Philosophical Review* 101, 791–825.

——1994: Self-movement and external causation. In M. L. Gill and J. G. Lennox (eds), *Self-Motion: from Aristotle to Newton*, Princeton, New Jersey: Princeton University Press.

——forthcoming: Moral Responsibility: Aristotle and after. In S. Everson (ed), *Companions to Ancient Thought*, Vol. 4, *Ethics*, Cambridge: Cambridge University Press.

Mingay, J. M. and Walzer, R. R. 1991: *Aristotelis Ethica Eudemia*. Oxford: Clarendon Press.

Moline, J. N. 1989: Aristotle on praise and blame. *Archiv für Geschichte der Philosophie*, 71, 283–302.

Mulhern, J. J. 1974: Aristotle and the Socratic paradoxes. *Journal of the History of Ideas*, 35, 293–9.

Nozick, R. 1969: Coercion. In S. Morgenbesser, P. Suppes and M. White (eds), *Philosophy, Science and Method*, New York: St Martin's Press.

Nussbaum, M. C. 1978: *Aristotle's De Motu Animalium*. Princeton: Princeton University Press.

——1982: Saving Aristotle's appearances. In M. Schofield and M. Nussbaum (eds), *Language and Logos*, Cambridge: Cambridge University Press.

——1983: The "common explanation" of animal motion. In P. Moraux and J. Wiesner (eds), *Symposium Aristotelicum, Zweifelhaftes im Corpus Aristotelicum*, Berlin: Walter de Gruyter.

——1986: *The Fragility of Goodness*. Cambridge: Cambridge University Press.

O'Brien, M. J. 1967: *The Socratic Paradoxes and the Greek Mind*. Chapel Hill: University of North Carolina.

Owen, G. E. L. 1961: Tithenai ta phainomena. In S. Mansion (ed.), *Aristote et les problèmes de méthode*, Papers of the Second Symposium Aristotelicum, Louvain: Publications Universitaires de Louvain. Reprinted in J. M. E. Moravcsik (ed.), *Aristotle*, Garden City, New York: Doubleday, 1957; and in *Articles on Aristotle*, Vol. 1, 113–25; and in G. E. L. Owen, *Logic, Science, and Dialectic*, Ithaca: Cornell University Press, 1986.

Pelling, C. 1990: *Characterization and Individuality in Greek Literature*. Oxford: Clarendon Press.

Prichard, H. A. 1935: The meaning of *agathon* in the *Ethics* of Aristotle. *Philosophy*, 10, 27–31. Reprinted in his *Moral Obligation*, Oxford: Clarendon Press, 1949.

Rackham, H. 1935: *Aristotle, The Athenian Constitution, The Eudemian Ethics, On Virtues and Vices*. Cambridge, Massachusetts: Harvard University Press.

Rassow, H. 1861: *Emendationes Aristoteleae*. Weimar: Druck der Hof-Buchdruckerei.

Rickert, G. 1989: *Hekon and akon in Early Greek Thought*. Atlanta, GA: Scholars Press.

Roberts, J. 1989: Aristotle on responsibility for action and character. *Ancient Philosophy*, 9, 23–36.

Ross, W. D. 1923: *Aristotle*. London: Methuen.

Rowe, C. J. 1971: *The Eudemian and Nicomachean Ethics. A study in the development of Aristotle's thought. Proceedings of the Cambridge Philological Society*, Supplement no. 2.

Sauvé, S. 1987: Unmoved movers, form and matter. *Philosophical Topics*, 15, 171–96.

——1988: Why involuntary actions are painful. *Southern Journal of Philosophy*, 27 (Supplement), 127–58.

Schofield, M. 1973: Aristotelian mistakes. *Proceedings of the Cambridge Philological Society*, 19, 66–70.

Sedley, D. 1983: Epicurus' refutation of determinism. In *Suzētēsis. Studi sull'epicureismo greco e latino offerti a Marcello Gigante*, Naples: G. Macchiaroli.

Sharples, R. 1982: *Alexander of Aphrodisias on Fate*. London: Duckworth.

——1990: *Alexander of Aphrodisias, Ethical Problems*. Ithaca: Cornell University Press.

Sherman, N. 1989: *The Fabric of Character*. Oxford: Clarendon Press.

Siegler, F. A. 1968: Voluntary and involuntary. *Monist*, 52, 268–87.

Solomon, J. 1915: *The Eudemian Ethics*. In *The Works of Aristotle Translated into English under the Editorship of Sir David Ross*, Vol. 19. Oxford: Oxford University Press.

Sorabji, R. 1973–4: Aristotle on the role of the intellect in virtue. *Proceedings of the Aristotelian Society*, 74, 107–29.

——1980: *Necessity, Cause and Blame: perspectives on Aristotle's theory*. Ithaca: Cornell University Press.

Stewart, J. A. 1892: *Notes on the Nicomachean Ethics of Aristotle*. Oxford: Clarendon Press.

Strawson, P. F. 1962: Freedom and resentment. *Proceedings of the British Academy*, 48, 187–211. Reprinted in G. Watson (ed.), *Free Will*, Oxford: Oxford University Press, 1980.

Susemihl, F. 1883: *Aristotelis Magna Moralia*. Leipzig: Teubner.

——1884: *Eudemi Rhodii Ethica Aristotelis Ethica Eudemia*. Leipzig: Teubner.

Susemihl, F. and Apelt, O. 1903: *Aristotelis Nicomachea Ethica*, Leipzig: Teubner.

Thomson, J. A. K. 1953: *The Ethics of Aristotle*. London: Geo. Allen & Unwin.

Urmson, J. O. 1988: *Aristotle's Ethics*. Oxford: Basil Blackwell.

Wallace, J. 1974: Excellences and Merit. *Philosophical Review*, 83, 182–99.

Walzer, R. 1929: *Magna Moralia und Aristotelische Ethik*. Berlin: Weidmann.

Watson, G. 1975: Free agency. *Journal of Philosophy*, 72, 205–20. Reprinted in G. Watson (ed.), *Free Will*, New York: Oxford University Press, 1982.

Williams, B. 1985: *Ethics and the Limits of Philosophy*. Cambridge: Harvard University Press.

Williams, B. 1986: How free does the will need to be? The Lindley Lecture, University of Kansas, 1985. Department of Philosophy, University of Kansas.

Wittmann, M. 1921: Aristoteles und die Willensfreiheit, eine historisch-kritische Untersuchung. Fulda: Fuldaer Actiendruckerei. *Philosophisches Jahrbuch,* 34, 5–30, 131–53.

Wolf, S. 1990: *Freedom within Reason.* New York: Oxford University Press.

Woods, M. 1982: *Aristotle's Eudemian Ethics (Books I, II, and VIII).* Oxford: Clarendon Press.

Woozley, A. D. 1978: Negligence and ignorance. *Philosophy,* 53, 293–306.

General Index

accidental and non-accidental, causation, 92n34, 101–10, 113–15, 116–18, 119n9, 119n10, 120n13, 120n14, 157–8, 158–61, 162, 163–4, 166, 168n11, 181–2; effects, 117, 120n13, 158; (in)justice, 101, 106, 109–10, 110–18, 158–66; properties, 103–4, 119n11; *see also* causal power, efficient cause

Ackrill, J. L., 34n21

action (*praxis*), 23, 33n11, 33n12; non-accidental, 109, 110–11

adikein see doing (in)justice

Adkins, A. W. H., 34n19, 55n14

agent-causation, 39, 152, 156

aitia, *aitios*, 37–8, 53n1, 170; *see also* cause

akousion see hekousion and *akousion*

Alexander of Aphrodisias, 167n2, 168n10

anger, 86–7, 167n7, 177

animals *see* children and animals

aporia (puzzle), 60, 62, 63; *see also* dialectical inquiry into voluntariness

appetite (*epithumia*), 63–5, 74, 75, 88n10, 88n12

Aquinas, 91n31, 91n32

archē see origin

argument against desire, 62–3, 63–76, 88n12; *see also* dialectical inquiry into voluntariness

Aspasius, 91n32

asymmetry thesis, 132–44 passim, 148n26

Austin, J. L., 87n1

bia see force

blame, blameworthiness, 32n6, 86, 94, 116–18, 175, 181–2; *see also* praise and blame, praise- and blameworthiness

Bondeson, W., 55n12

boulēsis see wish

Broadie, S., 55n12, 90n17, 146n3

carelessness, 135, 137, 147n21

causal power, 50, 57n29, 104–6, 114, 158, 166; character as, 105, 153–4; and efficient causes, 105; (non)accidental effects of, 104–6, 120n13, 162–4; and praiseworthiness, 44–6; *see also* cause, efficient cause

cause (*aitia*, *aition*); accidental *see* accidental and non-accidental; agent-, 39, 152, 156; Aristotelian vs. modern notions of, 38–9, 54n7, 54n10, 94; co-, 127, 146n5; efficient *see* efficient cause; event as, 38–9, 152; external, 77–8, 79, 83, 84, 91n32, 93, 95, 117–18, 156–61, 168n9, 168n13, 168n14; four kinds, 37; individuation of, 103, 117; substance as, 39, 153–4; *see also* causal power, efficient cause

character, 3–4, 19–24, 28–31, 35n28; causal power of, 45–50 passim, 153–5, 162–5; and ignorance, 175–6, 179; moral, 30, 154, 155, 156, 165, 175; reflected in voluntary action, 107–15 passim, 121n19; rel. virtue and vice, 30–1; responsibility for *see* responsibility for character; stability of, 29–30, 35n26, 147n20; as unmoved mover, 154–5;

Index Locorum